MINNESOTA CRIMINAL ELEMENTS HANDBOOK

BY

BRYAN R. LINDBERG
Assistant Anoka County Attorney
(763) 324-5386

Anoka County Government Center
2100 Third Avenue
Anoka, Minnesota 55303-2265

First Edition:	August 1992
Second Edition:	August 1993
Third Edition:	August 1994
Fourth Edition:	August 1995
Fifth Edition:	August 1996
Sixth Edition:	August 1997
Seventh Edition:	August 1998
Eighth Edition:	August 1999
Ninth Edition:	August 2000
Tenth Edition:	August 2001
Eleventh Edition:	August 2002
Twelfth Edition:	August 2003
Thirteenth Edition:	August 2004
Fourteenth Edition:	August 2005
Fifteenth Edition:	August 2006
Sixteenth Edition:	August 2007
Seventeenth Edition:	August 2008
Eighteenth Edition:	August 2009
Nineteenth Edition:	August 2010
Twentieth Edition:	August 2011
Twenty First Edition:	August 2012

Twenty Second Edition:	August 2013
Twenty Third Edition:	August 2014
Twenty Fourth Edition:	August 2015
Twenty Fifth Edition:	August 2016
Twenty Sixth Edition:	August 2017

MINNESOTA COUNTY ATTORNEYS ASSOCIATION
100 EMPIRE DRIVE, SUITE 200
ST. PAUL, MN 55103
PHONE: (651)641-1600
FAX (651)641-1666
www.mcaa-mn.org

Published by
*THE MINNESOTA COUNTY ATTORNEYS
ASSOCIATION*

MINNESOTA
CRIMINAL
ELEMENTS
HANDBOOK

2017

*Based on the Minnesota Criminal and
Traffic Codes, Including Prohibited Drugs
and Selected Gun Regulation Statutes*

INTRODUCTORY NOTE

This Criminal Elements Handbook includes changes in the law enacted by the 2017 Legislature. This codification is not official, and certain changes may be made by the Revisor of Statutes in the official version of the 2017 statutes. The official codification, however, will not be generally available until later this year. All new provisions become effective on or before August 1, 2017, unless otherwise noted.

This handbook was designed to provide law enforcement officers and attorneys with a compact, easy to use, reference guide to the basic statutory elements of most major felony offenses and selected misdemeanor and gross misdemeanor offenses.

Although this handbook does contain a comprehensive list of criminal offenses, it does not outline the elements for every crime and should be used as a supplement to the Minnesota Criminal and Traffic Codes, rather than as a substitute.

In order to simplify the complexity of our present criminal and traffic codes, this handbook has taken the statutory elements for each of the listed offenses and broken them down in outline form, into consecutively numbered paragraphs. When using this handbook, it is recommended you review each offense by following the numbers assigned to each element in sequence.

The shaded areas within the text represent changes in the law enacted by the 2017 Legislature.

ACKNOWLEDGMENT

Thank you to Traci Melberg, Paralegal, and Kim Holbrook, Paralegal, for all their hard work on this edition of the 2017 Minnesota Criminal Elements Handbook.

SPECIAL MENTION

A special thank you to the previous authors of the Criminal Elements Handbook: Former Judge Alan F. Pendleton, The Honorable Sean C. Gibbs, and The Honorable Michele A. Davis.

Bryan Lindberg

TABLE OF CONTENTS

Shaded areas indicate statutes changed by the 2017 Legislature. All new provisions become effective on or before August 1, 2017, unless otherwise noted.

3. BURGLARY AND RELATED OFFENSES

4. CONTROLLED SUBSTANCE CRIMES

1. ARSON AND RELATED OFFENSES

A.   ARSON IN THE FIRST DEGREE - Dwelling
M.S. § 609.561, subd. 1 (Felony)

Name
Date and Time of Offense
Location (Venue)

(1)   No person shall unlawfully
(2)   by means of fire or explosives
(3)   intentionally destroy or damage
(4)   a.   any building that is used as a dwelling at the time the act is committed, whether the inhabitant is present therein at the time of the act or not.
                 or
         b.   any building appurtenant to or connected with a dwelling.

<u>Note:</u> It doesn't matter whether the building belongs to the accused or another.

B.   ARSON IN THE FIRST DEGREE - Building, Non-Dwelling
M.S. § 609.561, subd. 3(a) (Felony)

Name
Date and Time of Offense
Location (Venue)

(1)   No person shall unlawfully
(2)   by means of fire or explosives
(3)   intentionally destroy or damage
(4)   any building not being used as a dwelling at the time the act is committed and is not appurtenant to or connected with a dwelling.
(5)   and uses a flammable material to start or accelerate the fire.

<u>Note:</u> It doesn't matter whether the property belongs to the accused or another.

Definition of **flammable material** is contained in M.S. § 609.561, subd. 3(b).

C. ARSON IN THE FIRST DEGREE - Occupied Building
M.S. § 609.561, subd. 2(a) & (b) (Felony)

Name

Date and Time of Offense

Location (Venue)

(1)   No person shall unlawfully

(2)   by means of fire or explosives

(3)   intentionally destroy or damage

(4)   any building that is not used as a dwelling at the time the act
is committed and is not appurtenant to or connected with a dwelling
IF

(5)   a.   another person who is not a participant in the crime is
present in the building at the time and the accused knows that.
or

        b.   the circumstances are such as to render the presence of such
a person therein a reasonable possibility.

<u>Note:</u> It doesn't matter whether the property belongs to the accused or another.

D. ARSON IN THE SECOND DEGREE - Unoccupied Building, Real or Personal Property Valued Over $1,000
M.S. § 609.562 (Felony)

Name

Date and Time of Offense

Location (Venue)

(1)   No person shall unlawfully

(2)   by means of fire or explosives

(3)   intentionally destroy or damage

(4)   a.   any building not covered by M.S. § 609.561 (Arson in the
1st Degree) no matter what its value.
or

        b.   any other real or personal property valued at more than
$1,000.

<u>Note:</u> It doesn't matter whether the property belongs to the accused or another.

E. **ARSON IN THE THIRD DEGREE - Real or Personal Property Valued Under $1,000**
M.S. § 609.563, subd. 1(a),(b),(c) (Felony)

Name

Date and Time of Offense

Location (Venue)

(1) No person shall unlawfully

(2) by means of fire or explosives

(3) intentionally destroy or damage

(4) any real or personal property

IF

(5)   a.   the property intended by the accused to be damaged or destroyed had a value of more than $300 but less than $1,000.
            or

        b.   property with a value of $300 or more was unintentionally damaged or destroyed, but such damage or destruction could reasonably have been foreseen.
            or

        c.   the property specified above in clauses a. and b. in the aggregate had a value of $300 or more.

F. **ARSON IN THE FOURTH DEGREE - Multiple Unit Residential or Public Building**
M.S. § 609.5631, subd. 2 (Gross Misdemeanor)

Name

Date and Time of Offense

Location (Venue)

(1) No person shall intentionally

(2) by means of fire or explosives

(3) set fire to or burn or cause to be burned

(4) any personal property

(5) in a multiple unit residential building or public building

(6) and Arson in the First, Second, or Third Degree was not committed.

G. **ARSON IN THE FIFTH DEGREE - Real or Personal Property of Value**
M.S. § 609.5632 (Misdemeanor)

Name
Date and Time of Offense
Location (Venue)
(1)   No person shall intentionally
(2)   by means of fire or explosives
(3)   set fire to or burn or cause to be burned
(4)   any real or personal property of value.

H. **NEGLIGENT FIRES - Great Bodily Harm, Property Damage $2,500 or more**
M.S. § 609.576, subd. 1(1)(2)(3) (Gross Misdemeanor - Felony)

Name
Date and Time of Offense
Location (Venue)
(1)   No person shall by gross negligence
(2)   cause a fire to burn or get out of control
(3)   thereby causing damage or injury to another
        IF
(4)   a.   as a result of this a human being is injured and great bodily harm incurred. **(Felony).**
               or
        b.   as a result of this a human being is injured and bodily harm incurred. **(Gross Misdemeanor).**
        c.   as a result of this property of another is injured and the value of the property <u>damaged</u> is $2,500 or more. **(Felony).**

Note: Because the legislative intention was that the extent of the damage, rather than the value of the overall property, should control the penalty, section (4)c. above should read "property damage" rather than "property damaged". (CRIMJIG 18.16)

I. **NEGLIGENT FIRES - Property Damage Under $2,500**
M.S. § 609.576, subd. 1(b)(1)(2) (Misdemeanor, Gross Misdemeanor)

Name
Date and Time of Offense
Location (Venue)
(1)   No person shall by gross negligence
(2)   cause a fire to burn or get out of control
(3)   thereby causing damage or injury to another

IF

(4)   a.   as a result thereof property of another is injured and the value of the property damage is under $300 **(misdemeanor).**
         or

       b.   the value of the property <u>damaged</u> is at least $300 but is less than $2,500 **(gross misdemeanor).**

<u>Note:</u> Because the legislative intention was that the extent of the damage, rather than the value of the overall property, should control the penalty, section (4)b. above should read "property damage" rather than "property damaged". (CRIMJIG 18.16).

J.   **NEGLIGENT FIRES - Dangerous Smoking**
         M.S. § 609.576, subd. 2 (Misdemeanor - Felony)

Name
Date and Time of Offense
Location (Venue)

(1)   No person shall

(2)   smoke in the presence of explosives or inflammable materials **(misdemeanor).**

<u>Enhancement:</u> Whoever violates the above section knowing that doing so creates a risk of death or bodily harm or serious property damage is guilty of a **felony.**

K.   **WILDFIRE ARSON - Setting Wildfires**
         M.S. § 609.5641, subd. 1, 1a, 2, 3 (Felony – Gross Misdemeanor)

Name
Date and Time of Offense
Location (Venue)

(1)   No person shall

       a.   intentionally set a fire to burn out of control on land of another containing timber, underbrush, grass, or other vegetative combustible material. **(Felony).**
          or

       b.   possess a flammable, explosive, or incendiary device, substance, or material with intent to use the device, substance, or material to set a fire to burn out of control on land of another containing timber, underbrush, grass, or other vegetative combustible material. **(Gross Misdemeanor).**

Penalties:

A person convicted under subd. 1, setting wildfires, is subject to the following penalties:

(a) A **five-year felony** and/or a $10,000 fine;

(b) A **ten-year felony** and/or a $15,000 fine if the fire:
>   (i)   threatens to damage or damages in excess of five buildings or dwellings; or
>   (ii)   burns 500 acres or more; or
>   (iii)   damages crops in excess of $100,000;

(c) A **twenty-year felony** and/or a $25,000 fine if the fire:
>   (i)   threatens to damage or damages in excess of 100 buildings or dwellings; or
>   (ii)   burns 1,500 acres or more; or
>   (iii)   damages crops in excess of $250,000

>   **or**

(d) A **ten-year felony** and/or a $15,000 fine if the fire causes another person to suffer demonstrable bodily harm.

L.   WILDFIRE ARSON - Possession of Flammables
M.S. § 609.5641, subd. 2, 3 (Gross Misdemeanor)
Name
Date and Time of Offense
Location (Venue)
(1)   No person shall
(2)   possess a flammable, explosive or incendiary device, substance, or material
(3)   with intent to use the device, substance, or material to set a wildfire, in violation of M.S. § 609.5641, subd. 1 (Setting Wildfires - See section K above).

M.   USE OF IGNITION DEVICES
M.S. § 609.5633 (Petty Misdemeanor)
Name
Date and Time of Offense
Location (Venue)
(1)   No student shall
(2)   use an ignition device, including a butane or disposable lighter or matches

(3)	inside an educational building
(4)	and under circumstances where there is an obvious risk of fire
(5)	and Arson in the First, Second, Third or Fourth Degree was not committed.

Exception: The above section does not apply if the student uses the device in a manner authorized by the school.

Definition of **student** (M.S. § 123B.41, subd. 11)   Student means a child enrolled in a school and is limited to children who are residents, or children of residents, of Minnesota.

N.	**DEFINITIONS:**	
(1)	**Bodily harm** (M.S. § 609.02, subd. 7)	
		"Bodily harm" means physical pain or injury, illness or any impairment of physical condition.
(2)	**Building** (M.S. § 609.556, subd. 3)	
		"Building," in addition to its ordinary meaning, includes any tent, watercraft, structure or vehicle that is customarily used for overnight lodging of a person or persons. If a building consists of two or more units separately secured or occupied, each unit shall be deemed a separate building.
(3)	**Great bodily harm** (M.S. § 609.02, subd. 8)	
		"Great bodily harm" means bodily injury which creates a high probability of death, or which causes serious permanent disfigurement, or which causes a permanent or protracted loss or impairment of the function of any bodily member or organ or other serious bodily harm.
(4)	**Gross negligence** (CRIMJIG 11.73)	
		"Gross negligence" means with very great negligence or without even scant care.
(5)	**Multiple unit residential building** (M.S. § 609.5631, subd. 1)	
		"Multiple unit residential building" means a building containing two or more apartments.
(6)	**Property of another** (M.S. § 609.556, subd. 2)	
		"Property of another" means a building or other property, whether real or personal, in which a person other than the accused has an interest which the accused has no authority to defeat or impair even though the accused may also have an interest in the building or property.

(7)   **Public building** (M.S. § 609.5631, subd. 1)

"Public building" means a building such as a hotel, hospital, motel, dormitory, sanitarium, nursing home, theatre, stadium, gymnasium, amusement park building, school or other building used for educational purposes, museum, restaurant, bar, correctional institution, place of worship, or other building of public assembly.

2. ASSAULT

A. ASSAULT IN THE FIRST DEGREE - Great Bodily Harm
M.S. § 609.221, subd. 1, 2 (Felony)

Name
Date and Time of Offense
Location (Venue)

Subd. 1
(1) No person shall
(2) assault another
(3) and inflict great bodily harm.

Subd. 2(a)
(1) No person shall
(2) assault a peace officer, prosecuting attorney, judge or correctional employee
(3) by using or attempting to use deadly force against the officer or employee
(4) while the officer or employee is engaged in the performance of a duty imposed by law, policy, or rule.
Note: A person convicted of the above section shall be committed to prison for not less than ten years, not more than 20 years. A defendant convicted and sentenced as required by this paragraph is not eligible for probation, parole, discharge, work release, or supervised release, until that person has served the full term of imprisonment as provided by law. See subd. 2(b)

Note: If the victim of the assault is a pregnant woman with resulting injury to her unborn child, see M.S. § 609.267 (Assault of an Unborn Child in the 1st Degree - Great Bodily Harm).

Jurisdiction - Child Victim: If the victim is a child (under 18), violations of the above section may be prosecuted in either the county where the incident occurred or where the child was found (M.S. § 627.15).

Enhanced Penalty: A person violating this section because of the victim's or another person's actual or perceived race, color, religion, sex, sexual orientation, disability, age, or national origin is subject to a statutory maximum penalty of 25 percent longer than the maximum penalty otherwise applicable (M.S. § 609.2233).

B. **ASSAULT IN THE SECOND DEGREE - Dangerous Weapon, Substantial Bodily Harm**
M.S. § 609.222, subds. 1, 2 (Felony)

Name
Date and Time of Offense
Location (Venue)
(1)   No person shall
(2)   assault another
(3)   with a dangerous weapon.

Enhancement: If an assault under the above section results in substantial bodily harm, increased felony penalties apply.

Jurisdiction - Child Victim: If the victim is a child (under 18), violations of the above section may be prosecuted in either the county where the incident occurred or where the child was found (M.S. § 627.15).

Enhanced Penalty: A person violating this section because of the victim's or another person's actual or perceived race, color, religion, sex, sexual orientation, disability, age, or national origin is subject to a statutory maximum penalty of 25 percent longer than the maximum penalty otherwise applicable (M.S. § 609.2233).

C. **ASSAULT IN THE THIRD DEGREE - Substantial Bodily Harm**
M.S. § 609.223, subd. 1 (Felony)

Name
Date and Time of Offense
Location (Venue)
(1)   No person shall
(2)   assault another
(3)   and inflict substantial bodily harm.

Note: If the victim of the assault is a pregnant woman with resulting injury to her unborn child, see M.S. § 609.2671 (Assault of an Unborn Child in the 2nd Degree - Substantial Bodily Harm).

Jurisdiction - Child Victim: If the victim is a child (under 18), violations of the above section may be prosecuted in either the county where the incident occurred or where the child was found (M.S. § 627.15).

Enhanced Penalty: A person violating this section because of the victim's or another person's actual or perceived race, color, religion, sex, sexual orientation, disability, age, or national origin is subject to a statutory maximum penalty of 25 percent longer than the maximum penalty otherwise applicable (M.S. § 609.2233).

D. **ASSAULT IN THE THIRD DEGREE - Child Abuse**
M.S. § 609.223, subd. 2 (Felony)

Name

Date and Time of Offense

Location (Venue)

(1) No person shall

(2) assault a minor (under 18 years of age)
  IF

(3) the perpetrator has engaged in a past pattern of child abuse against the minor.

Jurisdiction - Child Victim: Violations of the above section may be prosecuted in either the county where the incident occurred or where the child was found (M.S. § 627.15).

Enhanced Penalty: A person violating this section because of the victim's or another person's actual or perceived race, color, religion, sex, sexual orientation, disability, age, or national origin is subject to a statutory maximum penalty of 25 percent longer than the maximum penalty otherwise applicable (M.S. § 609.2233).

E. **ASSAULT IN THE THIRD DEGREE - Victim Under Four**
M.S. § 609.223, subd. 3 (Felony)

Name

Date and Time of Offense

Location (Venue)

(1) No person shall

(2) assault a victim under the age of four

(3) and cause bodily harm to the child's head, eyes, or neck, or otherwise cause multiple bruises to the body.

Jurisdiction - Child Victim: Violations of the above section may be prosecuted in either the county where the incident occurred or where the child was found. (M.S. § 627.15).

Enhanced Penalty: A person violating this section because of the victim's or another person's actual or perceived race, color, religion, sex, sexual orientation, disability, age, or national origin is subject to a statutory maximum penalty of 25 percent longer than the maximum penalty otherwise applicable (M.S. § 609.2233).

**F.   ASSAULT IN THE FOURTH DEGREE - Peace Officers
          M.S. § 609.2231, subd. 1 (Felony, Gross Misdemeanor)**

Name

Date and Time of Offense

Location (Venue)

(1)   No person shall

(2)   physically assault a peace officer licensed under M.S. § 626.845, subd.1

(3)   either:

      a.   when that officer is effecting a lawful arrest

          or

      b.   executing any other duty imposed by law.

Penalties: If the person physically assaults the officer and the assault inflicts demonstrable bodily harm, or the person intentionally throws or otherwise transfers bodily fluids or feces at or onto the officer, the penalty is a **three-year felony**. If the assault does not inflict demonstrable bodily harm or involve the transfer of bodily fluids or feces, the penalty is a **gross misdemeanor**.

**G.   ASSAULT IN THE FOURTH DEGREE - Firefighters, Emergency Medical Personnel, Health Care Providers, DNR Employees
          M.S. § 609.2231, subd. 2, 2a (Felony, Gross Misdemeanor)**

Name

Date and Time of Offense

Location (Venue)

(1)   No person shall

(2)   assault

      a.   a member of a municipal or volunteer fire department
          or emergency medical services personnel unit in the
          performance of the member's duty **(Felony)**

          or

      b.   a physician, nurse, or other person providing health care
          services in a hospital emergency department **(Felony)**

          or

      c.   an employee of the Department of Natural Resources who is
          engaged in forest fire activities **(Gross Misdemeanor)**

(3)   and inflict demonstrable bodily harm.

H. **ASSAULT IN THE FOURTH DEGREE** - **Correctional Employees; Prosecuting Attorneys; Judges; Probation Officers M.S. § 609.2231, subd. 3 (Felony)**

Name

Date and Time of Offense

Location (Venue)

(1)   No person shall

(2)   either:

    a.   assault an employee of a correctional facility, prosecuting attorney, judge, probation officer or other qualified person employed in supervising offenders and inflict demonstrable bodily harm

       or

    b.   intentionally throw or otherwise transfer bodily fluids or feces at or onto the employee, prosecuting attorney, judge, probation officer, or other qualified person employed in supervising offenders

(3)   while the employee, officer, or person is engaged in the performance of a duty imposed by law, policy or rule.

I. **ASSAULT IN THE FOURTH DEGREE – Secure Treatment Facility Personnel M.S. § 609.2231, subd. 3a (Felony)**

Name

Date and Time of Offense

Location (Venue)

(1)   No person, while committed under M.S. § 253B.185 or M.S. § 526.10, shall

(2)   either

    a.   assault an employee of a secure treatment facility or other individual who provides care or treatment at a secure treatment facility and inflict demonstrable bodily harm

       or

    b.   intentionally throw or otherwise transfer bodily fluids or feces at or onto the employee or individual providing care

(3)   while that employee or individual was engaged in the performance of a duty imposed by law, policy, or rule.

J. **ASSAULT IN THE FOURTH DEGREE - Motivated by Bias**
M.S. § 609.2231, subd. 4 (Gross Misdemeanor - Felony)

Name

Date and Time of Offense

Location (Venue)

(1) No person shall

(2) assault another

(3) because of the victim's or another's actual or perceived race, color, religion, sex, sexual orientation, disability, age or national origin **(gross misdemeanor)**.

Enhancement: Whoever violates the above section within five years of a previous conviction for the above offense, is guilty of a **felony**.

K. **ASSAULT IN THE FOURTH DEGREE - School Official**
M.S. § 609.2231, subd. 5 (Gross Misdemeanor)

Name

Date and Time of Offense

Location (Venue)

(1) No person shall

(2) assault a school official

(3) while the official is engaged in the performance of the official's duties

(4) and inflict demonstrable bodily harm.

L. **ASSAULT IN THE FOURTH DEGREE - Public Employees With Mandated Duties**
M.S. § 609.2231, subd. 6 (Gross Misdemeanor)

Name

Date and Time of Offense

Location (Venue)

(1) No person shall assault

(2) a. an agricultural inspector

  b. an occupational safety and health investigator

  c. a child protection worker

  d. a public health nurse

  e. animal control officer

  f. a probation or parole officer

(3) while the employee is engaged in the performance of a duty mandated by law, court order or ordinance

(4) and the accused knows that the victim is a public employee engaged in the performance of the official public duties of the office

(5) and inflict demonstrable bodily harm.

M. **ASSAULT IN THE FOURTH DEGREE - Community Crime Prevention Group Members**
M.S. § 609.2231, subd. 7 (Gross Misdemeanor)

Name

Date and Time of Offense

Location (Venue)

(1)   No person shall
(2)   assault a community crime prevention group member
(3)   while the community crime prevention group member is engaged in neighborhood patrol
(4)   the accused should reasonably know that the victim is a community crime prevention group member engaged in neighborhood patrol
(5)   and inflict demonstrable bodily harm.

N. **ASSAULT IN THE FOURTH DEGREE – Vulnerable Adult**
M.S. § 609.2231, subd. 8 (Gross Misdemeanor)

Name

Date and Time of Offense

Location (Venue)

(1)   No person shall
(2)   assault a vulnerable adult
(3)   knowing, or having reason to know, the victim is a vulnerable adult
(4)   and inflict demonstrable bodily harm.

O. **ASSAULT IN THE FOURTH DEGREE – Reserve Officer**
M.S. § 609.2231, subd. 9 (Gross Misdemeanor)

Name

Date and Time of Offense

Location (Venue)

(1)   No person shall
(2)   assault a reserve officer
(3)   while the reserve officer is engaged in the performance of official duties at the direction of, or on behalf of a peace officer or supervising law enforcement officer or agency
(4)   the accused should reasonably know the victim is a reserve officer who is engaged in the performance of official public duties of the peace office, or supervising law enforcement officer or agency.

P. **ASSAULT IN THE FOURTH DEGREE – Utility and Postal Service Employees and Contractors**
M.S. § 609.2231, subd. 10 (Gross Misdemeanor)

Name
Date and Time of Offense
Location (Venue)
(1)   No person shall
(2)   assault
    a.   an employee or contractor of a utility
       or
    b.   an employee or contractor of the United States Postal Service
(3)   while the employee or contractor is engaged in the performance of the employee's or contractor's duties
(4)   the accused should reasonably know that the victim is an employee or contractor of a utility or the postal service who is
    a.   performing duties of the victim's employment
       or
    b.   fulfilling the victim's contractual obligations
(5)   and inflict demonstrable bodily harm.

Q. **ASSAULT IN THE FOURTH DEGREE – Transit Operators**
M.S. § 609.2231, subd. 11 (Gross Misdemeanor)

Name
Date and Time of Offense
Location (Venue)
(1)   No person shall
(2)   either
    a.   assault a transit operator
       or
    b.   intentionally throw or otherwise transfer bodily fluids onto a transit operator
(3)   while the transit operator is acting in the course of the operator's duties
(4)   and the transit operator is
    a.   operating a transit vehicle
       or
    b.   aboard a transit vehicle
       or
    c.   otherwise responsible for a transit vehicle.

R. **ASSAULT IN THE FIFTH DEGREE - Fear, Bodily Harm**
M.S. § 609.224, subds. 1, 2, 4 (Misdemeanor - Gross Misdemeanor - Felony)

Name
Date and Time of Offense
Location (Venue)

(1)   No person shall
(2)   commit an act
(3)   a.   with intent to cause fear in another of immediate bodily harm or death **(misdemeanor).**
        or
        b.   intentionally inflict or attempt to inflict bodily harm upon another **(misdemeanor).**

Enhancement to Gross Misdemeanor and Felony:

a.   Same victim - prior conviction (GM): Whoever violates the above section against the same victim within ten years of a previous a qualified domestic violence-related offense conviction or adjudication of delinquency is guilty of a **gross misdemeanor.**
       or
b.   Any victim - prior conviction (GM): Whoever violates the above section (elements (1), (2), and (3) - Misdemeanor Assault) within three years of a previous a qualified domestic violence-related offense conviction or adjudication of delinquency is guilty of a **gross misdemeanor.**
       or
c.   Same victim - two prior convictions (F): Whoever violates the above section (elements (1), (2), and (3) - Misdemeanor Assault) against the same victim within ten years of the first of any combination of two or more previous qualified domestic violence-related offense convictions or adjudication of delinquency is guilty of a **felony.**
       or
d.   Any victim - two prior convictions (F): Whoever violates the above section (elements (1), (2), and (3) - Misdemeanor Assault) within three years of the first of two or more previous "qualified domestic violence-related offense" convictions or adjudications of delinquency is guilty of a **felony.**

Note: If the victim of the assault is a pregnant woman and her unborn child, see M.S. § 609.2672 (Assault of an Unborn Child in the 3rd Degree).

Jurisdiction - Child Victim: If the victim is a child (under 18), violations of the above section may be prosecuted in either the county where the incident occurred or where the child was found (M.S. § 627.15).

Note: For a list of Crimes Against Vulnerable Adults - see M.S. § 609.232.

S. DOMESTIC ASSAULT –
M.S. § 609.2242 (Misdemeanor - Gross Misdemeanor - Felony)
Name
Date and Time of Offense
Location (Venue)
(1)   No person shall
(2)   commit an act against a family or household member (as defined in section U. "Definitions" below)

(3)   a.   with intent to cause fear in another of immediate bodily harm or death (**misdemeanor**)
               or
          b.   intentionally inflict or attempt to inflict bodily harm upon another (**misdemeanor**).

Enhancement to Gross Misdemeanor and Felony:

a.   Prior Conviction (G.M.): Whoever violates the above section within ten years of a previous "qualified domestic violence-related offense" conviction or adjudication of delinquency, is guilty of a **gross misdemeanor**. (M.S. § 609.2242, subd. 2)

b.   Two prior convictions (F): Whoever commits Assault in the 5th Degree (M.S. § 609.224) or Domestic Assault (M.S. § 609.2242) within ten years of the first of two or more previous "qualified domestic violence-related offense" convictions or adjudication of delinquency, is guilty of
a **felony**.

T. DOMESTIC ASSAULT BY STRANGULATION
M.S. § 609.2247 (Felony)
Name
Date and Time of Offense
Location (Venue)
(1)   No person shall
(2)   assault a family or household member (as defined in section U. "Definitions" below)

(3)   by intentionally impeding normal breathing or circulation of the blood

(4)   a.   by applying pressure on the throat or neck
             or
           b.   by blocking the nose or mouth.

Penalty: Unless a greater penalty is provided elsewhere, the penalty is a three-year felony.

U.   **DEFINITIONS:**

(1)   **Assault** (M.S. § 609.02, subd. 10)

      "Assault" means:

      a.   an act done with intent to cause fear in another of immediate bodily harm or death;
          or
      b.   the intentional infliction of or attempt to inflict bodily harm upon another.

(2)   **Bodily harm** (M.S. § 609.02, subd. 7)

      "Bodily harm" means physical pain or injury, illness or any impairment of physical condition.

(3)   **Caregiver** (M.S. § 609.232, subd. 2)

      "Caregiver" means an individual or facility who has responsibility for the care of a vulnerable adult as a result of a family relationship, or who has assumed responsibility for all or a portion of the care of a vulnerable adult voluntarily, by contract, or by agreement.

(4)   **Child abuse** (M.S. § 609.185(5); 609.223, subd. 2; M.S. § 626.556, subd. 2)

      "Child abuse" means an act committed against a minor victim that constitutes a violation of M.S. § 609.221, § 609.222, § 609.223, § 609.224 (Assault in the 1st, 2nd, 3rd, and 5th Degree); M.S. § 609.342 to § 609.345 (Criminal Sexual Conduct in the 1st, 2nd, 3rd or 4th Degree); M.S. § 609.377 (Malicious Punishment of a Child); M.S. § 609.378 (Neglect or Endangerment of a Child); M.S. § 609.713 (Terroristic Threats).

(5)   **Community Crime Prevention Group** (M.S. § 609.2231, subd. 7(b))

      "Community crime prevention group" means a community group focused on community safety and crime prevention that is organized for the purpose of discussing community safety and patrolling community neighborhoods for criminal activity; is designated and trained by the local law enforcement agency as a community crime prevention group;

or interacts with local law enforcement regarding community safety issues.

(6)   **Correctional employee** (M.S. § 609.221, subd. 2(c)(1)

        "Correctional employee" means an employee of a public or private prison, jail, or workhouse.

(7)   **Correctional facility** (M.S. § 241.021, subd. 1(5))

        "Correctional facility" means any facility, including a group home, having a residential component, the primary purpose of which is to serve persons placed therein by a court, court services department, parole authority or other correctional agency having dispositional power over persons charged with, convicted or adjudicated to be guilty or delinquent.

(8)   **Dangerous weapon** (M.S. § 609.02, subd. 6)

        "Dangerous weapon" means any firearm, whether loaded or unloaded, or any device designed as a weapon and capable of producing death or great bodily harm, any combustible or flammable liquid or other device or instrumentality that, in the manner it is used or intended to be used, is calculated or likely to produce death or great bodily harm, or any fire that is used to produce death or great bodily harm. "Flammable liquid" means any liquid having a flash point below 100 degrees Fahrenheit and having a vapor pressure not exceeding 40 pounds per square inch (absolute) at 100 degrees Fahrenheit but does not include intoxicating liquor as defined in section 340A.101. "Combustible liquid" is a liquid having a flash point at or above 100 degrees Fahrenheit.

(9)   **Deadly force** (M.S. § 609.221, subd. 2(c)(2))

        "Deadly force" has the meaning given in section 609.066, subd. 1, which states, "deadly force" means force which the actor uses with the purpose of causing, or which the actor should reasonably know creates a substantial risk of causing, death or great bodily harm. The intentional discharge of a firearm in the direction of another person, or at a vehicle in which another person is believed to be, constitutes deadly force.

(10)   **Demonstrable bodily harm** (CRIMJIG 13.10)

        "Demonstrable bodily harm" is not defined by statute. It is a word of common usage. Webster's Dictionary defines "demonstrable" as "capable of being demonstrated" (i.e. cuts, scratches, visible bruises or nonvisible medically confirmed injuries).

(11) **Disability** (M.S. § 353.01, subd. 13)

"Disability" means any condition or characteristic that renders a person a disabled person. A disabled person is any person who (1) has a physical, sensory or mental impairment which materially limits one or more major life activities; (2) has a record of such an impairment; or (3) is regarded as having such an impairment.

(12) **Family or household members** (M.S. § 518B.01, subd. 2(b))

"Family or household members" means spouses and former spouses, parents and children, persons related by blood, persons who are presently residing together or who have resided together in the past, and persons who have a child in common regardless of whether they have been married or have lived together at any time. It also includes a man and woman if the woman is pregnant and the man is alleged to be the father, regardless of whether they have been married or have lived together at any time, and persons involved in a significant romantic or sexual relationship.

(13) **Great bodily harm** (M.S. § 609.02, subd. 8)

"Great bodily harm" means bodily injury which creates a high probability of death, or which causes serious permanent disfigurement, or which causes a permanent or protracted loss or impairment of the function of any bodily member or organ or other serious bodily harm.

(14) **Past pattern of child abuse**

This term is not defined by statute. Contact your county attorney's office for clarification.

(15) **Peace officer** (M.S. § 609.221, subd. 2(c)(3))

"Peace officer" has the meaning given in section 626.84, subd. 1. The full text of the definition is set out in chapter 13 "False Name to a Peace Officer".

(16) **Qualified Domestic Violence-Related Offense** (M.S. § 609.02, subd. 16)

"Qualified domestic violence-related offense" includes a violation of or an attempt to violate: § 518B.01, subd. 14 (Violation of Domestic Abuse Order for Protection); § 518B.01, subd 22 (Violation of a Domestic Abuse No Contact Order); § 609.185 (First Degree Murder); § 609.19 (Second Degree Murder; § 609.221 (First Degree Assault); § 609.22 (Second Degree Assault); § 609.223 (Third Degree Assault); § 609.2231 (Fourth Degree Assault); § 609.224 (Fifth Degree Assault); § 609.2242 (Domestic Assault); § 609.2245 (Female Genital Mutilation); § 609.2247 (Domestic Assault by Strangulation); § 609.342 (First Degree Criminal Sexual Conduct); § 609.343 (Second Degree Criminal Sexual

Conduct); § 609.344 (Third Degree Criminal Sexual Conduct); § 609.345 (Fourth Degree Criminal Sexual Conduct); § 609.377 (Malicious Punishment of a Child); § 609.713 (Terroristic Threats); § 609.748, subd. 6 (Violation of Harassment Restraining Order); § 609.749 (Harassment/Stalking); and § 609.78, subd. 2 (Interference with an Emergency Call); and similar laws of other states, the United States, the District of Columbia, tribal lands, and United States territories.

(17)   **Reserve officer** (M.S. § 626.84, subd. 1e)

"Reserve officer" means an individual whose services are utilized by a law enforcement agency to provide supplemental assistance at special events, traffic or crowd control, and administrative or clerical assistance.

(18)   **School official** (M.S. § 609.2231, subd. 5)

"School official" includes teachers, school administrators and other employees of a public or private school.

(19)   **Secure treatment facility** (M.S. § 253B.02, subd. 18(a))

"Secure treatment facility" means the Minnesota Security Hospital and the Minnesota sex offender program facility in Moose Lake and any portion of the Minnesota sex offender program operated by the Minnesota sex offender program at the Minnesota Security Hospital, but does not include services or programs administered by the secure treatment facility outside a secure environment.

(20)   **Strangulation** (M.S. § 609.2247, subd. 1(c))

"Strangulation" means intentionally impeding normal breathing or circulation of the blood by applying pressure on the throat or neck or by blocking the nose or mouth of another person.

(21)   **Substantial bodily harm** (M.S. § 609.02, subd. 7a)

"Substantial bodily harm" means bodily injury which involves a temporary but substantial disfigurement, or which causes a temporary but substantial loss or impairment of the function of any bodily member or organ, or which causes a fracture of any bodily member.

(22)   **Transit Operator** (M.S. § 609.2231, subd. 11)

"Transit Operator" means a driver or operator of a transit vehicle that is used to provide (1) public transit service, as defined by M.S. § 174.22, subd. 7; (2) light rail transit service; (3) special transportation service under M.S. § 473.386, whether provided by the Metropolitan Council or by other providers under contract with the council; or (4) commuter rail service.

(23)   **Utility** (M.S. § 609.594, subd. 1(3))
         "Utility" means an enterprise, carrier, company or utility that is formed for the purpose of providing electrical, gas, telephone, telecommunications, water, sewage, wastewater or other
         utility services and is owned or regulated by a governmental unit.

(24)   **Vulnerable Adult** (M.S. § 609.232, subd. 11)
         "Vulnerable adult" is a person 18 years of age or older who possesses a physical or mental infirmity or other physical, mental, or emotional dysfunction that impairs the individual's ability to provide adequately for the individual's own care without assistance, including provision of food, shelter, clothing, health care, or supervision and because of the dysfunction or infirmity and the need for assistance, the individual has an impaired ability to protect the individual from maltreatment.

3. BURGLARY AND RELATED OFFENSES

A. **BURGLARY IN THE FIRST DEGREE** - Occupied Dwelling, Dangerous Weapon, Assault
M.S. § 609.582, subd. 1 (Felony)

Name
Date and Time of Offense
Location (Venue)

(1)   No person shall
(2)   enter a building
(3)   without consent of the person in lawful possession
(4)   with intent to commit a crime **or** commits a crime while in the building, either directly or as an accomplice.

IF

(5)   a.   the building is a dwelling and another person, not an accomplice, is present in it when the burglar enters or at any time while the burglar is in the building.

or

         b.   when entering or at any time while in the building the burglar possesses a dangerous weapon, or any article used or fashioned in a manner to lead the victim to reasonably believe it to be a dangerous weapon, or an explosive.

or

         c.   the burglar assaults a person within the building or on the building's appurtenant property.

B. **BURGLARY IN THE SECOND DEGREE** - Unoccupied Dwelling, Business, Tool
M.S. § 609.582, subd. 2 (Felony)

Name
Date and Time of Offense
Location (Venue)

(1)   No person shall
(2)   a.   enter a building
               without consent of the person in lawful possession
               with intent to commit a crime **or** commits a crime while in the building, either directly or as an accomplice.

               IF

               1.   the building is a dwelling.

                      or

2.   the portion of the building entered contains a banking business or other business of receiving securities or other valuable papers for deposit or safekeeping and the entry is with force or threat of force.

or

3.   the portion of the building entered contains a pharmacy or other lawful business or practice in which controlled substances are routinely held or stored and the entry is forcible.

or

4.   when entering or while in the building the burglar possesses a tool to gain access to money or property.

(3)   b.   enter a government building, religious establishment, historic property or school building,

either directly or as an accomplice,

without consent

1.   with intent to commit a crime under § 609.52 or § 609.595

or

2.   commits a crime under § 609.52 or § 609.595 while in the building.

C.   BURGLARY IN THE THIRD DEGREE - Building
M.S. § 609.582, subd. 3 (Felony)

Name

Date and Time of Offense

Location (Venue)

(1)   No person shall

(2)   enter a building

(3)   without consent of the person in lawful possession

(4)   a.   with intent to steal or commit any felony or gross misdemeanor while in the building, either directly or as an accomplice.

or

b.   steals or commits a felony or gross misdemeanor while in the building, either directly or as an accomplice.

D.   BURGLARY IN THE FOURTH DEGREE - Building
M.S. § 609.582, subd. 4 (Gross Misdemeanor)

Name

Date and Time of Offense

Location (Venue)

(1)   No person shall

(2)   enter a building

(3)   without consent of the person in lawful possession

(4)   a.   with intent to commit a misdemeanor other than to steal, either directly or as an accomplice.

               or

             b.   commits a misdemeanor other than to steal while in the building, either directly or as an accomplice.

E.   POSSESSION OF BURGLARY OR THEFT TOOLS
M.S. § 609.59 (Felony)

Name

Date and Time of Offense

Location (Venue)

(1)   No person shall

(2)   have in their possession

(3)   any device, explosive or other instrumentality

(4)   with intent to use or permit the use of the same to commit burglary or theft.

F.   DEFINITIONS:

(1)   **Assault** (M.S. § 609.02, subd. 10)

             "Assault" means:

             a.   an act done with intent to cause fear in another of immediate bodily harm or death;

                 or

             b.   the intentional infliction of or attempt to inflict bodily harm upon another.

(2)   **Building** (M.S. § 609.581, subd. 2)

             "Building" means a structure suitable for affording shelter for human beings, including any appurtenant or connected structure (also includes detached garages).

(3)   **Dangerous weapon** (M.S. § 609.02, subd. 6)

             "Dangerous weapon" means any firearm, whether loaded or unloaded, or any device designed as a weapon and capable of producing death or great bodily harm, any combustible or flammable liquid or other device or instrumentality that, in the manner it is used or intended to be used, is calculated or likely to produce death or great bodily harm, or any fire that is used to produce death or great bodily harm. "Flammable liquid" means any liquid having a flash point below 100 degrees Fahrenheit and having a vapor pressure not exceeding 40 pounds per square inch (absolute) at 100 degrees Fahrenheit, but does not include intoxicating liquor as defined in section

340A.101. "Combustible liquid" is a liquid having a flash point at or above 100 degrees Fahrenheit.

(4) **Dwelling** (M.S. § 609.581, subd. 3)

"Dwelling" means a building used as a permanent or temporary residence.

(5) **Enters a building without consent** (M.S. § 609.581, subd. 4)

"Enters a building without consent" means:

a.   to enter a building without the consent of the person in lawful possession;

b.   to enter a building by using artifice, trick or misrepresentation to obtain consent to enter from the person in lawful possession; or

c.   to remain within a building without the consent of the person in lawful possession.

Whoever enters a building while open to the general public does so with consent except when consent was expressly withdrawn before entry.

(6) **Government Building** (M.S. § 609.581, subd. 5)

"Government building" means a building that is owned, leased, controlled or operated by a governmental entity for agovernmental purpose.

(7) **Historic Property** (M.S. § 609.581, subd. 8)

"Historic property" means any property identified as a historic site or historic place by sections 138.661 to 138.664 and clearly identified as such by a posted sign or other means.

(8) **Religious Establishment** (M.S. § 609.581, subd. 6)

"Religious establishment" means a building used for worship services by a religious organization and clearly identified as such by a posted sign or other means.

(9) **School Building** (M.S. §609.581, subd. 7)

"School building" means a public or private preschool, elementary school, middle school, secondary school, or post-secondary school building.

4. CONTROLLED SUBSTANCE CRIMES AND RELATED OFFENSES

A. CONTROLLED SUBSTANCE CRIME IN THE FIRST DEGREE
Sale Crimes
M.S. § 152.021, subd. 1 (Felony)

Name
Date and Time of Offense
Location (Venue)

(1)   No person shall

(2)   unlawfully sell

(3)   on one or more occasions within a 90-day period

(4)   one or more mixtures of a total weight of

(5)   a.   17 grams or more containing cocaine or methamphetamine

              or

        b.   10 grams or more containing cocaine or methamphetamine, **and**

              i.   the person or an accomplice possesses on their person or within immediate reach, or uses, whether brandishing, displaying, threatening with, or otherwise employing, a firearm

                      or

              ii.   the offense involves two aggravating factors (chapter 4. section Y. Definitions)

              or

        c.   10 grams or more containing heroin

              or

        d.   50 grams or more containing a narcotic drug other than cocaine, heroin, or methamphetamine

              or

        e.   50 grams or more containing amphetamine, phencyclidine, or hallucinogen, or, if the controlled substance is packaged in dosage units, equaling 200 or more dosage units

              or

        f.   25 kilograms or more containing marijuana or Tetrahydrocannabinol.

Aggregation: For sentencing purposes, separate sales on separate days are considered separate offenses. However, if separate sales within a 90-day period are aggregated under the above section, all sales are considered part of a single behavioral incident (M.S. § 609.035).

Jurisdiction: In a prosecution under the above section involving sales by the same person in two or more counties within a 90-day period, the person may be prosecuted for all of the sales in any county in which one of the sales occurred.

Sentence Enhancement: A person convicted under subparts (a) through (e) above where the person or an accomplice sold or possessed 100 or more grams or 500 or more dosage units of a mixture containing the controlled substance at issue may to subject to increased penalties, including mandatory commitments to prison, increased maximum fines, and/or increased maximum statutory sentence periods. M.S. § 152.021, subd. 3(c)

Subsequent Controlled Substance Conviction: A person convicted of Controlled Substance Crime in the First Degree may be subject to increased penalties, including mandatory commitments to prison, increased maximum fines, and/or increased maximum statutory sentence periods if the conviction is a subsequent controlled substance conviction (chapter 4, section Y, Definitions)

B.   CONTROLLED SUBSTANCE CRIME IN THE FIRST DEGREE
        Possession Crimes
        M.S. § 152.021, subd. 2 (Felony)
Name
Date and Time of Offense
Location (Venue)
(1)   No person shall
(2)   unlawfully possess

(3)	one or more mixtures of a total weight of
a.	50 grams or more containing cocaine or methamphetamine. **or**
b.	25 grams or more containing cocaine or methamphetamine, **and**
i.	the person or an accomplice possesses on their person or within immediate reach, or uses, whether by brandishing, displaying, threatening with, or otherwise employing, a firearm **or**
ii.	the offense involves two aggravating factors (chapter 4. section Y. Definitions) **or**
c.	25 grams or more containing heroin **or**
d.	500 grams or more containing amphetamine, phencyclidine, or hallucinogen, or if the substance is packaged in dosage units, equaling 500 or more dosage units

| | **or** |
| e. | 50 kilograms or more containing marijuana or Tetrahydrocannabinols. |

OR

| (4) | 500 or more marijuana plants. |

<u>Weight:</u> In a prosecution under the above possession crime section, the weight of fluid used in a water pipe may not be considered in measuring the weight of a mixture except in cases where the mixture contains four or more fluid ounces of fluid.

<u>Sentence Enhancement:</u> A person convicted under subparts (a) through (c) above where the person or an accomplice sold or possessed 100 or more grams or 500 or more dosage units of a mixture containing the controlled substance at issue may face increased penalties, including mandatory commitments to prison and/or increased maximum statutory sentence periods. M.S. § 152.021, subd. 3(c)

<u>Subsequent Controlled Substance Conviction:</u> A person convicted of Controlled Substance Crime in the First Degree may be subject to increased penalties, including mandatory commitments to prison, increased maximum fines, and/or increased maximum statutory sentence periods if the conviction is a subsequent controlled substance conviction (chapter 4, section Y, Definitions)

C.   AGGRAVATED CONTROLLED SUBSTANCE CRIME IN THE FIRST DEGREE
M.S. § 152.021, subd. 2b and subd. 3(d)
A person convicted of violating subpart (a) through (e) in Section A. above, or subpart (a) through (c) in Section B. above, when the person or an accomplice sells or possesses 100 or more grams or 500 or more dosage units of a mixture containing the controlled substance in question, **and**

(1)   the person or an accomplice possesses on their person or within immediate reach, or uses, whether by brandishing, displaying, threatening with, or otherwise employing, a firearm

or

(2)   the offense involves two aggravating factors (chapter 4. section X. Definitions) is subject to an increased mandatory prison sentence beyond that contemplated by an enhanced sentence under M. S. § 152.021, subd. 3(c).

<u>Jurisdiction:</u> In a prosecution under the above section involving sales by the same person in two or more counties within a 90-day period, the person may be prosecuted for all sales in any county in which one of the sales occurred.

D.   CONTROLLED SUBSTANCE CRIME IN THE FIRST DEGREE
Manufacture of Methamphetamine
M.S. § 152.021, subd. 2a (Felony)

Name
Date and Time of Offense
Location (Venue)

(1)	No person shall
(2)	manufacture
(3)	any amount of methamphetamine.

OR

(1)	No person shall
(2)	possess any chemical reagent or precursors
(3)	with the intent to manufacture methamphetamine.

E.   IMPORTING CONTROLLED SUBSTANCES ACROSS STATE BORDERS - First Degree Amount of Drugs and Use of a Minor
M.S. § 152.0261, subd. 1, 1a, 2, 3 (Felony)

Name
Date and Time of Offense
Location (Venue)

(1)	No person shall
(2)	cross a state or international border into Minnesota
(3)	while in possession of an amount of a controlled substance that constitutes a first degree controlled substance possession crime under M.S. § 152.021, subd. 2.

OR

(1)	No person shall
(2)	conspire with or employ a person
(3)	under the age of 18 years
(4)	to cross a state or international border into Minnesota
(5)	while that person or the person under the age of 18 is in possession of
(6)	an amount of controlled substance that constitutes a controlled substance crime in the 1st, 2nd, 3rd, 4th or 5th degree (M.S. §152.021 to § 152.025)
(7)	with the intent to obstruct the criminal justice process.

<u>Jurisdiction:</u> A violation of the above section may be charged, indicted, and tried in any county, but not more than one county, into or through which the actor has brought the controlled substance. M.S. § 152.0261, subd. 2.

F. **CONTROLLED SUBSTANCE CRIME IN THE SECOND DEGREE**
Sale Crimes
M.S. § 152.022, subd. 1 (Felony)

Name
Date and Time of Offense
Location (Venue)

(1)		No person shall
(2)		unlawfully sell
(3)		on one or more occasions within a 90-day period
(4)		one or more mixtures of a total weight of
(5)	a.	10 grams or more containing a narcotic drug other than heroin
		or
	b.	3 grams or more containing cocaine or methamphetamine, **and**
		i. the person or an accomplice possesses on their person or within immediate reach, or uses, whether by brandishing, displaying, threatening with, or otherwise employing, a firearm
		or
		ii. the offense involves three aggravating factors (chapter 4. section Y. Definitions)
		or
	c.	3 grams or more containing heroin
		or
	d.	10 grams or more containing amphetamine, phencyclidine (PCP), or hallucinogen <u>or</u> if the controlled substance is packaged in dosage units, equaling 50 or more dosage units
		or
	e.	10 kilograms or more containing marijuana or Tetrahydrocannabinols.

OR

(1)		No person shall unlawfully sell
(2)		any amount of a Schedule I or II narcotic drug
(3)	a.	to a person under the age of 18

		or
	b.	conspire with or employ a person under the age of 18 to unlawfully sell the substance.

OR

(1)		No person shall unlawfully sell
(2)		any of the following in a school zone, park zone, a public housing zone, or a drug treatment facility
	a.	any amount of a Schedule I or II narcotic drug or lysergic acid diethylamide (LSD), 3,4-methylenedioxy amphetamine, or 3,4-methylenedioxymethamphetamine.
		or
	b.	one or more mixtures containing methamphetamine or amphetamine.
		or
	c.	one or more mixtures of a total weight of five kilograms (11 lbs.) or more containing marijuana or Tetrahydrocannabinol (THC).

Aggregation: For sentencing purposes, separate sales on separate days are considered separate offenses. However, if separate sales within a 90-day period are aggregated under the above section, all sales are considered part of a single behavioral incident (M.S. § 609.035).

Jurisdiction: In a prosecution under any of the above sections involving sales by the same person in two or more counties within a 90-day period, the person may be prosecuted for all of the sales in any county in which one of the sales occurred.

Subsequent Controlled Substance Conviction: A person convicted of Controlled Substance Crime in the Second Degree may be subject to increased penalties, including mandatory commitments to prison, increased maximum fines, and/or increased maximum statutory sentence periods if the conviction is a subsequent controlled substance conviction (chapter 4, section Y, Definitions)

G. CONTROLLED SUBSTANCE CRIME IN THE SECOND DEGREE
Possession Crimes
M.S. § 152.022, subd. 2 (Felony)

Name

Date and Time of Offense

Location (Venue)

(1)   No person shall

(2)   unlawfully possess

(3)   one or more mixtures of a total weight of
a.   25 grams or more containing cocaine or methamphetamine
or

b.   10 grams or more containing cocaine or methamphetamine, **and**
i.   the person or an accomplice possesses on their person or within immediate reach, or uses, whether by brandishing, displaying, threatening with, or otherwise employing, a firearm
or
ii.   the offense involves three aggravating factors (Chapter 4, Section Y, Definitions)
or
c.   6 grams or more containing heroin
or
d.   50 grams or more containing a narcotic drug other than cocaine, heroin or methamphetamine
or
e.   50 grams or more containing amphetamine, phencyclidine (PCP), or hallucinogen <u>or</u> if the controlled substance is packaged in dosage units, equaling 100 or more dosage units
or
f.   25 kilograms or more containing marijuana or Tetrahydrocannabinol (THC).

OR

(4)   100 or more marijuana plants.

Weight: In a prosecution under the above possession crime section, the weight of fluid used in a water pipe may not be considered in measuring the weight of a mixture except in cases where the mixture contains four or more fluid ounces of fluid.

- 34 -

- <u>Subsequent Controlled Substance Conviction</u>: A person convicted of Controlled Substance Crime in the Second Degree may be subject to increased penalties, including mandatory commitments to prison, increased maximum fines, and/or increased maximum statutory sentence periods if the conviction is a subsequent controlled substance conviction (chapter 4, section Y, Definitions)

H. CONTROLLED SUBSTANCE CRIME IN THE THIRD DEGREE Sale Crimes
M.S. § 152.023, subd. 1 (Felony)

Name
Date and Time of Offense
Location (Venue)

(1)	No person shall	
(2)	unlawfully sell	
(3)	one or more mixtures	
	a.	containing a narcotic drug
		or
	b.	on one or more occasions within a 90-day period, the person unlawfully sells one or more mixtures containing phencyclidine (PCP) or hallucinogen if it is packaged in dosage units and equals 10 or more dosage units.
		or
	c.	containing a controlled substance classified in Schedule I, II, or III, except a Schedule I or II narcotic drug, to a person under the age of 18 (see section E. above, Controlled Substance Crime in the 2nd Degree).

OR

(1)	No person shall conspire with or employ a person
(2)	under the age of 18
(3)	to unlawfully sell one or more mixtures
(4)	containing a controlled substance listed in Schedule I, II, or III, except a Schedule I or II narcotic drug (see section E. above, Controlled Substance Crime in the 2nd Degree).

OR

(1)	On one or more occasions within a 90-day period, the person unlawfully sells
(2)	one or more mixtures of a total weight of

(3)	five kilograms (11 lbs.) or more containing marijuana or Tetrahydrocannabinol (THC).

Jurisdiction: In a prosecution under the above section involving sales or acts of possession by the same person in two or more counties within a 90-day period, the person may be prosecuted in any county in which one of the sales or acts of possession occurred.

I. CONTROLLED SUBSTANCE CRIME IN THE THIRD DEGREE Possession Crimes
M.S. § 152.023, subd. 2 (Felony)

Name
Date and Time of Offense
Location (Venue)

(1)	No person shall	
(2)	on one or more occasions within a 90-day period	
(3)	unlawfully possess	
(4)	one or more mixtures of a total weight of	
(5)	a.	three grams or more containing heroin
		or
	b.	10 grams or more containing a narcotic drug other than heroin
		or
	c.	10 kilograms (22 lbs.) or more containing marijuana or Tetrahydrocannabinol (THC).
Weight:	In a prosecution under the above possession crime section, the weight of fluid used in a water pipe may not be considered in measuring the weight of a mixture except in cases where the mixture contains four or more fluid ounces of fluid.	

OR

(1)	No person shall
(2)	on one or more occasions within a 90-day period
(3)	unlawfully possess
(4)	one or more mixtures
(5)	containing a narcotic drug if it is packaged in dosage units and equals 50 or more dosage units.

OR

(1)	No person shall

(2)	on one or more occasions within a 90-day period
(3)	unlawfully possess
(4)	any amount of a Schedule I or II narcotic drug or five or more dosage units of lysergic acid diethylamide (LSD), 3,4-methylenedioxy amphetamine, or 3,4-methylenedioxymethamphetamine
(5)	in a school zone, a park zone, a public housing zone, or a drug treatment facility.

OR

(1)	No person shall unlawfully possess
(2)	one or more mixtures
(3)	containing methamphetamine or amphetamine
(4)	in a school zone, a park zone, a public housing zone or a drug treatment facility.

Jurisdiction: In a prosecution under the above section involving sales or acts of possession by the same person in two or more counties within a 90-day period, the person may be prosecuted in any county in which one of the sales or acts of possession occurred.

Immunity from Prosecution (M.S. § 604A.05): A person acting in good faith who seeks medical assistance for another person who is experiencing a drug-related overdose may not be charged or prosecuted for the possession, sharing, or use of a controlled substance under M.S. § 152.023, subd. 2(4) and (6) (Controlled Substance Crime in the Third Degree – possession of any amount of Schedule I or II narcotic drug, five or more units of LSD, or one or more mixtures containing methamphetamine or amphetamine in a school zone, a park zone, a public housing zone, or a drug treatment facility), M.S. § 152.024 (Controlled Substance Crime in the Fourth Degree), M.S. § 152.025 (Controlled Substance Crime in the Fifth Degree) and M.S. § 152.092 (Possession of Drug Paraphernalia).

A person experiencing an overdose qualifies for the immunities provided only if:

a.	the evidence for the charge or prosecution was obtained as a result of the person seeking medical assistance for another person, and
b.	the person seeks medical assistance for another person who is in need of medical assistance for an immediate health or safety concern, provided that the person who seeks the

medical assistance is the first person to seek the assistance, provides a name and contact information, remains on the scene until assistance arrives or is provided, and cooperates with the authorities.

A person who experiences a drug-related overdose and is in need of medical assistance may not be charged or prosecuted for the possession, sharing, or use of a controlled substance under M.S. § 152.023, subd. 2(4) and (6) Controlled Substance Crime in the Third Degree – possession of any amount of a Schedule I or II narcotic drug, five or more units of LSD, or one or more mixtures containing methamphetamine or amphetamine in a school zone, a park zone, a public housing zone, or a drug treatment facility, M.S. § 152.024 (Controlled Substance Crime in the Fourth Degree), M.S. § 152.025 (Controlled Substance Crime in the Fifth Degree) and M.S. § 152.092 (Possession of Drug Paraphernalia).

A person experiencing an overdose qualifies for immunities provided only if the evidence of the charge or prosecution was obtained as a result of the drug-related overdose and the need for medical assistance.

J. **CONTROLLED SUBSTANCE CRIME IN THE FOURTH DEGREE**
Sale Crimes
M.S. § 152.024, subd. 1 (Felony)

Name
Date and Time of Offense
Location (Venue)

(1)	No person shall	
(2)	unlawfully sell	
(3)	one or more mixtures containing	
(4)	a.	a controlled substance classified in Schedule I, II or III <u>except</u> marijuana or Tetrahydrocannabinol (THC).
		or
	b.	a controlled substance classified in Schedule IV or V to a person under the age of 18.

OR

(1)	No person shall conspire with or employ a person
(2)	under the age of 18
(3)	to unlawfully sell a controlled substance classified in Schedule IV or V.

OR

> (1)   No person shall unlawfully sell
>
> (2)   any amount of marijuana or Tetrahydrocannabinol (THC)
>
> (3)   in a school zone, a park zone, a public housing zone, or a drug treatment facility, except a small amount for no remuneration (as defined in section X. "Definitions" below).

<u>Immunity from Prosecution (M.S. § 604A.05)</u>: A person acting in good faith who seeks medical assistance for another person who is experiencing a drug-related overdose may not be charged or prosecuted for the possession, sharing, or use of a controlled substance under M.S. § 152.023, subd. 2(4) and (6) (Controlled Substance Crime in the Third Degree – possession of any amount of Schedule I or II narcotic drug, five or more units of LSD, or one or more mixtures containing methamphetamine or amphetamine in a school zone, a park zone, a public housing zone, or a drug treatment facility), M.S. § 152.024 (Controlled Substance Crime in the Fourth Degree), M.S. § 152.025 (Controlled Substance Crime in the Fifth Degree) and M.S. § 152.092 (Possession of Drug Paraphernalia).

A person experiencing an overdose qualifies for the immunities provided only if:

    a.   the evidence for the charge or prosecution was obtained as a result of the person seeking medical assistance for another person, and

    b.   the person seeks medical assistance for another person who is in need of medical assistance for an immediate health or safety concern, provided that the person who seeks the medical assistance is the first person to seek the assistance, provides a name and contact information, remains on the scene until assistance arrives or is provided, and cooperates with the authorities.

A person who experiences a drug-related overdose and is in need of medical assistance may not be charged or prosecuted for the possession, sharing, or use of a controlled substance under M.S. § 152.023, subd. 2(4) and (6) Controlled Substance Crime in the Third Degree – possession of any amount of a Schedule I or II narcotic drug, five or more units of LSD, or one or more mixtures containing methamphetamine or amphetamine in a school zone, a park zone, a public housing zone, or a drug treatment facility, M.S. § 152.024 (Controlled Substance Crime in the Fourth Degree), M.S. § 152.025 (Controlled Substance Crime in the Fifth Degree) and M.S. § 152.092 (Possession of Drug Paraphernalia).

A person experiencing an overdose qualifies for immunities provided only if the evidence of the charge or prosecution was obtained as a result of the drug-related overdose and the need for medical assistance.

K.   CONTROLLED SUBSTANCE CRIME IN THE FOURTH DEGREE –
Possession Crimes
M.S. § 152.024, subd. 2 (Felony)

Name
Date and Time of Offense
Location (Venue)
(1)   No person shall
(2)   unlawfully possess
(3)   one or more mixtures
(4)   a.   containing phencyclidine (PCP) or hallucinogen, if it is packaged in dosage units, and equals 10 or more dosage units.
                 or
         b.   containing a controlled substance classified in Schedule I, II or III, <u>except</u> marijuana or Tetrahydrocannabinol (THC), with the intent to sell it.

L.   CONTROLLED SUBSTANCE CRIME IN THE FIFTH DEGREE - Sale Crimes
M.S. § 152.025, subd. 1 (Felony)

Name
Date and Time of Offense
Location (Venue)
(1)   No person shall
(2)   unlawfully sell
(3)   one or more mixtures
(4)   a.   containing marijuana or Tetrahydrocannabinol (THC), <u>except</u> a small amount of marijuana for no remuneration (as defined in section Y. "Definitions" below).
                 or
         b.   containing a controlled substance classified in Schedule IV.

<u>Immunity from Prosecution (M.S. § 604A.05)</u>: A person acting in good faith who seeks medical assistance for another person who is experiencing a drug-related overdose may not be charged or prosecuted for the possession, sharing, or use of a controlled substance under M.S. § 152.023, subd. 2(4) and (6) (Controlled Substance Crime in the Third Degree – possession of any amount of Schedule I or II narcotic drug, five or more units of LSD, or one or more mixtures containing methamphetamine or amphetamine in a school zone, a park

zone, a public housing zone, or a drug treatment facility), M.S. § 152.024 (Controlled Substance Crime in the Fourth Degree), M.S. § 152.025 (Controlled Substance Crime in the Fifth Degree) and M.S. § 152.092 (Possession of Drug Paraphernalia).

A person experiencing an overdose qualifies for the immunities provided only if:

    a.   the evidence for the charge or prosecution was obtained as a result of the person seeking medical assistance for another person, and

    b.   the person seeks medical assistance for another person who is in need of medical assistance for an immediate health or safety concern, provided that the person who seeks the medical assistance is the first person to seek the assistance, provides a name and contact information, remains on the scene until assistance arrives or is provided, and cooperates with the authorities.

A person who experiences a drug-related overdose and is in need of medical assistance may not be charged or prosecuted for the possession, sharing, or use of controlled substance under M.S. § 152.023, subd. 2(4) and (6) Controlled Substance Crime in the Third Degree – possession of any amount of a Schedule I or II narcotic drug, five or more units of LSD, or one or more mixtures containing methamphetamine or amphetamine in a school zone, a park zone, a public housing zone, or a drug treatment facility, M.S. § 152.024 (Controlled Substance Crime in the Fourth Degree), M.S. § 152.025 (Controlled Substance Crime in the Fifth Degree) and M.S. § 152.092 (Possession of Drug Paraphernalia).

A person experiencing an overdose qualifies for immunities provided only if the evidence of the charge or prosecution was obtained as a result of the drug-related overdose and the need for medical assistance.

M.   CONTROLLED SUBSTANCE CRIME IN THE FIFTH DEGREE - Possession and Other Crimes
M.S. § 152.025, subd. 2 (Felony – Gross Misdemeanor)

Name
Date and Time of Offense
Location (Venue)

(1)	No person shall
(2)	unlawfully possess
(3)	one or more mixtures
(4)	containing a controlled substance classified in Schedule I, II, III or IV, except a small amount of marijuana.

(1)	No person shall procure, attempt to procure, possess or have control over
(2)	a controlled substance
(3)	by any of the following means:
	a. fraud, deceit, misrepresentation or subterfuge
	or
	b. using a false name or giving false credit
	or

falsely assuming the title of, or falsely representing any person to be, a manufacturer, wholesaler, pharmacist, physician, doctor of osteopathy licensed to practice medicine, dentist, podiatrist, veterinarian, or other authorized person for the purpose of obtaining a controlled substance.

Potential gross misdemeanor sentence: A person who violates section M. – Controlled Substance Crime in the Fifth Degree – Possession, not including possession by fraud, false name, or false title as set forth in (3)a. – c. in box 2, and has not previously been convicted of a controlled substance offense under Minnesota Statutes Chapter 152 or similar offense in another jurisdiction, is guilty of a gross misdemeanor if: (1) the amount of the controlled substance possessed, other than heroin, is less than 0.25 grams or one dosage unit or less if the controlled substance was possessed in dosage units; or (2) the controlled substance possessed is heroin and the amount possessed is less than 0.05 grams. Jurisdiction for gross misdemeanors: Except in Hennepin and Ramsey Counties, only the county attorney shall prosecute gross misdemeanor Controlled Substance Crime in the Fifth Degree – Possession violations.

Immunity from Prosecution (M.S. § 604A.05): A person acting in good faith who seeks medical assistance for another person who is experiencing a drug-related overdose may not be charged or prosecuted for the possession, sharing, or use of a controlled substance under M.S. § 152.023, subd. 2(4) and (6) (Controlled Substance Crime in the Third Degree – possession of any amount of Schedule I or II narcotic drug, five or more units of LSD, or one or more mixtures containing methamphetamine or amphetamine in a school zone, a park zone, a public housing zone, or a drug treatment facility), M.S. § 152.024 (Controlled Substance Crime in the Fourth Degree), M.S. § 152.025 (Controlled Substance Crime in the Fifth Degree) and M.S. § 152.092 (Possession of Drug Paraphernalia).

A person experiencing an overdose qualifies for the immunities provided only if:

 a. the evidence for the charge or prosecution was obtained as a result of the person seeking medical assistance for another person, and

 b. the person seeks medical assistance for another person who is in need of medical assistance for an immediate health or safety concern, provided that the person who seeks the medical assistance is the first person to seek the assistance, provides a name and contact information, remains on the scene until assistance arrives or is provided, and cooperates with the authorities.

A person who experiences a drug-related overdose and is in need of medical assistance may not be charged or prosecuted for the possession, sharing, or use of a controlled substance under M.S. § 152.023, subd. 2(4) and (6) Controlled Substance Crime in the Third Degree – possession of any amount of a Schedule I or II narcotic drug, five or more units of LSD, or one or more mixtures containing methamphetamine or amphetamine in a school zone, a park zone, a public housing zone, or a drug treatment facility, M.S. § 152.024 (Controlled Substance Crime in the Fourth Degree), M.S. § 152.025 (Controlled Substance Crime in the Fifth Degree) and M.S. § 152.092 (Possession of Drug Paraphernalia).

A person experiencing an overdose qualifies for immunities provided only if the evidence of the charge or prosecution was obtained as a result of the drug-related overdose and the need for medical assistance.

N. **SALE OR POSSESSION OF SCHEDULE V CONTROLLED SUBSTANCE**
  M.S. § 152.027, subds. 1 and 2 (Gross Misdemeanor)

Name
Date and Time of Offense
Location (Venue)
(1) No person shall
(2) unlawfully sell or possess
(3) one or more mixtures
(4) containing a controlled substance classified in Schedule V.

Note: If defendant sells to, conspires with or employs a person under the age of 18 to unlawfully sell a Schedule IV or V Controlled Substance, defendant is

- 43 -

guilty of a **felony** – see section I. above, "Controlled Substance Crime in the Fourth Degree", M.S. § 152.024, subd. 1.

O. **SALE OR POSSESSION OF SALVIA DIVINORUM**
M.S. § 152.027, subd. 5 (Gross Misdemeanor, Misdemeanor)
Name
Date and Time of Offense
Location (Venue)
(1)   No person shall
        (a)   unlawfully sell any amount of salvia divinorum or savinorum A **(gross misdemeanor)**
              or
        (b)   unlawfully possess any amount of salvia divinorum or savinorum A **(misdemeanor).**

P. **SALE OR POSSESSION OF SYNTHETIC CANNABINOIDS**
M.S. § 152.027, subd. 6
(Felony, Gross Misdemeanor, Misdemeanor)
Name
Date and Time of Offense
Location (Venue)
(1)   No person shall
        (a)   unlawfully sell a synthetic cannabinoid **(felony)**
        (b)   unlawfully sell any amount of a synthetic cannabinoid **(gross misdemeanor)**
              or
        (c)   unlawfully possess any amount of a synthetic cannabinoid **(misdemeanor).**

Q. **POSSESSION OF MARIJUANA IN A MOTOR VEHICLE**
M.S. § 152.027, subd. 3 (Misdemeanor)
Name
Date and Time of Offense
Location (Venue)
(1)   No person shall
(2)   if the person is the owner of a private motor vehicle <u>or</u>
          is the driver of the motor vehicle if the owner is not present
(3)   possess on the person, <u>or</u>
          knowingly keep, <u>or</u>
          allow to be kept within the area of the vehicle normally occupied by the driver or passenger

(4)   more than 1.4 grams of marijuana (1.4 grams = approximately 3 to 5 marijuana cigarettes - see definition of "small amount of marijuana" in section X. "Definitions", below).

Note: The above section does not include the trunk of the motor vehicle if the vehicle is equipped with a trunk, or other area of the vehicle not normally occupied by the driver or passengers if the vehicle is not equipped with a trunk. The utility or glove compartment is deemed to be within the area occupied by the driver and passengers.

Note: Possession of controlled substance - drivers license revocation: If a suspect is convicted of or adjudicated for violating any of the above sections (A. to P.) or section Q. below, and if the suspect unlawfully sold or possessed the controlled substance while driving a motor vehicle, the Court shall order the Commissioner of Public Safety to revoke the defendant's drivers license for 30 days (M.S. § 171.172).

R.   POSSESSION OR SALE OF SMALL AMOUNTS OF MARIJUANA
M.S. § 152.027, subd. 4 (Petty Misdemeanor - Misdemeanor)

Name
Date and Time of Offense
Location (Venue)

(1)   No person shall
(2)   a.   unlawfully sell (give away) a small amount of marijuana for no remuneration (as defined in section X. "Definitions" below) **(petty misdemeanor).**
or
         b.   unlawfully possess a small amount of marijuana **(petty misdemeanor).**

Enhancement: Any person convicted of an unlawful sale under the above provision who is subsequently convicted of an unlawful sale under the above provision within two years is guilty of a **misdemeanor**, rather than a petty misdemeanor. ("Sell" is defined in section X. "Definitions" below.)

S.   POSSESSION OF DRUG PARAPHERNALIA PROHIBITED
M.S. § 152.092 (Petty Misdemeanor - Misdemeanor)

Name
Date and Time of Offense
Location (Venue)

(1)   No person shall
(2)   knowingly or intentionally
(3)   use or possess drug paraphernalia.

Enhancement: A person who violates this section and has previously violated this section on two or more occasions is guilty of a **misdemeanor**.

Immunity from Prosecution (M.S. § 604A.05): A person acting in good faith who seeks medical assistance for another person who is experiencing a drug-related overdose may not be charged or prosecuted for the possession, sharing, or use of a controlled substance under M.S. § 152.023, subd. 2(4) and (6) (Controlled Substance Crime in the Third Degree – possession of any amount of Schedule I or II narcotic drug, five or more units of LSD, or one or more mixtures containing methamphetamine or amphetamine in a school zone, a park zone, a public housing zone, or a drug treatment facility), M.S. § 152.024 (Controlled Substance Crime in the Fourth Degree), M.S. § 152.025 (Controlled Substance Crime in the Fifth Degree) and M.S. § 152.092 (Possession of Drug Paraphernalia).

A person experiencing an overdose qualifies for the immunities provided only if:

> a.   the evidence for the charge or prosecution was obtained as a result of the person seeking medical assistance for another person, and
>
> b.   the person seeks medical assistance for another person who is in need of medical assistance for an immediate health or safety concern, provided that the person who seeks the medical assistance is the first person to seek the assistance, provides a name and contact information, remains on the scene until assistance arrives or is provided, and cooperates with the authorities.

A person who experiences a drug-related overdose and is in need of medical assistance may not be charged or prosecuted for the possession, sharing, or use of a controlled substance under M.S. § 152.023, subd. 2(4) and (6) Controlled Substance Crime in the Third Degree – possession of any amount of a Schedule I or II narcotic drug, five or more units of LSD, or one or more mixtures containing methamphetamine or amphetamine in a school zone, a park zone, a public housing zone, or a drug treatment facility, M.S. § 152.024 (Controlled Substance Crime in the Fourth Degree), M.S. § 152.025 (Controlled Substance Crime in the Fifth Degree) and M.S. § 152.092 (Possession of Drug Paraphernalia).

A person experiencing an overdose qualifies for immunities provided only if the evidence of the charge or prosecution was obtained as a result of the drug-related overdose and the need for medical assistance.

T. MANUFACTURE OR DELIVERY OF DRUG PARAPHERNALIA PROHIBITED
M.S. § 152.093 (Misdemeanor)

Name

Date and Time of Offense

Location (Venue)

(1)   No person shall

(2)   knowingly or intentionally

(3)   a.   deliver drug paraphernalia.

           or

           b.   possess or manufacture drug paraphernalia for delivery.

Enhancement to Gross Misdemeanor:

Two or more prior convictions - Any person who violates the above section is guilty of a **gross misdemeanor** if the Court determines at the time of sentencing that the person has two or more prior convictions in this or any other state for any of the following misdemeanor-level crimes: manufacture or delivery of drug paraphernalia prohibited (§ 152.093); prostitution (§ 609.324); loitering with intent to participate in prostitution (§ 609.3243); motor vehicle tampering (§ 609.546); damage to property (§ 609.595); dangerous weapons (§ 609.66); trespass (misdemeanor-level violations of § 609.605); or violations of local ordinances prohibiting the unlawful sale or possession of controlled substances. M.S. § 609.153, subd. 1, 3.

U. DELIVERY OF DRUG PARAPHERNALIA TO A MINOR PROHIBITED
M.S. § 152.094 (Gross Misdemeanor)

Name

Date and Time of Offense

Location (Venue)

(1)   No person, 18 years of age or older, shall

(2)   violate M.S. § 152.093 (see section S. above)

(3)   by knowingly or intentionally

(4)   delivering drug paraphernalia to a person under 18 years of age

(5)   who is at least three years younger than the accused.

V.   SIMULATED CONTROLLED SUBSTANCES
M.S. § 152.097, subds. 1, 2, 3 (Felony)

Name

Date and Time of Offense

Location (Venue)

(1)   No person shall

(2)   knowingly manufacturer, sell, transfer or deliver or attempt to sell, transfer or deliver

(3)   a non-controlled substance upon:

    a.   the expressed representation that the non-controlled substance is a narcotic or non-narcotic controlled substance.

       or

    b.   the expressed representation that the substance is of such nature or appearance that the recipient of the delivery will be able to sell, transfer or deliver the substance as a controlled substance.

       or

    c.   under circumstances which would lead a reasonable person to believe that the substance was a controlled substance.

<u>Note:</u> Any of the following factors shall constitute relevant evidence:

    (i)   the non-controlled substance was packaged in a manner normally used for the illegal delivery of controlled substances, or

    (ii)   the delivery or attempted delivery included an exchange or demand for money or other valuable property as consideration for delivery of the non-controlled substance, and the amount of the consideration was substantially in excess of the reasonable value of the non-controlled substance, or

    (iii)   the physical appearance of the non-controlled substance is substantially identical to a specified controlled substance.

<u>No Defense:</u>   It is no defense that the accused believed the non-controlled substance to actually be a controlled substance.

<u>Exemption:</u> The above section does not apply to the prescribing and dispensing of placebos by licensed practitioners and licensed pharmacists.

W. RESTRICTIONS ON METHAMPHETAMINE PRECURSOR DRUGS
M.S. § 152.02, subd. 6 (Misdemeanor)

Name
Date and Time of Offense
Location (Venue)

(1)	No person shall
(2)	sell in a single over-the-counter sale
(3)	more than two packages of a methamphetamine precursor drug
	or
	a combination of methamphetamine precursor drugs
	or
	or any combination of packages exceeding a total weight of six grams.

OR

(1)	No business establishment that offers methamphetamine precursor drugs for sale shall fail to ensure that
	(a) all packages of the drugs are displayed behind a checkout counter where the public is not permitted; **and**
	(b) all drugs are offered for sale only by a licensed pharmacist, a registered pharmacy technician, or a pharmacy clerk.
(2)	The person making the sale shall ensure the buyer
	(a) provides a photographic identification showing the buyer's date of birth; **and**
	(b) signs a written or electronic document detailing the date of sale, name of buyer, and amount of drug sold.

OR

(1)	No person shall
(2)	acquire through over-the-counter sales more than six grams of methamphetamine precursor drugs
(3)	within a 30-day period.

OR

(1)	No person shall
(2)	sell in an over-the-counter sale
(3)	a methamphetamine precursor drug to a person under the age of 18 years.

Note: It is an affirmative defense if the defendant proves by a preponderance of the evidence that the defendant acted reasonably and in good faith relied on proof of age as described in M.S. § 340A.503, subd. 6.

Note: An owner, operator, supervisor, or manager of a business establishment whose employee is convicted for violating the above section is not subject to criminal penalties, if the person:

(a)   did not have prior knowledge of, participate in, or direct the employee or agent to commit the violation; **and**

(b)   documents that an employee training program was in place to provide the employee or agent with information on the state and federal laws and regulations regarding methamphetamine precursor drugs.

Note: Over-the-counter sales of methamphetamine precursor drugs are limited to:

(a)   packages containing not more than a total of three grams of one or more methamphetamine precursor drugs, calculated in terms of ephedrine base or pseudoephedrine base; **or**

(b)   for nonliquid products, sales in blister packs, where each blister contains not more than two dosage units, or, if the use of blister packs is not   technically feasible, sales in unit dose packets or pouches.

And the statute does not apply to:

(a)   pediatric products labeled pursuant to federal regulation primarily intended for administration to children under 12 years of age according to label instructions;

(b)   methamphetamine precursor drugs that are certified by the Board of Pharmacy as being manufactured in a manner that prevents the drug from being used to manufacture methamphetamine;

(c)   methamphetamine precursor drugs in gel capsule or liquid form; or

(d)   compounds, mixtures, or preparations in powder form where pseudoephedrine constitutes less than one percent of its total weight and is not its sole active ingredient.

Note: Wholesale drug distributors licensed and regulated by the Board of Pharmacy pursuant to M.S. § 151.42 to § 151.51 and registered with and regulated by the United States Drug Enforcement Administration are exempt from the methamphetamine precursor drug storage requirements of this section.

X. METHAMPHETAMINE-RELATED CRIMES INVOLVING CHILDREN AND VULNERABLE ADULTS
M.S. § 152.137, subd. 2a (Felony)

Name

Date and Time of Offense

Location (Venue)

(1)	No person shall
(2)	knowingly engage
	(a) in the presence of a child or vulnerable adult
	or
	(b) in the residence of a child or a vulnerable adult
	or
	(c) in a building, structure, conveyance, or outdoor location where a child or vulnerable adult might reasonably be expected to be present
	or
	(d) in a room offered to the public for overnight accommodation
	or
	(e) in any multiple unit residential building:
(3)	in any of the following activities
	(a) manufacturing or attempting to manufacture methamphetamine
	or
	(b) storing any chemical substance
	or
	(c) storing any methamphetamine waste products
	or
	(d) storing any methamphetamine paraphernalia.

OR

(1)	No person shall
(2)	knowingly cause or permit a child or vulnerable adult
(3)	to inhale, be exposed to, have contact with, or ingest
(4)	methamphetamine, a chemical substance, or methamphetamine paraphernalia.

<u>Note</u>: Notwithstanding M.S. § 609.035 and § 609.04, a prosecution for or conviction under this section is not a bar to conviction of or punishment for any other crime committed by the defendant as part of the same conduct.

Y.   DEFINITIONS:

(1) Aggravating Factor (M.S. § 152.01, subd. 24)

"Aggravating factor" includes

(a)   the defendant, within the previous ten years, has been convicted of a violent crime as defined in Section 34, Definitions, other than a violation of this section

(b)   the offense was committed for the benefit of a gang under M.S. § 609.229

(c)   the offense involved separate acts of sale or possession of a controlled substance in three or more counties

(d)   the offense involved the transfer of controlled substances across a state or international border and into Minnesota

(e)   the offense involved at least three separate transactions in which controlled substances were sold, transferred, or possessed with intent to sell or transfer

(f)   the circumstances of the offense reveal the offender to have occupied a high position in the drug distribution hierarchy

(g)   the defendant used a position or status to facilitate the commission of the offense, including positions of trust, confidence, or fiduciary relationships

(h)   the offense involved the sale of a controlled substance to a person under the age of 18 or a vulnerable adult as defined in M.S. § 609.232, subd. 11

(i)   the defendant or an accomplice manufactured, possessed, or sold a controlled substance in a school zone, park zone, correctional facility, or drug treatment facility

(j)   or, the defendant or an accomplice possessed equipment, drug paraphernalia, documents, or money evidencing that the offense involved the cultivation, manufacture, distribution, or possession of controlled substances in quantities substantially larger than the minimum threshold amount of the offense.

(2)   **Analog** (M.S. § 152.01, subd. 23)

"Analog" means a substance, chemical structure of which is substantially similar to the chemical structure of a controlled substance in Schedule I or II that has a stimulant, depressant, or hallucinogenic effect on the central nervous system that is substantially similar to or greater than the stimulant, depressant, or hallucinogenic effect on the central nervous system of a controlled substance in Schedule I or II; or with respect to a particular person, if the person represents or intends that the substance have a stimulant, depressant, or hallucinogenic effect on the central nervious system that is substantially similar to or greater than the stimulant, depressant, or hallucinogenic effect on the central nervous system of a controlled substance in Schedule I or II.

"Analog" does not include a controlled substance; any substance for which there is an approved new drug application under the Federal Food, Drug, and Cosmetic Act; or with respect to a particular person, if an exemption is in effect for investigational use, for that person, as provided by the Federal Code, and the person is registered as a controlled substance researcher as required by M.S. § 152.12, subd. 3 to the extent conduct with respect to the substance is pursuant to the exemption and registration.

(3)   **Chemical reagents or precursors** (M.S. § 152.01, subd. 2a)
"Chemical reagents or precursors" includes any of the following substances, or any similar substances that can be used to manufacture methamphetamine, or the salts, isomers, and salts of isomers of a listed or similar substances: ephedrine, pseudo-ephedrine, phenyl-2-propanone, phenylacetone, anhydrous ammonia, organic solvents, hydrochloric acid, lithium metal,sodium metal, ether, sulfuric acid, red phosphorus, iodine, sodium hydroxide, benzaldehyde, benzyl methyl ketone, benzyl cyanide, nitroethane, methylamine, phenylacetic acid, hydriodic acid, or hydriotic acid.

(4)   **Chemical substance** (M.S. § 152.137, subd.1b)
"Chemical substance" means a substance intended to be used as a precursor in the manufacture of methamphetamine or any other chemical intended to be used in the manufacture of methamphetamine.

(5)   **Child** (M.S. § 152.137, subd. 1c)
"Child" means any person under the age of 18 years.

(6)   **Controlled substance** (M.S. § 152.01, subd. 4)
"Controlled substance" means a drug, substance or immediate precursor in Schedules I-V of M.S. § 152.02. The term shall not include distilled spirits, wine, malt beverages, intoxicating liquors or tobacco.

(7)   **Drug paraphernalia** (M.S. § 152.01, subd. 18)
(a)   Except as otherwise provided in paragraph (b), "drug paraphernalia" means all equipment, products and materials of any kind, except those items used in conjunction with permitted uses of controlled substances in Chapter 152 (Prohibited Drugs) or the Uniform Controlled Substances Act, which are knowingly or intentionally used primarily in (1) manufacturing a controlled substance, (2) injecting, ingesting, inhaling or otherwise introducing into the human body a controlled substance, (3) testing the strength, effectiveness or purity of a controlled substance, or (4) enhancing the effect of a controlled substance.

(b) "drug paraphernalia" does not include the possession, manufacture, delivery, or sale of hypodermic needles or syringes in accordance with section 151.40, subd. 2.

(8) **Drug Treatment Facility** M.S. § 152.01, subd. 22)

"Drug treatment facility" means any facility in which a residential rehabilitation program licensed under Minnesota Rules, parts 9530.4100 to 9530.4450, is located, and includes any property owned, leased, or controlled by the facility.

(9) **Hallucinogen** (M.S. § 152.01, subd. 5a)

"Hallucinogen" means any hallucinogen listed in Schedule I, M.S. § 152.02, subd. 2, clause (3), or Minnesota Rules, Part 6800.4210, Item C, except marijuana and Tetrahydrocannabinol (THC). A nonexclusive list of hallucinogens includes the following: lysergic acid diethylamide (LSD and blotter acid), mescaline, psilocybin and psilocin (mushrooms), Dimethoxyamphetamine (DOM and STP), dimethyltryptamine (DMT), peyote, etc.

(10) **Marijuana** (M.S. § 152.01, subd. 9)

"Marijuana" means all parts of the plant of any species of the genus Cannabis, including all agronomical varieties, whether growing or not; the seeds thereof; the resin extracted from any part of such plant; and every compound, manufacture, salt, derivative, mixture or preparation of such plant, its seeds or resin, but shall not include the mature stalks of such plant, fiber from such stalks, oil or cake made from the seeds of such plant, any other compound, manufacture, salt, derivative, mixture or preparation of such mature stalks, except the resin extracted therefrom, fiber, oil or cake, or the sterilized seed of such plant which is incapable of germination.

(11) **Methamphetamine paraphernalia** (M.S. § 152.137, subd.1d)

"Methamphetamine paraphernalia" means all equipment, products, and materials of any kind that are used, intended for use, or designed for use in manufacturing, injecting, ingesting, inhaling, or otherwise introducing methamphetamine into the human body.

(12) **Methamphetamine precursor drug** (M.S. § 152.02, subd. 6)

"Methamphetamine precursor drug" means any compound, mixture, or preparation intended for human consumption contain-ing ephedrine or pseudoephedrine as its sole active ingredient or as one of its active ingredients.

(13) **Methamphetamine waste products** (M.S. § 152.137, subd. 1e)

"Methamphetamine waste products" means substances, chemicals, or items of any kind used in the manufacture of methamphetamine or any part of the manufacturing process, or the by-products or degradates of manufacturing methamphetamine.

(14)   **Mixture** (M.S. § 152.01, subd. 9a)

"Mixture" means a preparation, compound, mixture or substance containing a controlled substance, regardless of purity. Fluid used in a water pipe may not be considered in measuring the weight of a mixture except in cases where the mixture contains four or more fluid ounces of fluid.

(15)   **Narcotic drugs** (M.S. § 152.01, subds. 10,11)

A nonexclusive list of "narcotic" drugs includes the following: opium, coca leaves, cocaine, crack cocaine, codeine, morphine, heroin, percodan, methamphetamine and opiates which includes any dangerous substance having an addiction-forming or addiction-sustaining liability similar to morphine or being capable of conversion into a drug having such addiction-forming or addiction-sustaining liability.

(16)   **"Over-the-counter sale"** (M.S. § 152.02, subd. 6)

"Over-the-counter sale" means a retail sale of a drug or product but does not include the sale of a drug or product pursuant to the terms of a valid prescription.

(17)   **Park zone** (M.S. § 152.09, subd. 12a)

"Park zone" means an area designated as a public park by the federal government, the state, a local unit of government, a park district board or a park and recreation board in a city of the first class (population over 100,000). Park zone includes the area within 300 feet or one city block, whichever distance is greater, of the park boundary.

(18)   **Public housing zone** (M.S. § 152.01, subd. 19)

"Public housing zone" means any public housing project or development administered by a local housing agency, plus the area within 300 feet of the property's boundary, or one city block, whichever distance is greater.

(19)   **Remuneration** (State v. Hart, 393 N.W.2d 707 (Minn. App. 1986))

"Remuneration" means receiving money or other consideration for a controlled substance, whether or not the recipient realized any profit on the transaction.

(20)   **Sale of controlled substance**

(See #27 below defining "sell".)

(21)   **Schedule I controlled substance** (M.S. § 152.02, subds. 2,7)

A "Schedule I controlled substance" has a high potential for abuse, not currently accepted medical use in the United States and a lack of accepted safety for use under medical supervision. A nonexclusive list of Schedule I controlled substances includes the following: methacathinone, cathinone, lysergic acid diethylamide (LSD and blotter acid), mescaline, psilocybin and psilocin (mushrooms), marijuana, tetrahydrocannabinol (THC), morphine, heroin, codeine, peyote, etc.

(22)   **Schedule II controlled substance** (M.S. § 152.02, subds. 3,7)

A "Schedule II controlled substance" has a high potential for abuse, currently accepted medical use in the United States or currently accepted medical use with severe restrictions, and that abuse may lead to severe psychological or physical dependence. A nonexclusive list of Schedule II controlled substances includes: cocaine, crack cocaine, opium, codeine, morphine, poppy straw, coca leaves, methadone, amphetamine, methamphetamine, secobarbital (seconal), phencyclidine (PCP), etc.

(23)   **Schedule III controlled substance** (M.S. § 152.02, subds.4,7)

A "Schedule III controlled substance" has a potential for abuse less than the substances listed in Schedules I and II, currently accepted medical use and treatment in the United States, and that abuse may lead to moderate or low physical dependence or high psychological dependence. A nonexclusive list of Schedule III controlled substances includes: amphetamines, methamphetamines, codeine, opium, morphine, anabolic substances (steroids) and growth hormones, etc.

(24)   **Schedule IV controlled substance** (M.S. § 152.02, subds. 5,7)

A "Schedule IV controlled substance" has a low potential for abuse relative to the substances in Schedule III, currently accepted medical use and treatment in the United States, and that abuse may lead to limited physical dependence or psychological dependency relative to the substances in Schedule III. A nonexclusive list of Schedule IV controlled substances includes the following: Diazepam (Valium) and Phenobarbital, etc.

(25)   **Schedule V controlled substance** (M.S. § 152.02, subds. 6,7)

A "Schedule V controlled substance" has a low potential for abuse relative to the substances listed in Schedule IV, currently accepted medical use and treatment in the United States, and limited physical dependence and/or psychological dependence liability relative to the substances listed in Schedule IV. Schedule V controlled substances include compounds and/or mixtures that include certain narcotic drugs and one or more
non-narcotic active medicinal ingredients in sufficient proportion to confer upon the compound, mixture or preparation valuable medicinal qualities other than those possessed by the narcotic drug.

(26)   **School zone** (M.S. § 152.01, subd. 14a)

"School zone" means:

a.   any property owned, leased or controlled by a school district or an organization operating a nonpublic school, as defined in M.S. § 123.932, subd. 3, where an elementary, middle, secondary school, secondary vocational center or other school providing educational services in grade 1-12 is located, or used for educational purposes, or where extracurricular or cocurricular activities are regularly provided;

b.   the area surrounding school property as described in Clause (a) to a distance of 300 feet or one city block, whichever distance is greater, beyond the school property; and

c.   the area within a school bus when that bus is being used to transport one or more elementary or secondary school students.

(27)   **Sell (Sale)** (M.S. § 152.01, subd. 15a)

"Sell" (sale) means:

a.   to sell, give away, barter, deliver, exchange, distribute or dispose of to another, or to manufacture; or

b.   to offer or agree to perform an act listed in clause (a); or

c.   to possess with intent to perform an act listed in clause (a).

(28)   **Small amount of marijuana** (M.S. § 152.01, subd. 16)

"Small amount of marijuana" means 42.5 grams or less. This provision does not apply to the resinous form of marijuana. The weight of fluid used in a water pipe may not be considered in determining a small amount except in cases where the marijuana is mixed with four or more fluid ounces of fluid. (42.5 grams is equivalent to 1.5 ounces, excluding the weight of mature stalks. To determine exact quantities, officers should check with the B.C.A. or their local crime lab. However, as a general rule of thumb, a small amount of marijuana roughly translates to 84 to 127 marijuana cigarettes; 6 to 10 quarter-ounce baggies, or one full sandwich-size bag or less. One marijuana cigarette = approximately 1/2 to 1/3 of a gram.)

(29)   **Subsequent controlled substance conviction** (M.S. § 152.01, subd. 16a)

"Subsequent controlled substance conviction" means that before the commission of the offense for which the person is convicted under this chapter, the person was convicted of Controlled Substance Crime in the First Degree (152.021) or Controlled Substance Crime in the Second Degree (152.022), including an attempt or conspiracy, or was convicted of a similar offense by the United States or another state, provided that ten years have not elapsed since discharge from sentence.

(30) **Synthetic cannabinoid** (M.S. § 152.02, subd. 2(7))

"Synthetic cannabinoid" includes any natural or synthetic material, compound, or mixture, or preparation that contains any quantity of a substance that is a cannabinoid receptor agonist, including any of the substances listed in M.S. § 152.02, subd. 2(7) and their analogs.

(31) **Unlawfully** (M.S. § 152.01, subd. 20)

"Unlawfully" means selling or possessing a controlled substance in a manner not authorized by law.

(32) **Vulnerable adult** (M.S. § 152.137, subd. 1f)

"Vulnerable adult" has the meaning given in section 609.232, subd. 11.

COUNTERFEITING OF CURRENCY
M.S. § 609.632, subd. 1, 2, 3
(Gross Misdemeanor – Felony)
Name
Date and Time of Offense
Location (Venue)
(1)   No person shall
(2)   with the intent to defraud,

     a.   falsely make, alter, print, scan, image, or copy any United States postal money order, United States currency, Federal Reserve note, or other obligation or security of the United States so that it purports to be genuine or has different terms or provisions than that of the United States Postal Service or United States Treasury; (subd. 1)

         or

     b.   make, engrave, possess, or transfer a plate or instrument, computer, printer, camera, software, paper, cloth, fabric, ink or other material for the false reproduction of any United States postal money order, United States currency, Federal Reserve note, or other obligation or security of the United States; (subd. 2)

         or

     c.   utter or possess with intent to utter any counterfeit United States postal money order, United States currency, Federal Reserve note, or other obligation or security of the United States, having reason to know that the money order, currency, note or obligation or security is forged, counterfeited, falsely made, altered, or printed. (subd. 3)

Aggregation: In any prosecution under this section, the value of the counterfeited United States postal money orders, United States currency, Federal Reserve notes, or other obligations or securities of the United States, offered by defendant in violation of this section within any six-month period may be aggregated and defendant charged accordingly in applying the provisions of this section.

Jurisdiction: When two or more offenses are committed by the same person in two or more counties, the accused may be prosecuted in any county in which one of the counterfeited items was forged, offered, or possessed, for all of the offenses aggregated under this section.

Penalties:

If a person is convicted under subd. 1 or 2, the penalty is a **twenty-year felony**, with a maximum fine of $100,000.

A person convicted under subd. 3 is subject to the following penalties:

(a) A **twenty-year felony** and/or a $100,000 fine, if the counterfeited item is used to obtain property or services valued at more than $35,000, or the aggregate face value of the counterfeited item is more than $35,000;

(b) A **ten-year felony** and/or a $20,000 fine, if the counterfeited item is used to obtain property or services valued at more than $5,000, or the aggregate face value of the counterfeited item is more than $5,000;

(c) A **five-year felony** and/or a $10,000 fine, if:

  (i) the counterfeited item is used to obtain property or services valued at more than $1,000, or the aggregate face value of the counterfeited item is more than $1,000;

  OR

  (ii) the counterfeited item is used to obtain property or services valued at no more than $1,000, or the aggregate face value of the counterfeited item is no more than $1,000

    AND

    the person has been convicted within the last five years for an offense under this section, or M.S. § 609.24, § 609.245, § 609.52, § 609.53, § 609.582 (subd. 1, 2, or 3), § 609.625, § 609.63, or § 609.821; or a statute from another state or the United States in conformity with any of those sections;

    AND

    the person received a felony or gross misdemeanor sentence for the offense, or a sentenced stayed under § 609.135, if the offense pled to would have allowed a felony or gross misdemeanor sentence;

(d) A **gross misdemeanor** if the counterfeited item is used to obtain property or services valued at no more than $1,000, or the aggregate face value of the counterfeited item is no more than $1,000.

6. CRIMINAL SEXUAL CONDUCT

A. **CRIMINAL SEXUAL CONDUCT IN THE FIRST DEGREE -**
Sexual Penetration - Sexual Contact
M.S. § 609.342, subd. 1 (Felony)

Name

Date and Time of Offense

Location (Venue)

(1)   No person shall

(2)   engage in **sexual penetration** with another person
        or

(3)   engage in **sexual contact** with a person under 13 ("sexual contact" as
        used in this section has a special definition - see Section F, #15c
        below)

IF

(4)	a.	the complainant is under 13 years of age
	b.	and the defendant is more than 36 months older than the complainant.

Note: Neither mistake as to the complainant's age nor consent to
the act by the complainant is a defense.

OR

(5)	a.	the complainant is at least 13 but less than 16 years of age
	b.	and the defendant is more than 48 months older than the complainant
	c.	and in a position of authority over the complainant

Note: Neither mistake as to the complainant's age nor consent to
the act to the complainant is a defense.

OR

(6)	circumstances existing at the time of the act cause the complainant to have a reasonable fear of imminent great bodily harm to the complainant or another.

OR

(7)	a.	defendant is armed with a dangerous weapon or any article used or fashioned in a manner to lead the complainant to reasonably believe it to be a dangerous weapon
	b.	and uses or threatens to use the weapon or article to cause the complainant to submit.

OR

(8)		defendant causes personal injury to the complainant and either of the following circumstances exist:
	a.	defendant uses force or coercion to accomplish sexual penetration.
		or
	b.	defendant knows or has reason to know that complainant is mentally impaired, mentally incapacitated or physically helpless.

OR

(9)	a.	defendant is aided or abetted by one or more accomplices within the meaning of M.S. § 609.05
	b.	and either of the following circumstances exist:
	i.	an accomplice uses force or coercion to cause the complainant to submit.
		or
	ii.	an accomplice is armed with a dangerous weapon or any article used or fashioned in a manner to lead the complainant reasonably to believe it to be a dangerous weapon and uses or threatens to use the weapon or article to cause the complainant to submit.

OR

(10)	a.	defendant has a significant relationship to the complainant
	b.	and the complainant was under 16 years of age at the time of the sexual penetration.

Note: Neither mistake as to the complainant's age nor consent to the act by the complainant is a defense.

OR

(11)	a.	defendant has a significant relationship to the complainant,
	b.	the complainant was under 16 years of age at the time of the sexual penetration and;
	i.	defendant or an accomplice used force or coercion to accomplish the penetration.
		or
	ii.	the complainant suffered personal injury.
		or
	iii.	the sexual abuse involved multiple acts committed over an extended period of time.

Note: Neither mistake as to the complainant's age nor consent to the act by the complainant is a defense.

● Jurisdiction - Child Victim: If the victim is a child (under 18 years), violation of any of the above sections may be prosecuted in either the county where the incident occurred or where the child was found (M.S. § 627.15).

● **B.** **CRIMINAL SEXUAL CONDUCT IN THE SECOND DEGREE - Sexual Contact**
M.S. § 609.343, subd. 1 (Felony)

Note: The elements for Criminal Sexual Conduct in the Second Degree are exactly the same as for First Degree except for one important distinction:

      (a)   **First Degree:** "No person shall engage in **sexual penetration** with another" etc.

                    vs.

      (b)   **Second Degree:** "No person shall engage in **sexual contact** with another" etc.

Other than the distinction between "sexual penetration" and "sexual contact" the two statutes are identical.

● Jurisdiction - Child Victim: If the victim is a child (under 18 years), violations of the above section may be prosecuted in either the county where the incident occurred or where the child was found (M.S. § 627.15).

C. **CRIMINAL SEXUAL CONDUCT IN THE THIRD DEGREE - Sexual Penetration**
M.S. § 609.344, subd. 1 (Felony)

Name
Date and Time of Offense
Location (Venue)
(1)   No person shall
(2)   engage in **sexual penetration**
(3)   with another person
          IF

(4)	a.	the complainant is under 13 years of age
	b.	and defendant is no more than 36 months older than complainant.

Note: Neither mistake as to the complainant's age nor consent to the act by the complainant is a defense.

OR

(5)	a.	the complainant is at least 13 but less than 16 years of age
	b.	and defendant is more than 24 months older than complainant.

Defense: If the actor is no more than 120 months older than the complainant, it shall be an affirmative defense, which must be proved by a preponderance of the evidence, that defendant reasonably believed the complainant to be 16 years of age or older. In all other cases, mistake as to the complainant's age shall not be a defense. Consent by complainant is not a defense.

OR

(6)	defendant used force or coercion to accomplish the penetration.

OR

(7)	defendant knows or has reason to know that complainant is mentally impaired, mentally incapacitated or physically helpless.

OR

(8)	a.	the complainant is at least 16 but less than 18 years of age
	b.	and the defendant is more than 48 months older than the complainant
	c.	and in a position of authority over complainant

Note: Neither mistake as to the complainant's age nor consent to the act by the complainant is a defense.

OR

(9)	a.	defendant has a significant relationship to complainant
	b.	and the complainant was at least 16 but under 18 years of age at the time of the sexual penetration.

Note: Neither mistake as to the complainant's age nor consent to the act by the complainant is a defense.

OR

(10)	a.	defendant has a significant relationship to complainant
	b.	the complainant was at least 16 but under 18 years of age at the time of the sexual penetration and:
	i.	defendant or an accomplice used force or coercion to accomplish the penetration.
		or
	ii.	the complainant suffered personal injury.
		or

		iii.	the sexual abuse involved multiple acts committed over an extended period of time.
Note: Neither mistake as to the complainant's age nor consent to the act by the complainant is a defense.			

OR

(11)	a.	defendant is a psychotherapist
	b.	and the complainant is a patient of the psycho-therapist
	c.	and the sexual penetration occurred:
		i. during the psychotherapy session
		or
		ii. outside the psychotherapy session if an ongoing psychotherapist-patient relationship exists.
Note: Consent by the complainant is not a defense.		

OR

(12)	a.	defendant is a psychotherapist
	b.	and the complainant is a former patient of the psychotherapist
	c.	and the former patient is emotionally dependent upon the psychotherapist.

OR

(13)	a.	defendant is a psychotherapist
	b.	and complainant is a patient or former patient
	c.	and the sexual penetration occurred by means of therapeutic deception.
Note: Consent by the complainant is not a defense.		

OR

(14)	a.	defendant accomplishes the sexual penetration
	b.	by means of deception or false representation
	c.	that the penetration is for a bona fide medical purpose.
Note: Consent by the complainant is not a defense.		

OR

(15)	defendant is or purports to be a member of the clergy, the complainant is not married to the defendant, and:
	i. the sexual penetration occurred during the course of a meeting in which the complainant sought or received religious or spiritual advice, aid, or comfort from the defendant in private.
	or

| | ii. | the sexual contact occurred during a period of time in which the complainant was meeting on an ongoing basis with the defendant to seek or receive religious or spiritual advice, aid, or comfort in private. |

Note: Consent by the complainant is not a defense.

OR

| (16) | a. | defendant is an employee, independent contractor, or volunteer of a state, county, city, or privately operated adult or juvenile correctional system, or secure treatment facility, or treatment facility providing services to clients civilly committed as mentally ill and dangerous, sexually dangerous persons, or sexual psychopathic personalities, including, but not limited to, jails, prisons, detention centers, or work release facilities, **and** |
| | b. | The complainant is a resident of a facility or under supervision of the correctional system. |

Note: Consent by the complainant is not a defense.

OR

| (17) | a. | defendant provides or is an agent of an entity that provides special transportation service, the complainant used the special transportation service, and |
| | b. | the sexual penetration occurred during or immediately before or after the defendant transported the complainant. |

Note: Consent by the complainant is not a defense.

OR

(18) and	a.	defendant performs massage or other bodywork for hire,
	b.	the complainant was a user of those services, and
	c.	nonconsensual sexual penetration occurred during or immediately before or after the actor performed or was hired to perform one of the services for the complainant.

Jurisdiction - Child Victim: If the victim is a child (under 18 years), violation of any of the above sections may be prosecuted in either the county where the incident occurred or where the child was found (M.S. § 627.15).

D.   CRIMINAL SEXUAL CONDUCT IN THE FOURTH DEGREE -
Sexual Contact
M.S. § 609.345, subd. 1 (Felony)

Name

Date and Time of Offense

Location (Venue)

(1)   No person shall

(2)   engage in **sexual contact**

(3)   with another person

IF

(4)	a.	the complainant is under 13 years of age
	b.	and defendant is no more than 36 months older than complainant.

Note: Neither mistake as to the complainant's age nor consent to the act by the complainant is a defense. In a prosecution under this section, the State is not required to prove that the sexual contact was coerced.

OR

(5)	a.	the complainant is at least 13 but less than 16 years of age
	b.	and defendant is more than 48 months older than complainant.

Defense: If the actor is no more than 120 months older than complainant, it shall be an affirmative defense, which must be proved by a preponderrance of the evidence, that defendant reasonably believed the complainant to be 16 years of age or older. In all other cases, mistake as to the complainant's age shall not be a defense. Consent by complainant is not a defense.

OR

(6)	a.	the complainant is at least 13 but less than 16 years of age
	b.	and defendant is in a position of authority over complainant

Defense: If the actor is no more than 120 months older than complainant, it shall be an affirmative defense, which must be proved by a preponderance of the evidence, that defendant reasonably believed the complainant to be 16 years of age or older. In all other cases, mistake as to the complainant's age shall not be a defense. Consent by complainant is not a defense.

OR

(7)	defendant used force or coercion to accomplish the sexual contact.

OR

(8)	defendant knows or has reason to know that complainant is mentally impaired, mentally incapacitated or physically helpless.

OR

(9)	a.	the complainant is at least 16 but less than 18 years of age
	b.	and the defendant is more than 48 months older than the complainant
	c.	and in a position of authority over complainant

Note: Neither mistake as to the complainant's age nor consent to the act by the complainant is a defense.

OR

(10)	a.	defendant has a significant relationship to complainant
	b.	and the complainant was at least 16 but under 18 years of age at the time of the sexual contact.

Note: Neither mistake as to the complainant's age nor consent to the act by the complainant is a defense.

OR

(11)	a.	defendant has a significant relationship to complainant
	b.	the complainant was at least 16 but under 18 years of age at the time of the sexual contact, and:
	i.	defendant or an accomplice used force or coercion to accomplish the contact.
		or
	ii.	the complainant suffered personal injury.
		or
	iii.	the sexual abuse involved multiple acts committed over an extended period of time.

Note: Neither mistake as to the complainant's age nor consent to the act by the complainant is a defense.

OR

(12)	a.	defendant is a psychotherapist
	b.	and the complainant is a patient of the psycho-therapist
	c.	and the sexual contact occurred:
	i.	during the psychotherapy session.
		or
	ii.	outside the psychotherapy session if an ongoing psychotherapist-patient relationship exists.

Note: Consent by the complainant is not a defense.

OR

(13)	a.	defendant is a psychotherapist
	b.	and the complainant is a former patient of the psychotherapist
	c.	and the former patient is emotionally dependent upon the psychotherapist.

OR

(14)	a.	defendant is a psychotherapist
	b.	and complainant is a patient or former patient
	c.	and the sexual contact occurred by means of therapeutic deception.

<u>Note:</u> Consent by the complainant is not a defense.

OR

(15)	a.	defendant accomplishes the sexual contact
	b.	by means of deception or false representation
	c.	that the contact is for a bona fide medical purpose.

<u>Note:</u> Consent by the complainant is not a defense.

OR

(16)		defendant is or purports to be a member of the clergy, the complainant is not married to the defendant, and:
	a.	the sexual contact occurred during the course of a meeting in which the complainant sought or received religious or spiritual advice, aid, or comfort from the defendant in private.
		or
	b.	the sexual contact occurred during a period of time in which the complainant was meeting on an ongoing basis with the defendant to seek or receive religious or spiritual advice, aid, or comfort in private.

<u>Note:</u> Consent by the complainant is not a defense.

OR

(17)	a.	defendant is an employee, independent contractor, or volunteer of a state, county, city, or privately operated adult or juvenile correctional system, or secure treatment facility, or treatment facility providing services to clients civilly committed as mentally ill and dangerous, sexually dangerous persons, or sexual psychopathic personalities, including, but not limited to, jails, prisons, detention centers, or work release facilities, and
	b.	the complainant is a resident of a facility or under supervision of the correctional system.

Note: Consent by the complainant is not a defense.

OR

(18)	a.	defendant provides or is an agent of an entity that provides special transportation service, the complainant used the special transportation service, and
	b.	the sexual contact occurred during or immediately before or after the defendant transported the complainant.

Note: Consent by the complainant is not a defense.

OR

(19)	a.	defendant performs massage or other bodywork for hire, and
	b.	the complainant was a user of those services, and
	c.	nonconsensual sexual contact occurred during or immediately before or after the actor performed or was hired to perform one of those services for the complainant.

Jurisdiction - Child Victim: If the victim is a child (under 18 years), violation of any of the above sections may be prosecuted in either the county where the incident occurred or where the child was found (M.S. § 627.15).

E. **CRIMINAL SEXUAL CONDUCT IN THE FIFTH DEGREE -**
Sexual Contact
M.S. § 609.3451, subd. 1 (Gross Misdemeanor-Felony)

Name
Date and Time of Offense
Location (Venue)

(1) No person shall engage in nonconsensual sexual contact **(gross misdemeanor).**

Definition: For purposes of this section, **"sexual contact"** has the meaning given in M.S. § 609.341, subd. 11, paragraph (a), clauses (i), (iv) and (v): "the intentional touching by the actor of the complainant's intimate parts, the touching of the clothing covering the immediate area of the intimate parts, or the intentional touching with seminal fluid or sperm by the actor of the complainant's body or the clothing covering the complaint's body", but does not include the intentional touching of the clothing covering the immediate area of the buttocks. **"Sexual contact"** also includes the intentional removal or attempted removal of clothing covering the complainant's intimate parts or undergarments, and the nonconsensual touching by the complainant of the actor's intimate parts, effected by the actor, if the action is performed with sexual or aggressive intent. See section F. below, "Definitions", number 15.

OR

(2) Engage in masturbation or lewd exhibition of the genitals in the presence of a minor under the age of 16, knowing or having reason to know the minor is present. **(gross misdemeanor).**

Enhancement to **Felony**: Whoever violates the above section within seven years of:

a. A previous conviction for violating section (2) (masturbation or lewd exhibition in presence of a minor) above, or a statute from another state in conformity with this statute.

or

b. The first of two or more previous convictions for violating section (1) (nonconsensual sexual contact) above, or a statute from another state in conformity with this statute.

or

c. A previous conviction for violating M.S. § 609.342 (Criminal Sexual Conduct in the First Degree), M.S. § 609.343 (Criminal Sexual Conduct in the Second Degree), M.S. § 609.344 (Criminal Sexual Conduct in the Third Degree), M.S. § 609.345 (Criminal Sexual Conduct in the Fourth Degree), M.S. § 617.23, subd. 2, clause (2) (gross misdemeanor indecent exposure), or subd. 3 (felony indecent exposure), or M.S. § 617.247 (possession of pornographic work involving minors), is guilty of a **felony.**

<u>Jurisdiction:</u> The county attorney shall prosecute all violations of Criminal Sexual Conduct in the Fifth Degree (M.S. § 388.051, subd. 2(c)).

F. **DEFINITIONS:**

(1) **Accomplice** (M.S. § 609.05, subd. 1)

> "Accomplice" is any person who intentionally aids, advises, hires, counsels or conspires with or otherwise procures another person to commit a crime.

(2) **Coercion** (M.S. § 609.341, subd. 14)

> "Coercion" means the use by the actor of words or circumstances that cause the complainant reasonably to fear that the actor will inflict bodily harm upon, the complainant or another, or the use of the actor by confinement, or superior size or strength, against the complainant that causes the complainant to submit to sexual penetration or contact against the complainant's will. Proof of coercion does not require proof of a specific act or threat.

(3) **Consent** (M.S. § 609.341, subd. 4)

> "Consent" means words or overt actions by a person indicating a freely given present agreement to perform a particular sexual act with the actor. Consent does not mean the existence of a prior or current social relationship between the actor and the complainant or that the complainant failed to resist a particular sexual act. A person who is mentally incapacitated or physically helpless as defined by this section cannot consent to a sexual act. Corroboration of the victim's testimony is not required to show lack of consent.

(4) **Emotionally dependent** (M.S. § 609.341, subd. 19)

> "Emotionally dependent" means that the nature of the former patient's emotional condition and the nature of the treatment provided by the psychotherapist are such that the psychotherapist knows or has reason to know that the former patient is unable to withhold consent to sexual contact or sexual penetration by the psychotherapist.

(5) **Force** (M.S. § 609.341, subd. 3)

> "Force" means the infliction, attempted infliction or threatened infliction by the actor of bodily harm or commission or threat of any other crime by the actor against the complainant or another, which (a) causes the complainant to reasonably believe that the actor has the present ability to execute the threat and (b) if the actor does not have a significant relationship to the complainant, also causes the complainant to submit.

(6) **Mentally impaired** (M.S. § 609.341, subd. 6)

"Mentally impaired" means that a person, as a result of inadequately developed or impaired intelligence or a substantial psychiatric disorder of thought or mood, lacks the judgment to give a reasoned consent to sexual contact or to sexual penetration.

(7) **Mentally incapacitated** (M.S. § 609.341, subd. 7)

"Mentally incapacitated" means that a person under the influence of alcohol, a narcotic, anesthetic or any other substance, administered to that person without the person's agreement, lacks the judgment to give a reasoned consent to sexual contact or sexual penetration.

(8) **Patient** (M.S. § 609.341, subd. 16)

"Patient" means a person who seeks or obtains psychotherapeutic services.

(9) **Personal injury** (M.S. § 609.341, subd. 8)

"Personal injury" means bodily harm as defined in M.S. § 609.02, subd. 7 (i.e. physical pain or injury, illness or any impairment of physical condition) or severe mental anguish or pregnancy.

(10) **Physically helpless** (M.S. § 609.341, subd. 9)

"Physically helpless" means that a person is (a) asleep or not conscious, (b) unable to withhold consent or to withdraw consent because of a physical condition, or (c) unable to communicate nonconsent and the condition is known or reasonably should have been known to the actor.

(11) **Position of authority** (M.S. § 609.341, subd. 10)

"Position of authority" includes, but is not limited to any person who is a parent or acting in the place of a parent and charged with any of a parent's rights, duties or responsibilities to a child, or a person who is charged with any duty or responsibility for the health, welfare or supervision of a child, either independently or through another, no matter how brief, at the time of the act. Included in the definition of "sexual contact" (as defined in #15 below), "position of authority" includes a psychotherapist.

(12) **Psychotherapist** (M.S. § 609.341, subd. 17)

"Psychotherapist" means a person who is or purports to be a physician, psychologist, nurse, chemical dependency counselor, social worker, marriage and family therapist, licensed professional counselor or other mental health service provider, or other person, whether or not licensed by the state, who performs or purports to perform psychotherapy.

(13)   **Psychotherapy** (M.S. § 609.341, subd. 18)
         "Psychotherapy" means the professional treatment, assessment, or counseling of a mental or emotional illness, symptom or condition.

(14)   **Secure treatment facility** (M.S. § 609.341, subd. 23)
         "Secure treatment facility" means the Minnesota Security Hospital and the Minnesota sex offender program facility in Moose Lake and any portion of the Minnesota sex offender program operated by the Minnesota sex offender program at the Minnesota Security Hospital, but does not include services or programs administered by the secure treatment facility outside a secure environment.

(15)   **Sexual contact** (M.S. § 609.341, subd. 11)

    a.   No significant relationship: In cases where the actor does not have a significant relationship to complainant, "sexual contact" includes any of the following acts committed without the complainant's consent, except in those cases where consent is not a defense, and committed with sexual or aggressive intent:

        (i)   the intentional touching by the actor of the complainant's intimate parts, or

        (ii)   the touching by the complainant of the actor's, the complainant's or another's intimate parts effected by coercion, a person in a position of authority, or by inducement if the complainant is under 13 years of age or mentally impaired, or

        (iii)   the touching by another of the complainant's intimate parts effected by coercion, or by a person in a position of authority, or

        (iv)   in any of the cases above, the touching of the clothing covering the immediate area of the intimate parts.

        (v)   the intentional touching with seminal fluid or sperm by the actor of the complainant's body or the clothing covering the complainant's body.

    Note: **"Intimate parts"** includes the primary genital area, groin, inner thigh, buttocks or breast of a human being (M.S. § 609.341, subd. 5).

    b.   Significant relationship: In cases where the actor does have a significant relationship to complainant, "sexual contact" includes any of the following acts committed with sexual or aggressive intent:

(i)	the intentional touching by the actor of the complainant's intimate parts;
(ii)	the touching by the complainant of the actor's, the complainant's or another's intimate parts;
(iii)	the touching by another of the complainant's intimate parts; or
(iv)	in any of the cases listed above, touching of the clothing covering the immediate area of the intimate parts.
(v)	the intentional touching with seminal fluid or sperm by the actor of the complainant's body or the clothing covering the complainant's body.

Note: **"Intimate parts"** includes the primary genital area, groin, inner thigh, buttocks or breast of a human being (M.S. § 609.341, subd. 5).

c. With persons under 13 years of age: "Sexual contact with a person under 13" means the intentional touching of the complainant's bare genitals or anal opening by the actor's bare genitals or anal opening with sexual or aggressive intent or the touching by the complainant's bare genitals or anal opening of the actor's or another's bare genitals or anal opening with sexual or aggressive intent.

(16) **Sexual penetration** (M.S. § 609.341, subd. 12)

"Sexual penetration" means any of the following acts committed without the complainant's consent, except in those cases where consent is not a defense, whether or not emission of semen occurs:

a. sexual intercourse, cunnilingus, fellatio, or anal intercourse; or

b. any intrusion, however slight, into the genital or anal openings:

(i) of the complainant's body by any part of the actor's body or any object used by the actor for this purpose;

(ii) of the complainant's body by any part of the body of the complainant, by any part of the body of another person, or by any object used by the complainant or another person for this purpose, when effected by a person in a position of authority, or by coercion, or by inducement if the child is under 13 years of age or mentally impaired; or

(iii) of the body of the actor or another person by any part of the body of the complainant or by any object used by the complainant for this purpose, when effected by a person in a position of authority, or by coercion, or by inducement if the child is under 13 years of age or mentally impaired.

(17) **Significant relationship** (M.S. § 609.341, subd. 15)

"Significant relationship" means a situation in which the actor is:

a. the complainant's parent, stepparent or guardian;

b. any of the following persons related to the complainant by blood, marriage or adoption: brother, sister, stepbrother, stepsister, first cousin, aunt, uncle, nephew, niece, grandparent, great-grandparent, great-uncle, great-aunt; or

c. an adult who jointly resides intermittently or regularly in the same dwelling as the complainant and who is not the complainant's spouse.

(18) **Special Transportation Service** (M.S. § 609.341, subd. 21)

"Special Transportation Service" means motor vehicle transportation provided on a regular basis by a public or private entity or person that is intended exclusively or primarily to serve individuals who are vulnerable adults, handicapped, or disabled. Special transportation service includes, but is not limited to, service provided by buses, vans, taxis, and volunteers driving private automobiles.

(19) **Therapeutic deception** (M.S. § 609.341, subd. 20)

"Therapeutic deception" means a representation by a psychotherapist that sexual contact or sexual penetration by the psychotherapist is consistent with or part of the patient's treatment.

7. CRIMINAL VEHICULAR HOMICIDE

A. CRIMINAL VEHICULAR HOMICIDE
M.S. § 609.2112, subd. 1 (Felony)

Name
Date and Time of Offense
Location (Venue)

(1)   No person shall
(2)   Cause the death of a human being
(3)   As a result of operating a motor vehicle
(4)   a.   in a grossly negligent manner.

            or

       b.   in a negligent manner while under the influence of alcohol, a controlled substance or any combination of those elements.

            or

       c.   while having an alcohol concentration of 0.08 or more.

            or

       d.   while having an alcohol concentration of 0.08 or more, as measured within two hours of the time of driving.

            or

       e.   in a negligent manner while knowingly under the influence of a hazardous substance.

            or

       f.   in a negligent manner while any amount of a controlled substance listed in Schedule I or II, or its metabolite, other than marijuana or Tetrahydro cannabinols, is present in the person's body. (See Chapter 4 "Controlled Substance Crimes" Section X. (20) and (21) for a partial listing of Schedule I and II drugs),

            or

       g.   where the driver who causes the accident leaves the scene of the accident in violation of M.S. § 169.09, subd. 1 or 6. (See Chapter 19, "Hit and Run Traffic Accidents".)

            or

       h.   where the driver had actual knowledge that a peace officer had previously issued a citation or warning that the motor vehicle was defectively maintained, the driver had actual knowledge that remedial action was not taken, the driver had reason to know the defect created a present danger to others, and the injury or death was caused by the defective maintenance.

<u>Sentencing:</u>

A person who causes the death of a human being not constituting murder or manslaughter is guilty of a **felony.** The statutory maximum sentence is 15 years for a person who is sentenced for a violation under (b) – (f) above and has been convicted within the previous ten years of a qualified prior driving offense.

<u>Affirmative Defense:</u> It shall be an affirmative defense to a charge of Criminal Vehicular Homicide where the defendant was "driving in a negligent manner while any amount of a Schedule I or II controlled substance" was in the defendant's body, that the defendant used the controlled substance according to the terms of a prescription issued for the defendant.

B. CRIMINAL VEHICULAR OPERATION – BODILY HARM
M.S. § 609.2113, subds. 1, 2, and 3 (Felony – Gross Misdemeanor)

Name
Date and Time of Offense
Location (Venue)

(1) No person shall
(2) cause injury to another
(3) as a result of operating a motor vehicle

    a. in a grossly negligent manner.
       or
    b. in a negligent manner while under the influence of alcohol, a controlled substance or any combination of those elements.
       or
    c. while having an alcohol concentration of 0.08 or more.
       or
    d. while having an alcohol concentration of 0.08 or more, as measured within two hours of the time of driving.
       or
    e. in a negligent manner while knowingly under the influence of a hazardous substance.
       or
    f. in a negligent manner while any amount of a controlled substance listed in Schedule I or II, or its metabolite, other than marijuana or Tetrahydro cannabinols, is present in the person's body. (See Chapter 4 "Controlled Substance Crimes" Section X. (20) and (21) for a partial listing of Schedule I and II drugs),
       or
    g. where the driver who causes the accident leaves the scene of the accident in violation of M.S. § 169.09, subd. 1 or 6. (See Chapter 19, "Hit and Run Traffic Accidents".)
       or

h.   where the driver had actual knowledge that a peace officer had previously issued a citation or warning that the motor vehicle was defectively maintained, the driver had actual knowledge that remedial action was not taken, the driver had reason to know the defect created a present danger to others, and the injury or death was caused by the defective maintenance.

Sentencing: A person who causes great bodily harm to another not constituting attempted murder or assault is guilty of a **felony.** A person who causes substantial bodily harm to another is guilty of a **felony.** A person who causes bodily harm to another is guilty of a **gross misdemeanor.**

Affirmative Defense: It shall be an affirmative defense to a charge of Criminal Vehicular Operation – Bodily Harm where the defendant was "driving in a negligent manner while any amount of a Schedule I or II controlled substance" was in the defendant's body, that the defendant used the controlled substance according to the terms of a prescription issued for the defendant.

C.   CRIMINAL VEHICULAR OPERATION – UNBORN CHILD
M.S. § 609.2114, subds. 1,2 (Felony)

Name
Date and Time of Offense
Location (Venue)

(1)   No person shall
(2)   Cause
       a.   the death of an unborn child, **or**
       b.   great bodily harm to an unborn child subsequently born alive
(3)   As a result of operating a motor vehicle
       a.   in a grossly negligent manner.
           or
       b.   in a negligent manner while under the influence of alcohol, a controlled substance or any combination of those elements.
           or
       c.   while having an alcohol concentration of 0.08 or more.
           or
       d.   while having an alcohol concentration of 0.08 or more, as measured within two hours of the time of driving.
           or
       e.   in a negligent manner while knowingly under the influence of a hazardous substance.
           or
       f.   in a negligent manner while any amount of a controlled substance listed in Schedule I or II, or its metabolite, other than marijuana or Tetrahydro cannabinols, is present in the

person's body. (See Chapter 4 "Controlled Substance Crimes" Section X. (20) and (21) for a partial listing of Schedule I and II drugs),

or

g.   where the driver who causes the accident leaves the scene of the accident in violation of M.S. § 169.09, subd. 1 or 6. (See Chapter 19, "Hit and Run Traffic Accidents".)

or

h.   where the driver had actual knowledge that a peace officer had previously issued a citation or warning that the motor vehicle was defectively maintained, the driver had actual knowledge that remedial action was not taken, the driver had reason to know the defect created a present danger to others, and the injury or death was caused by the defective maintenance.

<u>Sentencing:</u>   The statutory maximum sentence is 15 years for a person who is sentenced for a violation under (b) – (f) above and has been convicted within the previous ten years of a qualified prior driving offense.

<u>Affirmative Defense:</u> It shall be an affirmative defense to a charge of Criminal Vehicular Operation – Unborn Child where the defendant was "driving in a negligent manner while any amount of a Schedule I or II controlled substance" was in the defendant's body, that the defendant used the controlled substance according to the terms of a prescription issued for the defendant.

D.   DEFINITIONS:

(1)   **Bodily harm** (M.S. § 609.02, subd. 7)

     "Bodily harm" means physical pain or injury, illness or any impairment of physical condition.

(2)   **Controlled substance** (M.S. § 152.01, subd. 4)

     "Controlled substance" means a drug, substance, or immediate precursor in Schedule I through V of section 152.02. The term shall not include distilled spirits, wine, malt beverages, intoxicating liquors or tobacco.

(3)   **Great bodily harm** (M.S. § 609.02, subd. 8)

     "Great bodily harm" means bodily injury which creates a high probability of death, or which causes serious permanent disfigurement, or which causes a permanent or protracted loss or impairment of the function of any bodily member or organ or other serious bodily harm.

(4)   **Gross negligence** (CRIMJIG 11.26)

"Gross negligence" means with very great negligence or without even scant care.

(5) **Hazardous substance** (M.S. § 609.21, subd. 5)

"Hazardous substance" means any chemical or chemical compound that is listed as a hazardous substance in rules adopted under chapter 182.

(6) **Motor vehicle** (M.S. § 609.52, subd. 1(10))

"Motor vehicle" means a self-propelled device for moving persons or property or pulling implements from one place to another, whether the device is operated on land, rails, water or in the air, including attached trailers.

(7) **Negligence** (JIG 101 and CRIMJIG 11.26)

Operating a motor vehicle in a negligent manner means to operate without using ordinary or reasonable care. Reasonable care is that care which a reasonable person would use under like circumstances. Negligence is the doing of something which a reasonable person would not do or the failure to do something which a reasonable person would do, under like circumstances.

(8) **Qualified prior driving offense** (Minn. Stat. § 609.2111(e))

"Qualified prior driving offense" means a prior conviction for

    i.   First Degree Driving While Impaired, Second Degree Driving While Impaired

    j.   Criminal Vehicular Homicide, excluding gross negligence, leaving the scene, and failure to take remedial action

    k.   Criminal Vehicular Operation –Great Bodily Harm, Substantial Bodily Harm, or Bodily Harm, excluding gross negligence, leaving the scene, and failure to take remedial action

    l.   Criminal Vehicular Operation – Death or Great Bodily Harm to an Unborn Child, excluding gross negligence, leaving the scene, and failure to take remedial action

(9) **Substantial bodily harm** (M.S. § 609.02, subd. 7a)

"Substantial bodily harm" means bodily injury which involves a temporary but substantial disfigurement, or which causes a temporary but substantial loss or impairment of the function of any bodily member or organ, or which causes a fracture of any bodily member.

(10) **Unborn child** (M.S. § 609.266(a))

"Unborn child" means the offspring of a human being conceived, but not yet born.

8. DAMAGE TO PROPERTY

A. DAMAGE TO PROPERTY OF CRITICAL PUBLIC SERVICE FACILITIES, UTILITIES, AND PIPELINES
M.S. § 609.594, Subd. 2 (Felony)

Name
Date and Time of Offense
Location (Venue)

(1)   No person shall
(2)   cause damage
(3)   to the physical property of a critical public service facility, utility, or pipeline
(4)   with intent to significantly disrupt the operation of or the provision of services by the facility, utility or pipeline
(5)   and without the consent of one authorized to give consent

Definition of "**critical public service facility**" (M.S. § 609.594, Subd. 1(1)) includes railroad yards and stations, bus stations, airports, and other mass transit facilities; oil refineries; storage areas or facilities for hazardous materials, hazardous substances, or hazardous wastes; and bridges.

Definition of "**pipeline**" (M.S. § 609.594, Subd. 1(2) and § 609.6055, subd. 1(c)) includes an aboveground pipeline and any equipment, facility, or building located in this state that is used to transport natural or synthetic gas, crude petroleum or petroleum fuels or oil or their derivatives, or hazardous liquids, to or within a distribution, refining, manufacturing, or storage facility that is located inside or outside of this state. Pipeline does not include service lines.

Definition of "**utility**" (M.S. § 609.594, Subd. 1(3)) includes: (i) any organization defined as a utility in section 216C.06, subdivision 5; (ii) any telecommunications carrier or telephone company regulated under chapter 237; and (iii) any local utility or enterprise formed for the purpose of providing electrical or gas heating and power, telephone, water, sewage, wastewater, or other related utility service, which is owned, controlled, or regulated by a town, a statutory or home rule charter city, a county, a port development authority, the metropolitan council, a district heating authority, a regional commission or other regional government unit, or a combination of these governmental units.

B. CRIMINAL DAMAGE TO PROPERTY IN THE FIRST DEGREE
M.S. § 609.595, subd. 1 (Felony)

Name

Date and Time of Offense

Location (Venue)

(1)   No person shall

(2)   intentionally cause damage

(3)   to physical property of another

(4)   without the other person's consent

     IF

(5)   a.   the damage to the property caused a reasonably foreseeable risk of bodily harm

            or

    b.   the property damaged was a public safety motor vehicle, the defendant knew the vehicle was a public safety motor vehicle, and the damage to the vehicle caused a substantial interruption or impairment of public safety service or a reasonably foreseeable risk of bodily harm

    c.   the property damaged belongs to a common carrier and the damage impairs the service to the public rendered by the carrier

            or

    d.   the damage reduces the value of the property by more than $1,000 measured by the cost of repair and replacement

            or

    e.   the damage reduces the value of the property by more than $500 measured by the cost of repair and replacement, and the defendant has been convicted within the preceding three years of criminal damage to property in the 1st, 2nd or 3rd degree (M.S.§ 609.595, subds. 1, 1a, 2)

Aggregation: In any prosecution under section (5)d. above charging damages over $1,000, the value of any property damaged by defendant in violation of that section within any six-month period may be aggregated and defendant charged accordingly in applying the provisions of this section.

Jurisdiction: When two or more offenses are committed by the same person in two or more counties, the accused may be prosecuted in any county in which one of the offenses was committed for all of the offenses aggregated under the above paragraph.

C. **CRIMINAL DAMAGE TO PROPERTY IN THE SECOND DEGREE**
M.S. § 609.595, subd. 1a (Felony)

Name

Date and Time of Offense

Location (Venue)

(1)   No person shall

(2)   intentionally cause damage

(3)   to another person's physical property

(4)   without the other person's consent

(5)   because of the property owner's or another's actual or perceived race, color, religion, sex, sexual orientation, disability, age or national origin
        IF

(6)   a.   the damage reduces the value of the property by more than $500 but not more than $1,000

          b.   measured by the cost of repair and replacement.

Aggregation: In any prosecution under the above section, the value of any property damaged by defendant in violation of the above section within any six-month period may be aggregated and defendant charged accordingly in applying the provisions of this section.

Jurisdiction: When two or more offenses are committed by the same person in two or more counties, the accused may be prosecuted in any county in which one of the offenses was committed for all of the offenses aggregated under the above paragraph.

D. **CRIMINAL DAMAGE TO PROPERTY IN THE THIRD DEGREE**
M.S. § 609.595, subd. 2 (Gross Misdemeanor)

Name

Date and Time of Offense

Location (Venue)

(1)   No person shall

(2)   intentionally cause damage

(3)   to another person's physical property

(4)   without the other person's consent
        IF

(5)   a.   the damage reduces the value of the property by more than $500 but not more than $1,000 measured by the cost of repair and replacement.

          b.   the damage was to a public safety motor vehicle and the defendant knew the vehicle was a public safety motor vehicle.
              or

      c.   because of the property owner's or another's actual or perceived race, color, religion, sex, sexual orientation, disability, age or national origin and the damage reduces the value of the property by not more than $500.

<u>Aggregation:</u> In any prosecution under section (5)a. above, the value of any property damaged by defendant in violation of that section within any six-month period may be aggregated and defendant charged accordingly in applying the above section.

<u>Jurisdiction:</u> When two or more offenses are committed by the same person in two or more counties, the accused may be prosecuted in any county in which one of the offenses was committed for all of the offenses aggregated under the above paragraph.

E.   CRIMINAL DAMAGE TO PROPERTY IN THE FOURTH DEGREE
M.S. § 609.595, subd. 3 (Misdemeanor, Gross Misdemeanor)

Name
Date and Time of Offense
Location (Venue)
(1)   No person shall intentionally cause damage
(2)   to another person's physical property
(3)   without the other person's consent
        IF
(4)   the damage reduces the value of the property by not more than $500.

<u>Enhancement to Gross Misdemeanor:</u>

If, in violating the above section, defendant was motivated by the property owner's or another's actual or perceived race, color, religion, sex, sexual orientation, disability, age or national origin, defendant is guilty of a **gross misdemeanor** rather than a misdemeanor.

F.   DEFINITIONS:

(1)   **Public Safety Motor Vehicle** (M.S. § 609.595, subd. 4(a))
        "Public Safety Motor Vehicle" includes:
        a.   marked vehicles used by law enforcement agencies and specially marked vehicles permitted under section 169.98, subd. 2a, owned or leased by the state or a political subdivision;
        b.   fire apparatuses, including fire-suppression support vehicles, owned or leased by the state or a political subdivision;

  c. ambulances owned or leased by the state or a political subdivision;

  d. vehicles owned by ambulance services licensed under section 144E.10 that are equipped and specifically intended for emergency response or providing ambulances services; and

  e. marked vehicles used by conservation officers of the Division of Enforcement and Field Service of the Department of Natural Resources.

(2) **Damage** (M.S. § 609.595, subd. 4(b))

"Damage" under sections B.(5)b. and D.5(b) above includes tampering with public safety motor vehicle and acts that obstruct or interfere with the vehicle's use.

9. DANGEROUS WEAPONS

A. DANGEROUS WEAPONS
  M.S. § 609.66, subd. 1 (Misdemeanor - Gross Misdemeanor)

Name

Date and Time of Offense

Location (Venue)

(1)	No person shall
(2)	recklessly handle or use a gun or other dangerous weapon or explosive so as to endanger the safety of another **(misdemeanor)**.

  OR

(1)	No person shall
(2)	intentionally point a gun of any kind, capable of injuring or killing a human being, whether loaded or unloaded, at or toward another **(misdemeanor)**.

  OR

(1)	No person shall
(2)	manufacture or sell for any unlawful purpose any weapon known as a slingshot or sand club **(misdemeanor)**.

  OR

(1)	No person shall
(2)	manufacture, transfer or possess metal knuckles or a switchblade knife opening automatically **(misdemeanor)**.

  OR

(1)	No person shall
(2)	possess any other dangerous article or substance for the purpose of being used unlawfully as a weapon against another **(misdemeanor)**.

> **OR**
> (1)   No person shall
> (2)   outside of a municipality and without the parent's or
> guardian's consent furnish a child under 14 years of age, or
> as a parent or guardian permit the child to handle or use, outside of
> the parent's or guardian's presence, a firearm or airgun of any kind,
> or any ammunition or explosive **(misdemeanor)**.
>
> Note: Possession of written evidence of prior consent signed by the minor's
> parent or guardian is a complete defense to a charge under the above section.

Enhancement to a Gross Misdemeanor:

If any of the above acts were committed in a public housing zone, a
school zone or a park zone, defendant is guilty of a **gross
misdemeanor**.

However

if any of the above acts were committed on residential premises within
a public housing zone, school zone or park zone as described above,
and if the offender was at the time an owner, tenant or invitee for a
lawful purpose with respect to those residential premises, defendant is
guilty of a **misdemeanor**, rather than a gross misdemeanor.

> **Transferring Firearms without Background Check - subd. 1f.**
> (1)   Whoever (other than a federally licensed firearms dealer)
> (2)   transfers a pistol or semi-automatic military-style assault weapon
> (3)   to another without complying with the transfer requirements of
> M.S. § 624.7132
>   **is guilty of a gross misdemeanor if:**
> (4)   The transferee possesses or uses the weapon within one
> year after the transfer in furtherance of a felony "crime of violence"
> (as defined in chapter 29, section H "Definitions")
> (5)   and the transferee was prohibited from possessing the weapon
> under M.S. § 624.713 at the time of the transfer
>   or
> it was reasonably foreseeable at the time of the transfer that the
> transferee was likely to use or possess the weapon in furtherance
> of a felony crime of violence.
>
> Note: What the above section means to law enforcement is that private
> transfer will most likely continue without the permit process; however, if
> someone does transfer a firearm without a permit, and the firearm is used in

the commission of a crime, then you go back to the initial transfer and it also becomes a crime.

> Note: Transfer to ineligible person - In addition to the above section, whoever transfers a pistol or an assault weapon to any person who is not eligible to possess the weapon is guilty of a **gross misdemeanor**. If the weapon is used in the furtherance of a crime of violence, the person is guilty of a **felony**. See M.S. § 624.7141 for the specific elements.

Note: This note applies to all of the above sections: Nothing in the above sections prohibits the possession of the articles mentioned by museums or collectors of art or for other lawful purposes of public exhibition.

B. DANGEROUS WEAPONS
M.S. § 609.66, subd. 1a, 1b, 1c, 1d, 1e, 1g (Felony)
Name
Date and Time of Offense
Location (Venue)

> (1) No person shall
> (2) sell or have in possession a suppressor that is not lawfully possessed under federal law.
>
> Note: If the above act is committed in a public housing zone, a school zone or a park zone, increased felony penalties apply (i.e. from a two year, $5,000 felony to a five year, $10,000 felony).
>
> Note: "Suppressor" is defined in Section F, "Definitions" below.
>
> Note: There is an exception for law enforcement purposes to the ban on silencers. See Minnesota Statutes § 609.66, subd. 1h.

OR

> (1) No person shall
> (2) intentionally discharge a firearm under circumstances that endanger the safety of another.
>
> Note: Violation of the above section is a five year, $10,000 felony regardless of whether the act is committed in a public housing zone, a school zone or a park zone.

OR

> (1) No person shall
> (2) recklessly discharge a firearm within a municipality.

> Note: If the above act is committed in a public housing zone, a school zone or a park zone, increased felony penalties apply (i.e. from a two year, $5,000 felony to a five year, $10,000 felony).

OR

(1)   No person shall

(2)   while in any municipality of the state, furnish a minor under 18 years of age with a firearm, airgun, ammunition or explosive without the prior consent of the minor's parent or guardian or the police department of the municipality.

> Note: Possession of written evidence of prior consent signed by the minor's parent or guardian is a complete defense to a charge under the above section.

OR

(1)   No person shall

(2)   recklessly furnish a person with a dangerous weapon in conscious disregard of a known substantial risk that the object will be possessed or used in furtherance of a felony crime of violence.

OR

Possession on School Property - subd. 1d.

(1)   No person shall

(2)   Possess, store, or keep a dangerous weapon while knowingly on school property. **(Felony)**

Exceptions: The above section does not apply to:

a.   licensed peace officers, military personnel, or students participating in military training, who are on duty performing official duties;

b.   Persons authorized to carry a pistol under section 624.714 while in a motor vehicle or outside of a motor vehicle to directly place a firearm in, or retrieve it from, the trunk or rear area of the vehicle;

c.   persons who keep or store in a motor vehicle pistols in accordance with section 624.714 or 624.715 (see chapter 29, section D.) or other firearms in accordance with section 97B.045 (Hunting);

d.   firearm safety or marksmanship courses or activities conducted on school property;

e.   possession of dangerous weapons, BB guns or replica firearms by a ceremonial color guard;

f.   a gun or knife show held on school property; or

g.   possession of dangerous weapons, BB guns or

replica firearms with written permission of the principal or other person having general control and supervision of the school or the director of a child care center; or

h.   persons who are on unimproved property owned or leased by a child care center, school, or school district unless the person knows that a student is currently present on the land for a school-related activity.

Note: Whoever uses or brandishes a replica firearm or a BB gun while knowingly on school property is guilty of a **gross misdemeanor**. (M.S. § 609.66, subd. 1d(b)) Whoever possesses, stores, or keeps a replica firearm or BB gun while knowingly on school property is guilty of a **misdemeanor.** (M.S. § 609.66, subd. 1d(c))

Note: "Dangerous weapon" and "school property" are defined in section F, "Definitions" below.

Note: **Misdemeanor** violation - Notwithstanding the above provisions, it is a misdemeanor for a person authorized to carry a firearm under the provisions of a permit or otherwise to carry a firearm on or about the person's clothes or person in a location the person knows is school property. (M.S. § 609.66, subd. 1d(d)) However, a firearm carried in violation of this law is not subject to forfeiture. (M.S. § 609.66, subd 1d(d)).

Definition of **"BB gun"** (M.S. § 609.66, subd. 1d(e)(1)) -
"BB gun" means a device that fires or ejects a shot measuring .18 of an inch or less in diameter.

Definition of **"Replica firearm"** (M.S. § 609.66, subd. 1d(e)(3); § 609.713)-
"Replica firearm" means a device or object that is not defined as a dangerous weapon, and that is a facsimile or toy version of, and reasonably appears to be a pistol, revolver, shotgun, sawed-off shotgun, rifle, machine gun, rocket launcher, or any other firearm. The term replica firearm includes, but is not limited to, devices or objects that are designed to fire only blanks.

OR

Drive By Shooting - subd. 1e(a)(b)
(1)   No person shall
(2)   while in or having just exited from a motor vehicle
(3)   recklessly discharge a firearm at or toward another motor vehicle, or a building.

Enhancement: If defendant fires at or toward a person, or if the motor vehicle or building is occupied, increased felony penalties apply.

Note: "Motor vehicle" and "building" are defined in section F, "Definitions" below.

OR

Possession in Courthouse or Certain State Buildings-subd. 1g.
(1)   No person shall
(2)   possess a dangerous weapon, ammunition or explosives

(3)   within any courthouse complex or state building within the capitol area described in M.S. § 15.50, other than the National Guard Armory.

Exceptions: The above section does not apply to:
    (a)   licensed peace officers or military personnel who are performing official duties;
    (b)   persons who carry pistols according to the terms of a permit issued under section 624.714 and who so notify the sheriff or the commissioner of public safety, as appropriate;
    (c)   persons who possess dangerous weapons for the purpose of display as demonstrative evidence during testimony at a trial or hearing or exhibition in compliance with advance notice and safety guidelines set by the sheriff or the commissioner of public safety; or
    (d)   persons who possess dangerous weapons in a courthouse complex with the express consent of the county sheriff or who possess dangerous weapons in a state building with the express consent of the commissioner of public safety.

Note: This note applies to all of the above sections: Nothing in the above sections prohibits the possession of the articles mentioned by museums or collectors of art or for other lawful purposes of public exhibition.

C. NEGLIGENT STORAGE OF FIREARMS
M.S. § 609.666, subds. 1, 2, 3 (Gross Misdemeanor)

Name

Date and Time of Offense

Location (Venue)

(1)   No person shall

(2)   negligently store or leave a loaded firearm

(3)   in a location where the person knows, or reasonably should know, that a child is likely to gain access

(4)   unless reasonable action is taken to secure the firearm against access by the child.

Exception: The above section does not apply to a child's access to firearms that was obtained as a result of an unlawful entry.

Note: The terms "firearm", "child" and "loaded" are defined in section F, "Definitions" below.

Cross Reference: See also "CHILD ENDANGERMENT BY FIREARM ACCESS", Chapter 23, section B. 4th box.

D. FIREARMS: REMOVAL OR ALTERATION OF SERIAL NUMBER
M.S. § 609.667 (Felony)

Name

Date and Time of Offense

Location (Venue)

(1)   No person shall

(2)   obliterate, remove, change or alter the serial number or other identification of a firearm,

(3)   or, receive or possess a firearm, the serial number or other identification of which has been obliterated, removed, changed, or altered,

(4)   or, receive or possess a firearm that is not identified by a serial number.

Note: As used in this section, "serial number or other identification" means the serial number and other information required under United States Code, title 26, section 5842, for the identification of firearms.

E. MACHINE GUNS AND SHORT-BARRELED SHOTGUNS
M.S. § 609.67, subd. 1, 2, 3 (Felony)

Name

Date and Time of Offense

Location (Venue)

(1)   No person shall

(2)   own, possess or operate

(3)   a machine gun, any trigger activator or machine gun conversation kit, or a short-barreled shotgun

Exemptions: The following persons may own or possess a machine gun or short-barreled shotgun provided the reporting provisions set forth in the note below are complied with:

(1)   law enforcement officers for use in the course of their duties;

(2)   chief executive officers of correctional facilities and other personnel thereof authorized by them and persons in charge of other institutions for the retention of persons convicted or accused of crime, for use in the course of their duties;

(3)   persons possessing machine guns or short-barreled shotguns which, although designed as weapons, have been determined by the superintendent of the BCA or the superintendent's delegate by reason of the date of manufacture, value, design or other characteristic to be primarily collector's items, relics, museum pieces or objects of curiosity, ornaments or keepsakes and are not likely to be used as weapons;

(4)   manufacturers of ammunition who possess and use machine guns for the sole purpose of testing ammunition manufactured for sale to federal and state agencies or political subdivisions; and

(5)   dealers and manufacturers who are federally licensed to buy and sell, or manufacture machine guns or short-barreled shotguns and who either use the machine guns or short-barreled shotguns in peace officer training under courses approved by the Board of Peace Officer Standards and Training, or are engaged in the sale of machine guns or short-barreled shotguns to federal and state agencies or political subdivisions.

Note: Reporting provisions - This note applies to all of the above exemptions: A person owning or possessing a machine gun or short-barreled shotgun as authorized by any of the above exemptions shall, within 10 days after acquiring such ownership or possession, file a written report with the BCA showing the person's name and address; the person's official title and position, if any; a description of the machine gun or short-barreled shotgun sufficient to enable identification thereof; the purpose for which it is owned or possessed; and such further information as the BCA may reasonably require. In addition, any dealer or manufacturer owning or having a machine gun or short-barreled shotgun as authorized by exemption (5) above shall, by the 10th day of each month, file a written report with the BCA showing the name and address of the dealer or manufacturer and the serial number of each machine gun or short-barreled shotgun acquired or manufactured during the previous month.

None of the above sections apply to members of the armed services of either the United States or the State of Minnesota for use in the course of their duties.

F.   **DEFINITIONS:**
(1)   **Building** (M.S. § 609.66, subd. 1e; § 609.581, subd. 2)
>   "Building" means a structure suitable for affording shelter for human beings, including any appurtenant or connected structure.

(2)   **Child** (M.S. § 609.666, subd. 1)
>   "Child" means a person under the age of 18 years.

(3)   **Dangerous weapon** (M.S. § 609.02, subd. 6)"Dangerous weapon" is defined in Chapter 2 (Assaults), section U.

(4)   **Firearm** (M.S. § 609.666, subd. 1)
>   "Firearm" means a device designed to be used as a weapon, from which is expelled a projectile by the force of any explosion or force of combustion.

(5)   **Loaded** (M.S. § 609.666, subd. 1)
>   "Loaded" means the firearm has ammunition in the chamber or magazine, if the magazine is in the firearm, unless the firearm is incapable of being fired by a child who is likely to gain access to the firearm.

(6)   **Machine gun** (M.S. § 609.67, subd. 1(a))
>   "Machine gun" means any firearm designed to discharge, or capable of discharging automatically more than once by a single function of the trigger.

(7)   **Machine gun conversion kit** (M.S. § 609.67, subd. 1(e))
>   "Machine gun conversion kit" means any part or combination of parts designed and intended for use in converting a weapon into a machine gun, and any combination of parts from which a machine gun can be assembled, but does not include a spare or replacement part for a machine gun that is possessed lawfully under section 609.67, subdivision 1 (see chapter 9, section E.).

(8)   **Motor vehicle** (M.S. § 609.66, subd. 1e; § 609.52, subd. 1)
>   "Motor vehicle" means a self-propelled device for moving persons or property or pulling implements from one place to another, whether the device is operated on land, rails, water, or in the air.

(9)   **Park zone** (M.S. § 152.01, subd. 12a)

"Park zone" is defined in chapter 4 (Controlled Substance Crimes), section X.

(10) **Public housing zone** (M.S. § 152.01, subd. 19)

"Public housing zone" is defined in chapter 4 (Controlled Substance Crimes), section X.

(11) **School property** (M.S. § 609.66, subd. 1d)

"School property" means:

a. a public or private elementary, middle, or secondary school building and its improved grounds, whether leased or owned by the school;

b. a child care center licensed under chapter 245A during the period children are present and participating in a child care program;

c. the area within a school bus when that bus is being used by a school to transport one or more elementary, middle, or secondary school students to and from school-related activities, including curricular, cocurricular, noncurricular, extracurricular, and supplementary activities; and

d. that portion of a building or facility under the temporary, exclusive control of a public or private school, a school district, or an association of such entities where conspicuous signs are prominently posted at each entrance that give actual notice to persons of the school-related use.

(12) **School zone** (M.S. § 152.01, subd. 14a)

"School zone" is defined in chapter 4 (Controlled Substance Crimes), section X, "Definitions".

(13) **Shotgun** (M.S. § 609.67, subd. 1(b))

"Shotgun" means a weapon designed, redesigned, made or remade which is intended to be fired from the shoulder and uses the energy of the explosive in a fixed shotgun shell to fire through a smooth bore either a number of ballshot or a single projectile for each single pull of the trigger.

(14) **Short-barreled shotgun** (M.S. § 609.67, subd. 1(c))

"Short-barreled shotgun" means a shotgun having one or more barrels less than 18 inches in length and any weapon made from a shotgun if such weapon as modified has an overall length less than 26 inches.

(15) **Suppressor** (M.S. § 609.66, subd. 1a(c))

"Suppressor" means any device for silencing, muffling, or diminishing the report of a portable firearm, including any combination of parts, designed or redesigned, and intended for use in assembling or fabricating a firearm silencer or firearm muffler, and any part intended only for use in such assembly or fabrication.

(16)   **Trigger activator** (M.S. § 609.67, subd. 1(d))

"Trigger activator" means a removable manual or power driven trigger activating device constructed and designed so that, when attached to a firearm, the rate at which the trigger may be pulled increases and the rate of fire of the firearm increases to that of a machine gun.

10. DEPRIVING ANOTHER OF CUSTODIAL
OR PARENTAL RIGHTS

DEPRIVING ANOTHER OF CUSTODIAL OR PARENTAL RIGHTS
M.S. § 609.26, subds. 1, 2, 3, 4, 5, 6 (Felony - Gross Misdemeanor)
Name
Date and Time of Offense
Location (Venue)

(1)   No person shall intentionally

(2)	a.	conceal a minor child from the child's parent
	b.	where the action manifests an intent substantially to deprive that parent of parental rights. **(Felony)**

OR

(3)	a.	conceal a minor child from another person having the right to visitation or custody
	b.	where the action manifests an intent to substantially deprive that person of rights to visitation or custody. **(Felony)**

OR

(4)	a.	take, obtain, retain or fail to return a minor child
	b.	in violation of a court order which has transferred legal custody under Chapter 260 to the Commissioner of Human Services, a child placement agency or the County Welfare Board. **(Felony)**

OR

(5)	a.	take, obtain, retain or fail to return a minor child from or to the parent
	b.	in violation of a court order
	c.	where the action manifests an intent to substantially deprive that parent of rights to visitation or custody. **(Felony)**

OR

(6)		take, obtain, retain or fail to return a minor child from or to a parent
	a.	after commencement of an action relating to child visitation or custody
	b.	but prior to the issuance of an order determining custody or visitation rights
	c.	where the action manifests an intent to substantially deprive that parent of parental rights. **(Felony)**

OR

(7)	a.	retain a child in this state
	b.	with the knowledge that the child was removed from another state
	c.	in violation of any of the above provisions. **(Felony)**

OR

(8)	a.	refuse to return a minor child to a parent or lawful custodian,
	b.	if the person is at least 18 years old and more than 24 months older than the child. **(Felony)**

OR

(9)	a.	cause or contribute to a child being a habitual truant (defined below)
	b.	if the person is at least 18 years old and more than 24 months older than the child. **(Gross Misdemeanor)**

Definition of **"Habitual Truant"** (M.S. § 260C.007, subd. 4(14).
"Habitual Truant" means a child under the age of 16 years who is absent from attendance at school without lawful excuse for seven school days if the child is in elementary school or for one or more class periods on seven school days if the child is in middle school, junior high school, or high school, or a child who is 16 or 17 years of age who is absent from attendance at school without lawful excuse for one or more class periods on seven school days and who has not lawfully withdrawn from school under § 120.101, subd. 5d.

Jurisdiction: The county attorney shall prosecute violations of the above section. M.S. § 609.26, subd. 6(b)

OR

(10)	a.	cause or contribute to a child being a runaway (defined below)
	b.	if the person is at least 18 years old and more than 24 months older than the child. **(Felony)**

Definition of **"Runaway"** (M.S. § 260C.007, subd. 4(13))
"Runaway" means an unmarried child under the age of 18 years who is absent from the home of a parent or other lawful placement with-out the consent of the parent, guardian, or lawful custodian.

OR

(11)	a.	reside with a minor child under the age of 16
	b.	without the consent of the minor's parent or lawful custodian
	c.	if the person is at least 18 years old. **(Felony)**

Defense: It is an affirmative defense if a person is charged under any of the above provisions that:

(1)	the person reasonably believed the action taken was necessary to protect the child from physical or sexual assault or substantial emotional harm.

OR

(2)	the person reasonably believed the action taken was necessary to protect the person taking the action from physical or sexual assault.

OR

(3)	the action taken is consented to by the parent, stepparent or legal custodian seeking prosecution. **Note:** Consent to custody or specific visitation is not consent to the action of failing to return or concealing a minor child.

OR

(4)	the action taken is otherwise authorized by court order issued prior to the violation of any of the above sections.

Jurisdiction: A person who violates any of the above sections may be prosecuted and tried either in the county in which the child was taken, concealed or detained, or in the county of lawful residence of the child.

Note: A child who has been concealed, obtained or retained in violation of any of the above sections shall be returned to the person having lawful custody of the child or shall be taken into custody pursuant to M.S. § 260C.175, subd. 1(b)(2) (i.e. Child Protection Statute).

Increased penalties (M.S. § 609.26, subd. 6): The penalty for violation of any of the above sections may be significantly increased if:

(1)   defendant committed the violation while possessing a dangerous weapon or caused substantial bodily harm to effect the taking; **or**

(2)   defendant abused or neglected the child during the concealment, detention or removal of the child; **or**

(3)   defendant inflicted or threatened to inflict physical harm on a parent or lawful custodian of the child or on the child with intent to cause the parent or lawful custodian to discontinue criminal prosecution; **or**

(4)   defendant demanded payment in exchange for return of the child or demanded to be relieved of the financial or legal obligation to support the child in exchange for return of the child; **or**

(5)   defendant has previously been convicted under any of the above sections or a similar statute of another jurisdiction.

Dismissal of charge (M.S. § 609.26, subd. 5): A felony charge brought under any of the above sections shall be dismissed if:

(1)   The defendant voluntarily returns the child within 48 hours after taking, detaining or failing to return the child in violation of any of the above sections.

             Note: The above section does not apply if defendant returns the child as a result of being located by law enforcement authorities.

             or

(2)   The defendant and the child have not left the State of Minnesota and within a period of seven days after taking the action:

         a.   defendant files a motion or commences an action affecting custody or visitation of the child pursuant to Chapters 518, 518B, 518C, or 518D; or

         b.   defendant's attorney consents to service of process by the party whose rights are being deprived, for any motion or action affecting custody or visitation of the child pursuant to Chapters 518, 518A, 518B or 518C.

11. DISORDERLY CONDUCT

DISORDERLY CONDUCT
M.S. § 609.72 (Misdemeanor- Gross Misdemeanor)
Name
Date and Time of Offense
Location (Venue)
(1)   No person shall
(2)   a.   engage in brawling or fighting
               or
        b.   disturb an assembly or meeting, not unlawful in its character
               or
        c.   engage in offensive, obscene, abusive, boisterous or noisy conduct or in offensive, obscene or abusive language tending reasonably to arouse alarm, anger or resentment in others
(3)   if the acts are committed in a public or private place, including on a school bus,
(4)   knowing or having reasonable grounds to know that it will or will tend to alarm, anger or disturb others or provoke an assault or breach of the peace.

Note: A person does not violate the above section if the person's disorderly conduct was caused by an epileptic seizure.

Enhancement to Gross Misdemeanor: A caregiver (as defined in Chapter 2, Section U, "Definitions".), who violates the above section against a vulnerable adult, (as defined in M.S. § 609.232, subd. 11) is guilty of a **gross misdemeanor**.
Note: For an additional list of crimes against vulnerable adults see M.S. § 609.232.

12. DRIVING WHILE IMPAIRED AND RELATED OFFENSES

A. **DRIVING WHILE IMPAIRED CRIME; MOTOR VEHICLE**
M.S. § 169A.20, Subd. 1
Name
Date and Time of Offense
Location (Venue)

(1)   No person shall

(2)   drive, operate, or be in physical control

(3)   of any motor vehicle

(4)   within this state or on any boundary water of this state

    IF

(5)   a.   the person is under the influence of alcohol

        or

        b.   the person is under the influence of controlled substance

        or

        c.   the person is knowingly under the influence of a hazardous substance that affects the nervous system, brain or muscles of the person so as to substantially impair the person's ability to drive or operate the motor vehicle

        or

        d.   the person is under the influence of a combination of any two or more of the following:

                (i)   alcohol

                (ii)   controlled substance

                (iii)   a hazardous substance that affects the nervous system, brain or muscles of the person so as to substantially impair the person's ability to drive or operate the motor vehicle.

        or

        e.   the person's alcohol concentration at the time, or as measured within two hours of the time, of driving, operating, or being in physical control of the motor vehicle is 0.08 or more

        or

        f.   when the vehicle is a commercial motor vehicle and the person's alcohol concentration at the time, or as measured within two hours of the time, of driving, operating, or being in physical control of the commercial motor vehicle is 0.04 or more

        or

        g.   when the person's body contains any amount of a controlled substance listed in Schedule I or II, or its

- 102 -

metabolite, other than marijuana or tetrahydrocannabinols.

B. **DRIVING WHILE IMPAIRED CRIME; MOTORBOAT IN OPERATION**
M.S. § 169A.20, Subd. 1a
Name
Date and Time of Offense
Location (Venue)

(1)   No person shall
(2)   operate, or be in physical control
(3)   of a motorboat in operation
(4)   on any waters or boundary water of this state
IF
(5)   a.   the person is under the influence of alcohol
             or
          b.   the person is under the influence of controlled substance
             or
          c.   the person is knowingly under the influence of a hazardous substance that affects the nervous system, brain or muscles of the person so as to substantially impair the person's ability to drive or operate the motorboat
             or
          d.   the person is under the influence of a combination of any two or more of the following:
                (i)   alcohol
                (ii)   controlled substance
                (iii)   a hazardous substance that affects the nervous system, brain or muscles of the person so as to substantially impair the person's ability to drive or operate the motorboat.
             or
          e.   the person's alcohol concentration at the time, or as measured within two hours of the time, of driving, operating, or being in physical control of the motorboat is 0.08 or more
             or
          f.   the person's body contains any amount of controlled substance listed in Schedule I or II, or its metabolite, other than marijuana or tetrahydrocannabinols.

C. **DRIVING WHILE IMPAIRED CRIME; SNOWMOBILE OR ALL-TERRAIN VEHICLE**
M.S. § 169A.20, Subd. 1b

Name
Date and Time of Offense
Location (Venue)

(1)   No person shall
(2)   drive, operate, or be in physical control
(3)   of any snowmobile or all-terrain vehicle
(4)   within this state or on any boundary water of this state
      IF
(5)   a.   the person is under the influence of alcohol
          or
      b.   the person is under the influence of controlled substance
          or
      c.   the person is knowingly under the influence of a hazardous substance that affects the nervous system, brain or muscles of the person so as to substantially impair the person's ability to drive or operate the snowmobile or all-terrain vehicle
          or
      d.   the person is under the influence of a combination of any two or more of the following:
          (i)   alcohol
          (ii)   controlled substance
          (iii)   a hazardous substance that affects the nervous system, brain or muscles of the person so as to substantially impair the person's ability to drive or operate the snowmobile or all-terrain vehicle
          or
      e.   the person's alcohol concentration at the time, or as measured within two hours of the time, of driving, operating, or being in physical control of the the snowmobile or all-terrain vehicle is 0.08 or more
          or
      f.   the person's body contains any amount of controlled substance listed in Schedule I or II, or its metabolite, other than marijuana or tetrahydrocannabinols.

D. **DRIVING WHILE IMPAIRED CRIME; OFF-HIGHWAY MOTORCYCLE AND OFF-ROAD VEHICLE**
M.S. § 169A.20, Subd. 1c

Name

Date and Time of Offense

Location (Venue)

(1)   No person shall

(2)   drive, operate, or be in physical control

(3)   of any

(4)   within this state or on any boundary water of this state

IF

(5)   a.   the person is under the influence of alcohol

        or

      b.   the person is under the influence of controlled substance

        or

      c.   the person is knowingly under the influence of a hazardous substance that affects the nervous system, brain or muscles of the person so as to substantially impair the person's ability to drive or operate the motor vehicle

        or

      d.   the person is under the influence of a combination of any two or more of the following:

          (i)   alcohol

          (ii)   controlled substance

          (iii)   a hazardous substance that affects the nervous system, brain or muscles of the person so as to substantially impair the person's ability to drive or operate the motor vehicle.

        or

      e.   the person's alcohol concentration at the time, or as measured within two hours of the time, of driving, operating, or being in physical control of the off-highway motorcycle or off-road vehicle is 0.08 or more

        or

      f.   the person's body contains any amount of controlled substance listed in Schedule I or II, or its metabolite, other than marijuana or tetrahydrocannabinols.

Note: "**Alcohol - Related School Bus or Head Start Bus Driving**" It is a crime (misdemeanor) for any person to drive, operate or be in physical control of any class of school bus or Head Start bus within this state when there is physical evidence present in the person's body of the consumption of any alcohol. It is a gross misdemeanor crime if the violation occurs while a child under the age of 16 is in the vehicle if the child is more than 36 months younger than the violator or the violation occurs within ten years of a qualified prior impaired driving incident. (M.S. § 169A.31)

DRIVING WHILE IMPAIRED CRIME; DEGREE DETERMINED

A. **FIRST DEGREE DRIVING WHILE IMPAIRED**
M.S. § 169A.20, Subd. 1a-d; § 169A.24 (Felony)

A person who violates M.S. § 169A.20, subd. 1a-d (Driving While Impaired; Motor Vehicle, Driving While Impaired; Motorboat in Operation, Driving While Impaired; Snowmobile and All-Terrain Vehicle, Driving While Impaired; Off-Highway Motorcycle and Off-Road Vehicle) is guilty of First Degree Driving While Impaired if:

(1)   The violation is committed within ten years of the first of three or more qualified prior impaired driving incidents
OR
(2)   The person has previously been convicted of a felony under M.S. § 169A.
OR
(3)   The person has previously been convicted of a felony under:
   a.   M.S. § 609.21 (criminal vehicular homicide and injury, substance-related offenses, specifically M.S. § 609.21, subd. 1, clauses (2) to (6))
   b.   M.S. 2006 § 609.21 (criminal vehicular homicide and injury, substance-related offenses, specifically M.S. 2006 § 609.21, subd. 1, clauses (2) to (6); subd. 2, clauses (2) to (6); subd. 2a, clauses (2) to (6); subd. 3, clauses (2) to (6); or subd. 4, clauses (2) to (6))

B. **SECOND DEGREE DRIVING WHILE IMPAIRED**
M.S. § 169A.20, Subd. 1a-d; M.S. § 169A.26 (Gross Misdemeanor)
A person who violates M.S. § 169A.20, Subd. 1a-d (Driving While Impaired; Motor Vehicle, Driving While Impaired; Motorboat in Operation, Driving While Impaired; Snowmobile and All-Terrain Vehicle, Driving While Impaired; Off-Highway Motorcycle and Off-Road Vehicle) is guilty of Second Degree Driving While Impaired if:

(1)   Two or more aggravating factors were present when the violation was committed.

C. **THIRD DEGREE DRIVING WHILE IMPAIRED**
M.S. § 169A.20, Subd. 1a-d; M.S. § 169A.26 (Gross Misdemeanor)

A person who violates M.S. § 169A.20, Subd. 1a-d (Driving While Impaired; Motor Vehicle, Driving While Impaired; Motorboat in Operation, Driving While Impaired; Snowmobile and All-Terrain Vehicle, Driving While Impaired; Off-Highway Motorcycle and Off-Road Vehicle) is guilty of Third Degree Driving While Impaired if:

(1) One aggravating factor was present when the violation was committed.

D. **FOURTH DEGREE DRIVING WHILE IMPAIRED**
M.S. § 169A.20, Subd. 1a-d; MS. § 169A.27 (Misdemeanor)

A person who violates M.S. § 169A.20, Subd. 1a-d (Driving While Impaired; Motor Vehicle, Driving While Impaired; Motorboat in Operation, Driving While Impaired; Snowmobile and All-Terrain Vehicle, Driving While Impaired; Off-Highway Motorcycle and Off-Road Vehicle) is guilty of Fourth Degree Driving While Impaired if:

(1) No aggravating factors were present when the violation was committed.

E. **FIRST DEGREE REFUSAL TO SUBMIT TO CHEMICAL TESTING**
M.S. § 169A.20, Subd. 2; § 169A.24 (Felony)

Name
Date and Time of Offense
Location (Venue)
(1) No person shall
(2) refuse to submit to a chemical test
(3) a. of the person's breath under MS § 169A.51 (chemical tests for intoxication), or § 169A.52 (test refusal or failure; revocation of license; Implied Consent);

OR

b. of the person's blood or urine as required by a search warrant under M.S. §§ 626.04 to 626.18 and 171.177;

AND
(4) a. the violation was committed within ten years of the first of three or more qualified prior impaired driving incidents;

OR

b. the person has previously been convicted of a felony under M.S. § 169A.

F. **SECOND DEGREE REFUSAL TO SUBMIT TO CHEMICAL TESTING**
M.S. § 169A.20, Subd. 2; § 169A.25 (Gross Misdemeanor)

Name
Date and Time of Offense
Location (Venue)
(1) No person shall
(2) refuse to submit to a chemical test
(3) a. of the person's breath under Minnesota Statutes section
    169A.51 (chemical tests for intoxication), or 169A.52
    (test refusal or failure; revocation of license; Implied
    Consent);
  OR
  b. of the person's blood or urine as required by a search
    warrant under M.S. §§ 626.04 to 626.18 and 171.177;
(4) and one aggravating factor was present when the violation
  was committed.

G. **THIRD DEGREE REFUSAL TO SUBMIT TO CHEMICAL TESTING**
M.S. § 169A.20, Subd. 2; § 169A.26 (Gross Misdemeanor)

Name
Date and Time of Offense
Location (Venue)
(1) No person shall
(2) refuse to submit to a chemical test
(3) a.of the person's breath under Minnesota Statutes section
    169A.51 (chemical tests for intoxication), or 169A.52
    (test refusal or failure; revocation of license; Implied
    Consent);
  OR
  b. of the person's blood or urine as required by a search
    warrant under M.S. §§ 626.04 to 626.18 and 171.177.

H. **UNDERAGE DRINKING AND DRIVING**
M.S. § 169A.33 (Misdemeanor)

Name
Date and Time of Offense
Location (Venue)
(1) No person under the age of 21 years

(2) shall drive, operate or be in physical control of a motor vehicle
(3) while consuming alcoholic beverages, or after having consumed alcoholic beverages while there is physical evidence of consumption present in the person's body.

Note: As used in this section, "motor vehicle" does NOT include motorboats in operation or off-road recreational vehicles. (M.S. § 169A.33, Subd. 1)

Exception: If the person's conduct violates M.S. § 169A.20, "Driving While Impaired, " the penalties and license sanctions in those laws or M.S. § 169A.54 (impaired driving convictions and adjudications; administrative penalties) apply instead of the license sanction in found in M.S. § 169A.33, subd. 4.

Jurisdiction: The above offense may be prosecuted either in the jurisdiction where consumption occurs or the jurisdiction where the evidence of consumption is observed.

I. UNDERAGE DRINKING
M.S. § 340A.503, subds. 1,2 (Misdemeanor)

Name
Date and Time of Offense
Location (Venue)
(1)   No person under the age of 21 years
(2)   shall <u>consume</u> any alcoholic beverage.

Definition of "**consume**": Following the 1993 legislative session, the term "consume" includes "the ingestion of an alcoholic beverage and the physical condition of having ingested an alcoholic beverage". As a result of this new definition, the act of "underage drinking" is now an ongoing crime and is not limited to the place where initial consumption of alcohol occurred.

Jurisdiction: A violation of the "underage drinking" statute may be prosecuted either in the jurisdiction where consumption occurs or the jurisdiction where evidence of consumption is observed. There is no requirement that officers actually observe the person drinking.

Affirmative defense: If proven by a preponderance of the evidence, it is an affirmative defense to a violation of the above section that defendant consumed the alcoholic beverage in the household of the defendant's parent or guardian with the consent of the parent or guardian.

J. OPEN BOTTLE LAW
M.S. § 169A.35   (Misdemeanor)

Name
Date and Time of Offense
Location (Venue)

(1)	No person shall
(2)	drink or consume intoxicating liquors or 3.2 percent malt liquor
(3)	in a motor vehicle
(4)	when such vehicle is upon a public highway.

OR

(1)	No person shall
(2)	have in possession while in a private motor vehicle upon a street or highway
(3)	any bottle or receptacle containing intoxicating liquor or 3.2 percent malt liquor
(4)	which has been opened, or the seal broken, or the contents which have been partially removed.

Definition of "**Possession**" means either that the person had actual possession of the bottle or receptacle or that the person consciously exercised dominion and control over the bottle or receptacle. (M.S. § 169A.035, Subd. 1(2)).

OR

(1)	The owner of any private motor vehicle or the driver, if the owner is not present in the motor vehicle
(2)	shall not keep or allow to be kept in a motor vehicle
(3)	when the vehicle is upon a street or highway
(4)	any bottle or receptacle containing intoxicating liquor or 3.2 percent malt liquor
(5)	which has been opened, or the seal broken or the contents of which have been partially removed.

Note: The above provisions do not apply to a bottle or receptacle that is in the trunk of the vehicle if it is equipped with a trunk, or that is in another area of the vehicle not normally occupied by the driver and passengers if the vehicle is not equipped with a trunk. However, a utility compartment or glove compartment is deemed to be within the area occupied by the driver and passengers.

Note: As used in this section, the term "motor vehicle" does not include motorboats in operation or off-road recreational vehicles. (M.S. § 169A.35, subd. 1(1)).

Exceptions: None of the above sections apply to the possession or consumption of alcoholic beverages by passengers in:

      i.   a bus that is operated by a motor carrier of passengers, as defined in § 221.011, subd. 48.

      ii.   a vehicle that is operated for commercial purposes in a manner similar to a bicycle as defined in § 169.01, subd. 51, with five or more passengers who provide pedal power to the drive train of the vehicle; or

      iii.   a vehicle providing limousine service, as defined in

§ 221.84, subd. 1.

K. LICENSE PLATE IMPOUNDMENT VIOLATION CRIME
M.S. § 169A.37   (Misdemeanor)

Name
Date and Time of Offense
Location (Venue)

(1)   No person shall
(2)   (a)   fail to comply with an impoundment order under section 169A.60 (administrative plate impoundment)
                or
        (b)   file a false statement under section 169A.60, subd. 7 or 8
                or
        (b)   operate a self-propelled motor vehicle on a street or highway when the vehicle is subject to an impoundment order issued under section 169A.60
                or
        (d)   fail to notify the commissioner of the impoundment order when requesting new plates.

L. DEFINITIONS:

(1)   **Aggravating Factor** (M.S. § 169A.03, Subd. 3)
        "Aggravating factor" includes:
        (1)   a qualified prior impaired driving incident within the ten years immediately preceding the current offense;
        (2)   having an alcohol concentration of 0.16 or more as measured at the time, or within two hours of the offense;
        (3)   having a child under the age of 16 in the motor vehicle at the time of the offense if the child is more than 36 months younger than the offender.

        Note: When determining the number of aggravating factors present, each qualified prior impaired driving incident within ten years immediately preceding the current offense is counted as a separate aggravating factor. (M.S. § 169A.095)

(2)   **All-Terrain Vehicle** (M.S. § 84.787, Subd. 7)
        "All-Terrain Vehicle" means a motorized flotation-tired vehicle of not less than three low pressure tires, but not more than six tires, that is limited in engine displacement of less than 800 cubic centimeters and total dry weight less than 900 pounds.

(3)   **Commercial motor vehicle** (M.S. § 169A.03, subd. 4; § 169.01, subd. 75)

"Commercial motor vehicle" means a motor vehicle or combination of motor vehicles used to transport passengers or property if the motor vehicle:

(a)   has a gross vehicle weight of more than 26,000 pounds;

(b)   has a towed unit with a gross vehicle weight of more than 10,000 pounds and the combination of vehicles has a combined gross vehicle weight of more than 26,000 pounds;

(c)   is a bus;

(d)   is of any size and is used in the transportation of hazardous materials except for those vehicles having a gross vehicle weight of 26,000 pounds or less while carrying in bulk tanks a total of not more than 200 gallons of petroleum products and liquid fertilizer; or

(e)   is outwardly equipped and identified as a school bus (except for school buses as defined in M.S.§ 169.01, subd. 6(c));

(f)   For purposes of sections 169.1211, 169.1215, and 169.123, subdivisions 2 and 4, commercial motor vehicle does not include a farm truck, firefighting equipment, or recreational equipment being operated by a person within the scope of section 171.02, subd. 2(a); and a commercial motor vehicle includes a vehicle capable of or designed to meet the standards described in paragraph (b) above, whether or not the towed unit is attached to the truck-tractor at the time of the violation or stop.

(4)   **Control Analysis** (M.S. § 169A.03, subd. 5a)

"Control Analysis" means a procedure involving a solution that yields a predictable alcohol concentration reading.

(5)   **Controlled substance** (M.S. § 169A.03, subd. 6; § 152.01, subd. 4)

"Controlled substance" means a drug, substance, or immediate precursor in Schedule I through V of section 152.02. The term shall not include distilled spirits, wine, malt beverages, intoxicating liquors or tobacco.

(6)   **Drive a motor vehicle** (CRIMJIG 29.08)

A person "drives" a motor vehicle when the person exercises physical control over the speed and direction of a motor vehicle while it is in motion.

(7) **Hazardous substance** (M.S. § 169A.03, subd. 9)

"Hazardous substance" means any chemical or chemical compound that is listed as a hazardous substance in rules adopted under chapter 182.

(8) **Intoxicating liquor** (M.S. § 340A.101, subd. 14)

"Intoxicating liquor" is ethyl alcohol, distilled, fermented, spirituous, vinous and malt beverages containing more than 3.2% of alcohol by weight.

(9) **Limousine service** (M.S. § 221.84, subd. 1)

"Limousine service" means a service that:

(a)   is not provided on a regular route;

(b)   is provided in an unmarked luxury passenger automobile that is not a van or station wagon and has a seating capacity of not more than 12 persons, excluding the driver;

(c)   provides only prearranged pickup; and

(d)   charges more than a taxi cab fare for a comparable trip.

(10) **Motor carrier of passengers** (M.S. § 221.011, subd. 48)

"Motor carrier of passengers" means a person engaged in the for-hire transportation of passengers in vehicles designed to transport eight or more persons, including the driver.

(11) **Motor Vehicle** (M.S. § 169A.03, Subd. 15)

"Motor Vehicle" means every vehicle that is self-propelled and every vehicle that is propelled by electric power obtained from overhead trolley wires. The term includes motorboats in operation and off-road recreational vehicles, but does not include a vehicle moved solely by human power.

(12) **Nonintoxicating malt liquor** (M.S. § 340A.101, subd. 19)

"Nonintoxicating malt liquor" is malt liquor containing not less than 1/2 of one percent alcohol by volume nor more than 3.2% alcohol by weight.

(13) **Off-Highway Motorcycle** (M.S. 84.787, Subd. 7)

"Off-Highway Motorcycle" means a motorized, off-highway vehicle traveling on two wheels and having a seat or saddle designed to be straddled by the operator and handlebars for steering control, including a vehicle that is registered under chapter 168 for highway use if it is also used for off-highway operation on trails or unimproved terrain.

(14) **Off-Road Recreational Vehicle** (M.S. § 169A.03, Subd. 16)

"Off-road recreational vehicle" means an off-highway motorcycle as defined in section 84.787, subd. 7; off-road vehicle as defined in section 84.797, subd. 7; snowmobile as defined in section 84.81, subd. 3; and all-terrain vehicle as defined in section 84.92, subd. 8.

(15)   **Off-Road Vehicle** (M.S. § 84.797, Subd. 7)

"Off-Road Vehicle" means a motor-driven recreational vehicle capable of cross-country travel on natural terrain without benefit of a road or trail. "Off-Road Vehicle" does not include a snowmobile; an all-terrain vehicle; a watercraft; a farm vehicle being used for farming; a vehicle used for military, fire, emergency, or law enforcement purposes; a construction of logging vehicle used in the performance of its common function; a motor vehicle owned by or operated under contract with a utility, whether publicly or privately owned, when used for work on utilities; a commercial vehicle being used for its intended purpose; snow-grooming equipment when used for its intended purpose; or an aircraft.

(16)   **Operating a motor vehicle** (CRIMJIG 29.08)

A person "operates" a motor vehicle when the person manipulates or activates any of the controls of a motor vehicle necessary to put the vehicle into motion.

(17)   **Physical control of a motor vehicle** (CRIMJIG 29.08)

A person is in "physical control" of a motor vehicle when the person is present in a vehicle and is in a position to either direct the movement of the vehicle or keep the vehicle in restraint. It is not necessary for the engine to be running in order for a person to be in physical control of a motor vehicle.

(18)   **Possession of liquor** (M.S. § 169A.035, subd. 1(2))

"Possession" means either that the person had actual possession of the bottle or receptacle or that the person consciously exercised dominion and control over the bottle or receptacle.

(19)   **Prior Impaired Driving Conviction** (M.S. § 169A.03, Subd. 20)

"Prior impaired driving conviction" includes a prior conviction under any of the following sections:

    a.   M.S. § 169A.20 (driving while impaired and refusal to submit to testing)

    b.   M.S. § 169A.31 (alcohol related school bus or Head Start bus driving)

    c.   M.S. § 360.0752 (impaired aircraft operation)

    d.   M.S. § 609.21 (criminal vehicular homicide and injury, substance-related offenses, specifically § 609.21, subd. 1, clauses (2) to (6)

    e.   Minnesota Statutes 1998, § 169.21 (driver under influence of alcohol or controlled substance)

    f.   Minnesota Statutes 1998, § 169.1211 (alcohol related driving by commercial drivers)

    g.   Minnesota Statutes 1998, § 169.129 (aggravated DWI-related violations, penalty)

h.	Minnesota Statutes 1996, § 84.91, subd. 1(a) (operating snowmobile or all-terrain vehicle while impaired)
i.	Minnesota Statutes 1996, § 86B.331, subd. 1(a) (operating a motorboat while impaired)
j.	M.S. 2006 § 609.21 (criminal vehicular homicide and injury, substance-related offenses, specifically M.S. 2006 § 609.21, subd. 1, clauses (2) to (6); subd. 2, clauses (2) to (6); subd. 2a, clauses (2) to (6); subd. 2b, clauses (2) to (6); subd. 3, clauses (2) to (6); or subd. 4, clauses (2) to (6))
k.	An ordinance from this state, or a statute or ordinance from another state, in conformity with any of the above listed provisions (a) through (j).

Note: a **"prior impaired driving conviction"** also includes a prior juvenile adjudication that would have been a prior impaired driving conviction if committed by an adult.

(20) **Prior Impaired Driving-Related Loss of License** (M.S. § 169A.03, subd. 21)

"Prior impaired driving-related loss of license" includes a driver's license suspension, revocation, cancellation, denial or disqualification under any of the following provisions:

[Note: the following listed prior impaired driving related loss of license provisions (a) through (i) must be a loss of license because of an *alcohol related incident.*]

(a)	M.S. § 169A.31 (alcohol-related school bus or Head Start bus driving)
(b)	M.S. § 169A.50 to § 169A.53 (implied consent law)
(c)	M.S. § 169A.54 (impaired driving convictions and adjudications; administrative penalties)
(d)	M.S. § 171.04 (persons not eligible for driver's licenses)
(e)	M.S. § 171.14 (cancellation)
(f)	M.S. § 171.16 (court may recommend suspension)
(g)	M.S. §171.165 (commercial driver's license disqualification)
(h)	M.S. § 171.17 (revocation)
(i)	M.S. § 171.177 (revocation; pursuant to search warrant)
(j)	M.S. § 171.18 (suspension)
(k)	M.S. § 609.21 (criminal vehicular homicide and injury, substance-related offenses, specifically 609.21, subd. 1, clauses (2) to (6); subd. 2

(l)   Minnesota Statutes 1998, § 169.121 (driver under influence of alcohol or controlled substance)

(m)   Minnesota Statutes 1998, § 169.1211 (alcohol related driving by commercial drivers)

(n)   Minnesota Statutes 1998, § 169.123 (chemical tests for intoxication)

(o)   M.S. 2006 § 609.21 (criminal vehicular homicide and injury, substance related offenses, specifically §§ 609.21, subd. 1, clauses (2) to (6); subd. 2, clauses (2) to (6); subd. 2a, clauses (2) to (6); subd. 2b, clauses (2) to (6); subd. 3, clauses (2) to (6); or subd. 4, clauses (2) to (6))

(p)   M.S. § 609.2112, subd. 1, clauses (2) to (6); subd. 2, clauses (2) to (6), or subd. 3, clauses (2) to (6); or § 609.2114, subd. 1, clauses (2) to (6), or subd. 2, clauses (2) to (6)

(q)   an ordinance from this state, or a statute or ordinance from another state, in conformity with any of the above listed provisions (a) through (n).

"**Prior impaired driving-related loss of license**" also includes the revocation of snowmobile or all-terrain vehicle operating privileges under section 84.911 (chemical testing), or motorboat operating privileges under section 86B.335 (testing for alcohol and controlled substances), for violations that occurred on or after August 1, 1994; the revocation of snowmobile or all-terrain vehicle operating privileges under section 84.91 (operation of snowmobiles and all-terrain vehicles by persons under the influence of alcohol or controlled substances); or the revocation of motorboat operating privileges under section 86B.331 (operation while using alcohol or drugs with a physical or mental disability.

"**Prior impaired driving-related loss of license**" **does not include** any license action stemming solely from a violation of section 169A.33 (underage drinking and driving), 171.09 (conditions of a restricted license), or 340A.503 (persons under the age of 21, illegal acts).

(21)   **Qualified Prior Impaired Driving Incident** (M.S. § 169A.03, subd. 22)

"Qualified prior impaired driving incident" includes prior impaired driving convictions and prior impaired driving-related losses of license.

Note: Prior impaired driving convictions and prior impaired driving-related losses of license must arise out of a separate course of conduct to be considered as multiple qualified prior impaired driving incidents under this chapter. When a person has a prior impaired driving conviction and a prior impaired driving-related loss of license based on the same course of conduct, either conviction or the loss of license may be considered a qualified prior impaired driving incident, but not both. (M.S. § 169A.09)

(22)   **Snowmobile** (M.S. § 84.81, Subd. 3):
"Snowmobile" means a self-propelled vehicle designed for travel on snow or ice steered by skis or runners.

13. FALSE NAME TO PEACE OFFICER OR COURT OFFICIAL

GIVING PEACE OFFICER FALSE NAME
M.S. § 609.506, subd. 1, 2 (Misdemeanor - Gross Misdemeanor)
Name
Date and Time of Offense
Location (Venue)
(1)   No person shall
(2)   with intent to obstruct justice
(3)   give a fictitious name other than a nickname
          or give a false date of birth
          or false or fraudulently altered identification card
(4)   to a peace officer, as defined in M.S. § 626.84, subd. 1(c)
(5)   when that officer makes inquiries incident to a lawful investigatory stop or lawful arrest or inquiries incident to executing any other duty imposed by law. **(Misdemeanor)**

Enhancement: Whoever violates the above section by giving the name and date of birth of another person to a peace officer is guilty of a **gross misdemeanor** rather than a misdemeanor.

Definition of **peace officer** (M.S. § 626.84, subd. 1(c)) - "Peace officer" means an employee or an elected or appointed official of a political subdivision or law enforcement agency who is licensed by the board, charged with the prevention and detection of crime and the enforcement of the general criminal laws of the state and who has the full power of arrest, and shall also include the Minnesota State Patrol, agents of the Division of Gambling Enforcement, state conservation officers, and Metropolitan Transit police officers; and a peace officer who is employed by a law enforcement agency of a federally recognized tribe, as defined in United States code, title 25, section 450b(e), and who is licensed by the board.

* * * * *

GIVING COURT OFFICIAL FALSE NAME
M.S. § 609.506, subd. 3
(Misdemeanor - Gross Misdemeanor)
Name
Date and Time of Offense
Location (Venue)
(1)   No person shall
(2)   in any criminal proceeding
(3)   with intent to obstruct justice
(4)   give a fictitious name, other than a nickname, or give a false date of birth to a court official. **(Misdemeanor)**

Enhancement: Whoever violates the above section by giving the name and date of birth of another person to a court official is guilty of a **gross misdemeanor** rather than a misdemeanor.

Definition of **court official** - "Court official" includes a judge, referee, court administrator, or any employee of the court.

14. FINANCIAL TRANSACTION CARD FRAUD

FINANCIAL TRANSACTION CARD FRAUD
M.S. § 609.821, subd. 1, 2, 3 (Gross Misdemeanor - Felony)

Name
Date and Time of Offense
Location (Venue)

A.	**Use without consent** (subd. 2(1))
(1)	No person shall
(2)	without the consent of the cardholder and knowing that the cardholder has not given consent
(3)	use or attempt to use a card to obtain the property of another, or a public assistance benefit issued for the use of another.

Penalty: To determine if offense is a gross misdemeanor or felony, see Section J, "Special Sentencing Considerations".

OR

B.	**Use of forged or false cards** (subd. 2(2))
(1)	No person shall
(2)	use or attempt to use a card
(3)	knowing it to be forged, false, fictitious or obtained based upon a false application (see Section G. "False Application" below.

Penalty: To determine if offense is a gross misdemeanor or felony, see Section J, "Special Sentencing Considerations".

OR

C.	**Fraudulent providers of goods and services** (subd. 2(5))	
(1)	No person who is authorized by a card issuer to furnish money, goods, services, or anything else of value, shall	
(2)	knowingly and with intent to defraud the issuer or the cardholder	
(3)	a.	furnish money, goods, services, or anything else of value upon presentation of a financial transaction card knowing it to be forged, expired, or revoked, or knowing that it is presented by a person without authority to use the card; **or**
	b.	represents in writing to the issuer that the person has furnished money, goods, services, or anything else of value which has not, in fact, been furnished.

Penalty: To determine if offense is a gross misdemeanor or felony, see Section J, "Special Sentencing Considerations".

OR

D.	**False documents pertaining to card transactions** (subd. 2(8))
(1)	No person shall
(2)	without the consent of the cardholder and knowing that the cardholder has not given consent
(3)	falsely alter, make, or sign any written documents pertaining to a card transaction
(4)	to obtain or attempt to obtain the property of another.
Penalty: To determine if offense is a gross misdemeanor or felony, see Section J, "Special Sentencing Considerations".	

OR

E.	**Sale or transfer of cards** (subd. 2(3))
(1)	No person shall
(2)	sell or transfer a card
(3)	a. knowing that the cardholder and issuer have not authorized the person to whom the card is sold or transferred to use the card; **or** b. knowing that the card is forged, false, fictitious, or was obtained based upon a false application. (See Section G. "False Application" below.)
Penalty: Whoever violates the above section is guilty of a 3-year **felony**.	

OR

F.	**Possession with intent to use, sell or transfer cards** (subd. 2(4))
(1)	No person shall
(2)	without a legitimate business purpose
(3)	and without the consent of the cardholder,
(4)	receive or possess with intent to use, or with intent to sell or transfer in violation of Section E. above
(5)	a. two or more cards issued in the name of another; **or** b. two or more cards knowing the cards to be forged, false, fictitious, or obtained based upon a false application (See Section G. "False Application" below.)
Penalty: Whoever violates the above section is guilty of a 3-year **felony**.	

OR

G.   **False card application** (subd. 2(6))
(1)   No person shall
(2)   upon applying for a financial transaction card to an issuer, or for a public assistance benefit which is distributed by means of a financial transaction card.
(3)   a.   knowingly give a false name or occupation;
         or
      b.   knowingly and substantially overvalue assets or substantially undervalue indebtedness for the purpose of inducing the issuer to issue a financial transaction card;
         or
      c.   knowingly make a false statement or representation for the purpose of inducing an issuer to issue a financial transaction card used to obtain a public assistance benefit.

Penalty: If no property, other than a financial transaction card, has been obtained by means of the false statement, then whoever violates the above section is guilty of a **gross misdemeanor**. However, if property, other than a financial transaction card, is so obtained then to determine if offense is a gross misdemeanor, or felony, see section J "Special Sentencing Considerations".

OR

H.   **False card theft or loss report** (subd. 2(7))
(1)   No person shall
(2)   with intent to defraud
(3)   falsely notify the issuer or any other person
(4)   of a theft, loss, disappearance, or non-receipt of a financial transaction card.

Penalty: If no property, other than a financial transaction card, has been obtained by means of the false report, then whoever violates the above section is guilty of a **gross misdemeanor**. However, if property, other than a financial transaction card, is so obtained then to determine if offense is a gross misdemeanor, or felony, see section J "Special Sentencing Considerations".

OR

I.   Trafficking of SNAP benefits (subd. 2(9))
(1)   No person shall
(2)   Engage in trafficking of SNAP benefits

Penalty: To determine if offense is a gross misdemeanor or felony, see Section J, "Special Sentencing Considerations."

J. SPECIAL SENTENCING CONSIDERATIONS

20-Year Felony
(1)   If the value of the property defendant obtained or attempted to obtain is more than $35,000, or the aggregate amount of the transactions under this chapter is more than $35,000.

10-Year Felony
(1)   If the value of the property the defendant obtained or attempted to obtain is more than $2,500, or the aggregate amount of the transactions under this chapter is more than $2,500.

5-Year Felony
(1)   If the value of the property defendant obtained or attempted to obtain was more than $250 but not more than $2,500, or the aggregate amount of the transactions under this chapter was more than $250 but not more than $2,500;
        or
(2)   The value of the property defendant obtained or attempted to obtain is not more than $250, or the aggregate amount of the transactions under this chapter is not more than $250, and defendant has been convicted of and received a felony or gross misdemeanor sentence, within the preceding five years, for any of the following offenses:
        a.   Financial Transaction Card Fraud (M.S. § 609.821, subd. 2(1-8))
        b.   Simple Robbery (M.S. § 609.24)
        c.   Aggravated Robbery (M.S. § 609.245)
        d.   Theft (M.S. § 609.52)
        e.   Receiving Stolen Property (M.S. § 609.53)
        f.   Burglary, 1st, 2nd or 3rd Degree (M.S. § 609.582, subd. 1, 2 or 3)
        g.   Aggravated Forgery (M.S. § 609.625)
        h.   Forgery (M.S. § 609.63)
        i.   Check Forgery; Offering a Forged Check (M.S. § 609.631)
        j.   or a statute from another state in conformity with any of the above sections.

Note: In order for any of the above convictions to apply for enhancement purposes, the defendant must have received a felony or gross misdemeanor sentence for the offense, or a sentence that was stayed under M.S. § 609.135 if the offense to which a plea was entered would allow imposition of a felony or gross misdemeanor sentence.

Gross Misdemeanor

(1) If the value of the property defendant obtained or attempted to obtain is not more than $250, or the aggregate amount of the transactions under this chapter is not more than $250.

Aggregation: In any prosecution for Financial Transaction Card Fraud under section A (Use without consent), section B (Use of forged or false card), section C (Fraudulent providers of goods and services), or section D (False documents pertaining to card transactions), the value of the transactions made or attempted within any six-month period may be **aggregated** and the defendant charged accordingly in applying the provisions of this section.

Jurisdiction: When two or more offenses are committed by the same person in two or more counties, the accused may be prosecuted in any county in which one of the card transactions occurred for all of the transactions aggregated under the above paragraph.

K.   DEFINITIONS:

(1)   **Cardholder** (M.S. § 609.821, subd. 1(b))
"Cardholder" means a person in whose name a card is issued.

(2)   **Financial transaction card** (M.S. § 609.821, subd. 1(a))
"Financial transaction card" means any instrument or device, whether known as a credit card, credit plate, charge plate, courtesy card, bank service card, banking card, check guarantee card, debit card, electronic benefit system (EBS) card, electronic benefit transfer (EBT) card, assistance transaction card, or by any other name, issued with or without fee by an issuer for the use of the cardholder in obtaining credit, money, goods, services, public assistance benefits, or anything else of value, and includes the account or identification number or symbol of a financial transaction card.

(3)   **Issuer** (M.S. § 609.821, subd. 1(c))
"Issuer" means a person, firm, or governmental agency, or a duly authorized agent, or designee, that issues a financial transaction card.

(4)   **Property** (M.S. § 609.821, subd. 1(d))
"Property" includes money, goods, services, public assistance benefit, or anything else of value.

(5)   **Public assistance benefit** (M.S. § 609.821, subd. 1(e))
"Public assistance benefit" means any money, goods or services, or anything else of value, issued under M.S. § 256 (AFDC), M.S. § 256B (Medical Assistance), M.S. § 256D (General Assistance), or M.S. § 393.07, subd. 10 (Food Stamps).

(6)   **Trafficking of SNAP benefits** (M.S. § 609.821, subd. 1(f))
"Trafficking of SNAP benefits" means:

(a)   The buying, selling, stealing, or otherwise effecting an exchange of Supplemental Nutrition Assistance Program (SNAP) benefits issued and accessed via an electronic benefit number and personal identification number (PIN), or manual voucher and signature, for cash or consideration other than eligible food, either directly, indirectly, in complicity or collusion with others, or acting alone;

(b)   The exchange of one of the following for SNAP benefits: firearms, ammunition, explosives, or controlled substances as defined in United States Code, title 21, section 802;

(c)   Purchasing a product with SNAP benefits that has a container requiring a return deposit with the intent of obtaining cash by discarding the product and returning the container for the deposit amount, intentionally discharging the product and intentionally returning the container for the deposit amount;

(d)   Purchasing a product with SNAP benefits with the intent of obtaining cash or consideration other than eligible food by reselling the product, and intentionally reselling the product purchased with SNAP benefits in exchange for cash or consideration other than eligible food;

(e)   Intentionally purchasing products originally purchased with SNAP benefits in exchange for cash or consideration other than eligible food; or

(f)   Attempting to buy, sell, steal, or otherwise effect an exchange of SNAP benefits issued and accessed via an EBT card, card number and PIN number, or manual voucher and signature, for cash or consideration other than eligible food, either directly, indirectly, in complicity or collusion with others, or acting alone.

15. FLEEING A PEACE OFFICER

A. **FLEEING A PEACE OFFICER IN A MOTOR VEHICLE**
M.S. § 609.487, subd. 1, 2, 3, 4 (Felony)

Name
Date and Time of Offense
Location (Venue)
(1)   No person shall
(2)   by means of a motor vehicle
(3)   flee or attempt to flee
(4)   a peace officer
(5)   who is acting in the lawful discharge of an official duty
(6)   and the person knows or should reasonably know the same to be a peace officer. **(felony - up to 3 years and/or $5,000)**

Enhancement:

a.   Death - Whoever violates the above section (elements 1-6) and during the course of fleeing in a motor vehicle or subsequently by other means causes the death of a human being not constituting murder or manslaughter is guilty of a **felony** up to 10 years and/or $20,000.

b.   Great bodily harm - Whoever violates the above section (elements 1-6) and during the course of fleeing in a motor vehicle or subsequent-ly by other means causes great bodily harm of a human being not constituting murder or manslaughter is guilty of a **felony** up to 7 years and/or $14,000.

c.   Substantial bodily harm - Whoever violates the above section (elements 1-6) and during the course of fleeing in a motor vehicle or subsequently by other means causes substantial bodily harm of a human being not constituting murder or manslaughter is guilty of a **felony** up to 5 years and/or $10,000.

Sentencing: A conviction for "fleeing a peace officer" is not a bar to conviction of or punishment for any other crime committed by the defendant as part of the same conduct. It is not a departure from the sentencing guidelines for a court to impose consecutive sentences for these crimes. M.S. § 609.035, subd. 5.

Note: Possession of Police Radio - Whoever has in possession or uses a radio or device capable of receiving or transmitting a police radio signal, message, or transmission of information used for law enforcement purposes, while committing or attempting to commit a felony or fleeing a peace officer in a motor vehicle is guilty of a **felony**. A prosecution for or conviction of the crime of use or possession of a police radio is not a bar to conviction for any other crime committed while possessing or using the police radio (M.S. § 609.856).

Definition of **"flee"** (M.S. § 609.487, subd. 1) - means to increase speed, extinguish motor vehicle headlights or taillights, refuse to stop the vehicle, or to use other means with intent to attempt to elude a peace officer following a signal given by any peace officer to the driver of a motor vehicle.

Definition of **"motor vehicle"** (M.S. § 609.487, subd. 2a) - "Motor vehicle" means every vehicle which is self-propelled or every vehicle which is propelled by electric power obtained from overhead trolley wires. Motor vehicle does not include a vehicle moved solely by human power. (See M.S. § 169.01, subd. 3). For purposes of the above section it also includes a snowmobile, as defined in section 84.81.

Definition of **"motor vehicle forfeiture"** (M.S. § 609.5312, subd. 4(a)) -any motor vehicle used to commit the crime of "fleeing a peace officer" is subject to seizure or forfeiture if the act of fleeing endangered life or property. If the motor vehicle is seized (without a judicial forfeiture order) by officers incident to the driver's arrest or otherwise during a lawful search, a hearing before a judge must be held within 96 hours of the seizure. Because there are special notification, procedural and forfeiture requirements that must be complied with, it is very important that you notify the local prosecuting authority of the motor vehicle seizure as soon as possible. (M.S. § 609.5312, subd. 4(b)) - "The Department of Corrections' Fugitive Apprehension Unit shall not seize real property for the purposes of forfeiture under paragraphs (a) to (g)."

Definition of **"peace officer"** (M.S. § 609.487, subd. 2) - an employee of a political subdivision or state law enforcement agency who is licensed by the Minnesota Board of Peace Officer Standards and Training, charged with the prevention and detection of crime and the enforcement of the general criminal laws of the state and who has the full power of arrest, and shall also include the Minnesota State Patrol and Minnesota Conservation officers; or a member of a duly organized state, county or municipal law enforcement unit of another state charged with the duty to prevent and detect crime and generally enforce criminal laws, and granted full powers of arrest.

Driver License Revocation: When a person is convicted of operating a motor vehicle in violation of the above section or an ordinance in conformity with the above section, the Court shall notify the Commissioner of Public Safety and order the Commissioner to revoke the driver's license of the person (M.S. § 609.487, subd. 5).

B.   FLEEING, OTHER THAN VEHICLE
M.S. § 609.487, subd. 6 (Misdemeanor)

Name

Date and Time of Offense

Location (Venue)

(1)   No person shall

(2)   a.   for the purpose of avoiding arrest, detention, or investigation
        or
        b.   in order to conceal or destroy potential evidence related to the commission of a crime

(3)   attempt to evade or elude

(4)   a peace officer

(5)   who was acting in the lawful discharge of an official duty

(6)   by means of running, hiding, or by any other means except fleeing in a motor vehicle.

16. FORGERY AND RELATED OFFENSES

A. FORGERY
M.S. § 609.63, subds. 1, 2 (Felony)

Name
Date and Time of Offense
Location (Venue)

(1)		No person shall
(2)		with intent to injure or defraud
(3)	a.	use a false writing
	b.	knowing it to be false
	c.	for the purpose of identification or recommendation.

OR

(1)		No person shall
(2)		with intent to injure or defraud
(3)	a.	without consent
	b.	place, or possess with intent to place,
	c.	upon any merchandise
	d.	an identifying label or stamp
	e.	which is or purports to be that of another craftsperson, tradesperson, packer or manufacturer,
	f.	or dispose or possess with intent to dispose of any merchandise so labeled or stamped.

OR

(1)		No person shall
(2)		with intent to injure or defraud
(3)	a.	falsely make or alter
	b.	a membership card purporting to be that of a fraternal, business, professional or other association, or of any labor union, or
	c.	possess any such card knowing it to have been thus falsely made or altered.

OR

(1)		No person shall
(2)		with intent to injure or defraud
(3)	a.	falsely make or alter a writing
	b.	or possess a falsely made or altered writing
	c.	evidencing a right to transportation on a common carrier.

OR

(1)	No person shall	
(2)	with intent to injure or defraud	
(3)	a.	destroy, mutilate or by alteration, false entry or omission
	b.	falsify any record, account or other document relating to a private business.

OR

(1)	No person shall	
(2)	with intent to injure or defraud	
(3)	a.	without authority of law
	b.	destroy, mutilate or by alteration, false entry or omission
	c.	falsify any record, account or other document
	d.	relating to a person, corporation or business,
	e.	or filed in the office of, or deposited with, any public office or officer.

OR

(1)	No person shall	
(2)	with intent to injure or defraud	
(3)	a.	destroy a writing or object
	b.	to prevent it from being produced at a trial, hearing or other proceeding authorized by law.

OR

(1)	No person shall
(2)	with knowledge that it is forged,
(3)	offer in evidence
(4)	in any trial, hearing or other proceeding authorized by law, as genuine,
(5)	any forged writing or object.

B.   AGGRAVATED FORGERY
M.S. § 609.625, subd. 1, 2, 3 (Felony)

Name
Date and Time of Offense
Location (Venue)

Making or altering a writing or object (subd. 1)
(1)   No person shall

(2)		with intent to defraud
(3)		falsely make or alter a writing or object of any of the following kinds:
(4)	a.	a writing or object whereby, when genuine, legal rights, privileges or obligations are created, terminated, transferred or evidenced, or any writing normally relied upon as evidence of debt or property rights, other than a check as defined in M.S. § 609.631 (Check Forgery - See Section C below) or a financial transaction card as defined in chapter 14, section J. "Definitions"; or
	b.	an official seal or the seal of a corporation; or
	c.	a public record or an official authentication or certification of a copy thereof; or
	d.	an official return or certificate entitled to be received as evidence of its contents; or
	e.	a court order, judgment, decree or process; or
	f.	the records or accounts of a public body, office or officer; or
	g.	the records or accounts of a bank or person, with whom funds of the state or any of its agencies or subdivisions are deposited or entrusted, relating to such funds
(5)	a.	so that it purports to have been made by another
	b.	or by the maker or alterer under an assumed or fictitious name
	c.	or at another time
	d.	or with different provisions or by authority of one who did not give such authority.

OR

Means for false reproduction (subd. 2)

(1)	No person shall
(2)	with intent to defraud
(3)	make, engrave, possess or transfer
(4)	a plate or instrument for the false reproduction of a writing or object mentioned above (see **Making or altering a writing or object**), or a check as defined in section C. below, or a financial transaction card as defined in chapter 14, section J, "Definitions".

OR

<table>
<tr><td>

Uttering or possessing (subd. 3)
(1)   No person shall
(2)   with intent to defraud
(3)   utter or possess with intent to utter
(4)   any forged writing or object mentioned above (see **Making or altering a writing or object**) not including a check as defined in Section C below, or a financial transaction card as defined in Chapter 14, section J, "Definitions".
(5)   knowing it to have been so forged.
</td></tr>
</table>

C.   CHECK FORGERY; OFFERING A FORGED CHECK
M.S. § 609.631, subds. 1, 2, 3 (Gross Misdemeanor - Felony)

Name
Date and Time of Offense
Location (Venue)

<table>
<tr><td>

Check forgery
(1)   No person shall
(2)   with intent to defraud
(3)   falsely make or alter a check
(4)   a.   so that it purports to have been made by another
        b.   or by the maker under an assumed or fictitious name
        c.   or at another time
        d.   or with different provisions
        e.   or by the authority of one who did not give authority
        f.   or falsely endorse or alter a check so that it purports to have been endorsed by another.

Penalty: See Section D, "Sentencing Considerations" below.
</td></tr>
</table>

OR

<table>
<tr><td>

Offering a forged check
(1)   No person shall
(2)   with intent to defraud
(3)   offer or possess with intent to offer
(4)   a forged check
(5)   whether or not it is accepted.

Penalty: See Section D, "Sentencing Considerations" below.
</td></tr>
</table>

Definition of "**check**": (M.S. § 609.631, subd. 1(b)) - means a check, draft, order of withdrawal, or similar negotiable or non-negotiable instrument.

D. **SENTENCING CONSIDERATIONS**

20-Year Felony

(1)　If the forged check or checks are used to obtain, or in an attempt to obtain, property or services of more than $35,000, or the aggregate amount of the forged checks is more than $35,000.

10-Year Felony

(1)　If the forged check or checks are used to obtain, or in an attempt to obtain, property or services of more than $2,500, or the aggregate amount of the forged checks is more than $2,500.

5-Year Felony

(1)　If the forged check or checks are used to obtain, or in an attempt to obtain, property or services of more than $250 but not more than $2,500, or the aggregate face amount of the forged checks is more than $250 but not more than $2,500.

　　or

(2)　If the forged check or checks are used to obtain, or in an attempt to obtain, property or services of no more than $250, or have an aggregate face value of no more than $250, and defendant has been convicted of and received a felony or gross misdemeanor sentence, within the preceding five years, for any of the following offenses:

a.　Check Forgery (M.S. § 609.631)

b.　Robbery (M.S. § 609.24)

c.　Aggravated Robbery (M.S. § 609.245)

d.　Theft (M.S. § 609.52)

e.　Receiving Stolen Property (M.S. § 609.53)

f.　Burglary - 1st, 2nd or 3rd Degree (M.S. § 609.582, subds. 1, 2, 3)

g.　Aggravated Forgery (M.S. § 609.625)

h.　Forgery (M.S. § 609.63)

i.　Financial Transaction Card Fraud (M.S. § 609.821)

j.　or a statute from another state in conformity with any of the above sections

Gross Misdemeanor

(1)　　　If the forged check or checks are used to obtain, or in an attempt to obtain, property or services of no more than $250, or the aggregate face amount of the forged checks is no more than $250.

Aggregation:　The value of the checks forged or offered by defendant in violation of any of the above sections within any six-month period may be aggregated and the defendant charged accordingly in applying the provisions of the above sections.

Jurisdiction:　When two or more offenses are committed by the same defendant in two or more counties, the defendant may be prosecuted in any county in which one of the checks was forged or offered for all of the offenses aggregated under the above paragraph.

17. FRAUDULENT DRIVER'S LICENSES AND IDENTIFICATION CARDS

A. **FRAUDULENT DRIVER'S LICENSES AND
IDENTIFICATION CARDS
M.S. § 609.652, subds. 1, 2, 3 (Gross Misdemeanor - Felony)**

Name
Date and Time of Offense
Location (Venue)

(1)		No person shall for consideration
(2)		with intent to manufacture, sell, issue, publish, or pass more than one fraudulent driver's license or identification card
(3)	a.	have control, custody, or possession of any plate, block, press, stone, digital image, computer software program, encoding equipment, computer optical scanning equipment, digital photo printer, or other implement, or part of such item, designed to assist in making a fraudulent driver's license or identification card
	or	
	b.	engrave, make, or amend, or begin to engrave, make, or amend, any plate, block, press, stone, or other implement for the purpose of producing a fraudulent driver's license or identification card
	or	
	c.	use a photocopier, digital camera, photographic image, or computer software to generate a fraudulent driver's license or identification card
	or	
	d.	have control, custody, or possession or make or provide paper or other material adapted and designed for the making of a fraudulent driver's license or identification card
	or	
	e.	print, photograph, or in any manner make or execute an engraved photograph, print, or impression purporting to be a driver's license or identification card

OR

(1)	No person shall for consideration
(2)	cause or permit to be used in forging or making more than one false or counterfeit driver's license or identification card

      a.   a plate, block, press, stone, digital image, computer software program, encoding equipment, computer optical scanning equipment, digital photo printer, or other implement, or any part thereof, designed to assist in making a fraudulent driver's license or identification card

    or

      b.   a photocopier, digital camera, photographic image, or paper or other material adapted or designed for the making of a fraudulent driver's license or identification card.

B. **DEFINITIONS**

(1) **Driver's license or identification card** (M.S. § 609.652, subd. 1(1))

"Driver's license or identification card" means a driver's license or identification card issued by the driver and vehicle services division of the department of public safety or receipts issued by its authorized agents or those of any state as defined in M.S. § 171.01 that issues licenses recognized in this state for the operation of a motor vehicle or that issues identification cards recognized in this state for the purpose of indicating a person's legal name and age.

(2) **Fraudulent driver's license or identification card** (M.S. § 609.652, subd 1(2))

"Fraudulent driver's license or identification card" means a document purporting to be a driver's license or identification card, but that is not authentic.

(3) **Sell** (M.S. § 609.652, subd 1(3))

"Sell" means to sell, barter, deliver, exchange, distribute, or dispose of to another.

Penalty: Whoever violates either of the above sections is guilty of a **gross misdemeanor.** A second or subsequent conviction for this offense may be sentenced as a 5-year **felony.** (M.S. § 609.652, subd 3)

18. FRAUDULENT OR OTHERWISE IMPROPER FINANCING STATEMENTS

FRAUDULENT OR OTHERWISE IMPROPER FINANCIAL STATEMENTS
M.S. § 609.7475, subd. 2, 3 (Gross Misdemeanor – Felony)
Name
Date and Time of Offense
Location (Venue)

(1) No person shall
(2) knowingly cause a record to be presented for filing
(3) or promote the filing of a record

(4)	that is not
	a. related to a valid lien or security agreement
	or
	b. filed pursuant to M.S. § 336.9-502(d)

OR

(5)	that contains a forged signature or is based on a document containing a forged signature.

OR

(6)	files, or presents for filing, a record with the intent that is be used to defraud or harass any other person.

Penalties:
A violation of subd. 2 is a **gross misdemeanor**. A violation of subd. 3 is a **five-year felony**, with a maximum fine of $10,000, if the person:

(a) commits the offense with the intent to influence or otherwise tamper with a juror or a judicial proceeding, or with intent to retaliate against a judicial officer, prosecutor, defense attorney, or officer of the court, because of that person's performance of official duties in connection with a judicial proceeding;
    OR
(b) commits the offense after having been previously convicted of a violation under this section.

19. HIT AND RUN TRAFFIC ACCIDENTS

HIT AND RUN TRAFFIC ACCIDENTS
M.S. § 169.09, subd. 1 to 15 (Misdemeanor, Gross Misdemeanor, Felony)
Name
Date and Time of Offense
Location (Venue)

A.	**Personal Injury Accident (subds. 1,3,6,7,14,15)**
(1)	The driver of any vehicle involved in an accident
(2)	resulting in immediately demonstrable bodily injury to, or death of any person
(3)	shall immediately stop the vehicle at the scene of the accident or as close to the same as possible, without unnecessarily obstructing traffic, but shall then return to the scene
(4)	and in every event, shall remain at the scene of the accident until the driver has provided information as required by M.S. § 169.09, subd. 7 (i.e. driver's name, address, date of birth, registration number of the vehicle being driven and, upon request and if available, exhibit the drivers license or drivers permit to the person struck or to the driver, occupant of, or person attending any vehicle collided with).
(5)	after complying with the above provisions, the driver of a vehicle involved in an accident resulting in bodily harm to or death of any person shall, by the quickest means of communication, give notice of the accident to the local police department, state patrol officer or sheriffs office.

Penalty:
a.   **Driver Who Causes Accident (M.S. § 609.21)** - Any driver who <u>causes</u> an accident which results in bodily injury, substantial bodily harm, great bodily harm or death to any person and who then leaves the scene of an accident in violation of the above section is subject to the criminal penalties in M.S. § 609.21 "Criminal Vehicular Homicide and Injury". See chapter 7.

b.   **Driver Who Does Not Cause Accident (subd. 14)** - Any driver who is involved in, but does not cause, an accident resulting in bodily injury, substantial bodily harm, great bodily harm or death to any person and who then violates the above section is guilty of:

(i)   if accident results in the death of any person (**3-year felony**)

(ii)   if accident results in great bodily harm to any person (**2-year felony**)

(iii)   if accident results in bodily injury or substantial bodily harm to any person (**gross misdemeanor**).

Note: Rendering Reasonable Assistance (subd. 3) - The driver of any vehicle involved in an accident resulting in bodily injury to any person shall render reasonable assistance to any person injured in the accident. Violation of this section is a **misdemeanor**.

Affirmative Defense (subd. 15): It is an affirmative defense that the driver left the scene of the accident to take any person suffering immediately demonstrable bodily injury in the accident to receive emergency medical care if the driver of the involved vehicle gives notice to a law enforcement agency as required by the above section as soon as reasonably feasible after the emergency medical care has been undertaken.

OR

B.   Property Damage, Occupied Vehicle (subds. 2,3,7,14)

(1)   The driver of any vehicle involved in an accident to a vehicle (not resulting in bodily injury or death)

(2)   which is driven or attended by any person

(3)   shall immediately stop such vehicle at the scene of the accident or as close thereto as possible without obstructing traffic more than is necessary, but shall forthwith return to the accident scene

(4)   and, in every event, shall remain at the scene of the accident until the driver has provided information as required by M.S. § 169.09 (i.e. driver's name, address, date of birth, registration number of the vehicle being driven, and, upon request and if available, exhibit the drivers license or drivers permit to the person struck or the driver or occupant of or person attending any vehicle collided with or to any peace officer at the scene or who is investigating the accident).

Penalty: Any driver who violates the above section is guilty of a **misdemeanor**.

OR

C.   **Property Damage, Unattended Vehicle (subds. 4 & 7)**
(1)   The driver of any vehicle which collides with and damages
(2)   any vehicle which is unattended
(3)   shall immediately stop and either:
a.   locate and notify the driver or owner of the vehicle, of the name and address of the driver and owner of the vehicle striking the unattended vehicle, **or**
b.   shall report the same to a police officer **or**
c.   shall leave in a conspicuous place in or secured to the vehicle struck a written notice giving the name and address of the driver and of the owner of the vehicle doing the striking.
Penalty: Whoever violates the above section is guilty of a **misdemeanor**.

OR

D.   **Property Damage, Non-vehicle (subd. 5)**
(1)   The driver of any vehicle involved in an accident
(2)   resulting only in damage to fixtures legally upon or adjacent to a highway
(3)   shall take reasonable steps to:
a.   locate and notify the owner or person in charge of such property of such fact and of the driver's name and address and of the registration number of the vehicle being driven, **and**
b.   shall, upon request and if available, exhibit the drivers or chauffeur's license, **and**
c.   make a report of such accident in every case to the Commissioner of Public Safety within ten days thereof (regardless of the amount of property damage).
Penalty: Whoever violates the above section is guilty of a **misdemeanor**.

Note: Filing Accident Report (subd. 7 & 8) - The driver of a vehicle involved in an accident resulting in bodily injury to or death of any person or total property damage to an apparent extent of $1,000 or more, shall forward a written report of the accident to the Commission of Public Safety within ten days thereof. On the required report, the driver shall provide the Commissioner with the name and policy number of the insurer providing vehicle liability coverage at the time of the accident. The ten day filing requirement for accident reports also applies to law enforcement officers investigating the accident. Violation of this section is a **misdemeanor**.

<u>Note:</u> Insurance Information (subd. 3) - If not given at the scene of the accident, the driver, within 72 hours thereafter, shall give, upon request to any person involved in the accident or to a peace officer investigating the accident, the name and address of the insurer providing automobile liability insurance coverage and the local insurance agent for the insurer. Violation of this section is a **misdemeanor**.

E.   DEFINITIONS:
(1)   **Bodily injury** (M.S. § 609.02, subd. 7)
          "Bodily injury" means physical pain or injury, illness or any impairment of physical condition.
(2)   **Demonstrable bodily injury** (CRIMJIG 13.10)
          "Demonstrable bodily injury" is not defined by statute. It is a word of common usage. Webster's Dictionary defines "demonstrable" as "capable of being demonstrated" (i.e. cuts, scratches, visible bruises or non-visible medically confirmed injuries).
(3)   **Great bodily harm** (M.S. § 609.02, subd. 8)
          "Great bodily harm" means bodily injury which creates a high probability of death, or which causes serious permanent disfigurement, or which causes a permanent or protracted loss or impairment of the function of any bodily member or organ or other serious bodily harm.
(4)   **Substantial bodily harm** (M.S. § 609.02, subd. 7a)
          "Substantial bodily harm" means bodily injury which involves a temporary but substantial disfigurement, or which causes a temporary but substantial loss or impairment of the function of any bodily member or organ, or which causes a fracture of any bodily member.
(5)   **Vehicle** (M.S. § 169.01, subd. 2)
          "Vehicle" means every device in, upon, or by which any person or property is or may be transported or drawn upon a highway, excepting devices used exclusively upon stationary rails or tracks.

20. IDENTITY THEFT

A. IDENTITY THEFT
M.S. § 609.527, subds. 1, 2, 3 (Misdemeanor - Gross Misdemeanor - Felony)
Name
Date and Time of Offense
Location (Venue)
(1)   No person shall
(2)   with intent to commit, aid, or abet any unlawful activity
(3)   transfer, possess, or use an identity that is not the person's own

Definitions: **"Direct victim"** means any person or entity whose identity has been transferred, used, or possessed in violation of this section. **"Identity"** means any name, number, or data transmission that may be used, alone or in conjunction with any other information, to identify a specific individual or entity including a name, social security number, date of birth, official government-issued driver's license, or identification number, government passport number, employer or taxpayer identification number, unique electronic identification number, address, account number, routing code, telecommunication identification information, or access device. **"Indirect victim"** means any person or entity other than a direct victim. **"Loss"** means value obtained and expenses incurred by a direct or indirect victim as a result of a violation of this section. **"Unlawful activity"** means any felony violation of the laws of this state or any felony violation of a similar law of another state or the United States and any non-felony violation of the laws of this state involving theft, theft by swindle, forgery, fraud, or giving false information to a public official, or any other non-felony violation of a similar law of another state or the United States.

Penalties: If the offense involves a single direct victim and the total, combined loss to the direct victim and any indirect victims is $250 or less, the penalty is a **misdemeanor**. If the offense involves a single direct victim and the total, combined loss to the direct victim and any indirect victims is more than $250 but not more than $500, the penalty is a **gross misdemeanor**. If the offense involves two or three direct victims or the total, combined loss to the direct and indirect victims is more than $500 but not more than $2,500, the penalty is a **five-year felony**. If the offense involves more than three but not more than seven direct victims, or if the total, combined loss to the direct and indirect victims is more than $2,500, the penalty is a **ten-year felony**. If the offense involves eight or more direct victims, or if the total, combined loss to the direct and indirect victims is more than $35,000, or if the offense relates to the possession or distribution of pornographic work, the penalty is a twenty-year felony.

Aggregation: In any prosecution for identity theft, the value of the money or property or services the defendant receives or the number of direct or indirect victims within any six-month period may be aggregated and the defendant charged accordingly in applying the penalty provisions; provided that when two or more offenses are committed by the same person in two or more counties, the accused may be prosecuted in any county in which one of the offenses was committed for all of the offenses aggregated under this statute.

Venue: An offense may be prosecuted in the county where the offense occurred or the county of residence or place of business of the direct or indirect victim.

B. CRIME OF ELECTRONIC USE OF FALSE PRETENSE TO OBTAIN PROPERTY
M.S. § 609.527, Subd. 5(a) (Felony)

Name
Date and Time of Offense
Location (Venue)
(1)   No person shall
(2)   with intent to obtain the identify of another
(3)   use a false pretense
(4)   a.   in an e-mail to another person,
        or
        b.   in a Web page, electronic communication, advertisement, or any other communication on the Internet.

Definition of "**False Pretense**" – means any false, fictitious, misleading, or fraudulent information or pretense or pretext depicting or including or deceptively similar to the name, logo, Web site address, e-mail address, postal address, telephone number, or any other identifying information of a for-profit or not-for-profit business or organization or of a governmental agency, to which the user has no legitimate claim of right.

Note: It is **not** a defense that the person committing the offense did not obtain the identity of another person, did not use the identity of another person, or the offense did not result in financial loss or any other to any person.

Venue: An offense may be prosecuted in the county where the offense occurred or the county of residence of the person whose identity was obtained or sought.

C.   UNLAWFUL POSSESSION OR USE OF SCANNING DEVICE OR REENCODER
M.S. § 609.527, Subd. 5(b) (Felony)

Name

Date and Time of Offense

Location (Venue)

(1)	No person shall
(2)	with intent to commit, aid, or abet any unlawful activity
(3)	use a scanning device or reencoder without the permission of the cardholder of the card from which with information is being scanned or reencoded.

OR

(1)	No person shall
(2)	with intent to commit, aid, or abet any unlawful activity
(3)	possess any device, apparatus, equipment, software, material, good, property, or supply that is designed or adapted for use as a scanning device or reencoder.

Definitions: **"Scanning device"** means a scanner, reader, or any other electronic device that is used to access, read, scan, obtain, memorize, or store, temporarily or permanently, information encoded on a computer chip or magnetic strip or stripe of a payment card, driver's license, or state-issued identification card. **"Reencoder"** means an electronic device that places encoded information from the computer chip or magnetic strip or stripe of a payment card, driver's license, or state-issued identification card, onto the computer chip or magnetic strip or stripe of a different payment card, driver's license, or state-issued identification card, or any electronic medium that allows an authorized transaction to occur. **"Payment card"** means a credit card, charge card, debit card, or any other card that: (1) is issued to an authorized card user; and (2) allows the user to obtain, purchase, or receive credit, money, a good, a service, or anything of value.

21. KIDNAPPING AND FALSE IMPRISONMENT

A.   KIDNAPPING
   M.S. § 609.25 (Felony)

Name
Date and Time of Offense
Location (Venue)
(1)   No person shall
(2)   confine or remove from one place to another
(3)   a.   any person without the person's consent
                 or
         b.   if the person is under the age of 16 years, without the consent
                 of the person's parents or other legal custodian
(4)   for any of the following purposes:
         a.   to hold for ransom or reward for release, or as shield or
                 hostage.
                 or
         b.   to facilitate commission of any felony or flight thereafter.
                 or
         c.   to commit great bodily harm or to terrorize the victim or
                 another.
                 or
         d.   to hold in involuntary servitude.

Increased penalty: If the victim is not released in a safe place or if the victim
suffers great bodily harm during the course of the kidnapping, or if the person
kidnapped is under the age of 16, the penalties may be significantly increased.

Jurisdiction: Violations of the above section may be prosecuted either in the
county where the offense was committed or in any county through or in which
the person kidnapped was taken or kept while under confinement or restraint
(Rule of Criminal Procedure 24.02, Subd. 6).

B.   FALSE IMPRISONMENT - Intentional Restraint
   M.S. § 609.255, subd. 2 (Felony)

Name
Date and Time of Offense
Location (Venue)
(1)   No person shall
(2)   knowingly lacking lawful authority to do so
(3)   a.   intentionally confine or restrain someone else's child under
                 the age of 18 years without consent of the child's parent or
                 legal custodian

- 144 -

or

b.   any other person without the person's consent.

C.   FALSE IMPRISONMENT - Unreasonable Restraint of Children M.S. § 609.255, subd. 3 (Gross Misdemeanor - Felony)

Name

Date and Time of Offense

Location (Venue)

(1)   No parent, legal guardian or caretaker shall

(2)   intentionally subject a child under the age of 18 years

(3)   to unreasonable physical confinement or restraint

(4)   by means including but not limited to tying, locking, caging or chaining for a prolonged period of time and in a cruel manner which is excessive under the circumstances. **(gross misdemeanor)**

Enhancement: If the confinement or restraint results in demonstrable bodily harm, defendant is guilty of a **felony**.

Jurisdiction: In Anoka, Carver, Dakota, Hennepin, Ramsey, Scott and Washington Counties, the county attorney shall prosecute all felony and gross misdemeanor violations of the above section (M.S. § 388.05, Subd. 2(a),(b).

Definition of **caretaker** (M.S. § 609.255, subd. 1) - "caretaker" means an individual who has responsibility for the care of a child as a result of a family relationship, or who has assumed responsibility for all or a portion of the care of a child.

- 145 -

22. MAIL THEFT

A. MAIL THEFT
    M.S. § 609.529 (Felony)

Name
Date and Time of Offense
Location (Venue)

(1)   No person shall

(2)   intentionally and without claim of right remove mail from a mail depository; or

(3)   intentionally and without claim of right take mail from a mail carrier; or

(4)   obtain custody of mail by intentionally deceiving a mail carrier, or other person who rightfully possesses or controls the mail, with a false representation which is known to be false, made with intent to deceive and which does deceive a mail carrier or other person who possesses or controls the mail or

(5)   intentionally and without claim of right remove the contents of mail addressed to another; or

(6)   intentionally and without claim of right take mail, or the contents of mail, that has been left for collection on or near a mail depository; or

(7)   receive, possess, transfer, buy, or conceal mail obtained by acts described above, knowing or having reason to know the mail was obtained illegally.

Definitions: "**Mail**" means a letter, postal card, package, bag or other sealed article addressed to another. "**Mail depository**" means a mail box, letter box, or mail receptacle; a post office or station of a post office; a mail route; or a postal service vehicle.

Venue: Mail theft may be prosecuted in the county where the offense occurred or the county of residence or place of business of the direct or indirect victim. (M.S. § 609.529, subd. 4).

- 146 -

23. MALICIOUS PUNISHMENT, NEGLECT OR ENDANGERMENT OF A CHILD

A.   MALICIOUS PUNISHMENT OF A CHILD
M.S. § 609.377 (Gross Misdemeanor - Felony)

Name
Date and Time of Offense
Location (Venue)
(1)   No parent, legal guardian or caretaker shall
(2)   by an intentional act or a series of intentional acts with respect to a child (under 18 years)
(3)   use unreasonable force or cruel discipline
(4)   that is excessive under the circumstances.

Enhancement: Whoever violates the above section during the period of time between a previous conviction or adjudication for delinquency under this section or M.S. § 609.221 to § 609.224 (Assault in the First through Fifth Degrees) or M.S. § 609.2242 (Domestic Assault) or M.S. § 609.342 to § 609.345 (Criminal Sexual Conduct in the First through Fourth Degrees) or M.S. § 609.713 (Terroristic Threats) and the end of five years following discharge from sentence or disposition for that conviction or adjudication may be sentenced to a five-year felony.

Penalties: If the punishment results in less than substantial bodily harm, the penalty is a **gross misdemeanor**. If the punishment results in substantial bodily harm, the penalty is a **five-year felony**. If the punishment results in great bodily harm, the penalty is a **ten-year felony**. If the punishment is to a child under the age of 4 and causes bodily harm to the head, eyes, neck, or otherwise causes multiple bruises to the body, the penalty is a **five-year felony**.

Jurisdiction - Gross misdemeanor: In Anoka, Carver, Dakota, Hennepin, Ramsey, Scott and Washington Counties, the county attorney shall prosecute all felony and gross misdemeanor violations of the above section (M.S. § 388.051, Subd. 2(a), (b).

Jurisdiction - Child victim: If the victim is a child (under 18 years), violations of the above section may be prosecuted in either the county where the incident occurred or where the child was found (M.S. § 627.15).

B. NEGLECT OR ENDANGERMENT OF A CHILD
M.S. § 609.378, subds. 1, 2 (Gross Misdemeanor - Felony)

Name
Date and Time of Offense
Location (Venue)

Neglect
(1)   No parent, legal guardian or caretaker shall
(2)   willfully deprive a child (under 18 years) of necessary food, clothing, shelter, health care, or supervision appropriate to the child's age
(3)   when the parent, guardian or caretaker is reasonably able to make the necessary provisions
(4)   and the deprivation harms or is likely to substantially harm the child's physical, mental, or emotional health. **(gross misdemeanor)**

Enhancement: If the deprivation results in substantial harm to the child's physical, mental, or emotional health, defendant is guilty of a **felony**.

"Substantial harm" is not defined by statute; consult with your county attorney for clarification.

Note on health care: If a parent, guardian or caretaker responsible for the child's care in good faith selects and depends upon spiritual means or prayer for treatment or care of disease or remedial care of the child, this treatment or care is "health care" for purposes of the above section.

OR

Neglect - Physical or Sexual Abuse
(1)   No parent, legal guardian or caretaker shall
(2)   knowingly permit the continuing physical or sexual abuse of a child (under 18 years). **(gross misdemeanor)**

Defense: It is a defense to a prosecution under the above section that at the time of the neglect there was a reasonable apprehension in the mind of the defendant that acting to stop or prevent the neglect would result in substantial bodily harm to the defendant or the child in retaliation.

OR

- 148 -

Endangerment
(1)   No parent, legal guardian or caretaker shall
(2)   endanger a child's (under 18 years) person or health by:
(3)   a.   intentionally or recklessly causing or permitting a child to be placed in a situation likely to substantially harm the child's physical, mental, or emotional health or cause the child's death.

                      or

          b.   by knowingly causing or permitting the child to be present where any person is selling, manufacturing, possessing immediate precursors or chemical substances with intent to manufacture or possessing a controlled substance, as defined in M.S. § 152.01, subd. 4, in violation of M.S. § 152.021, 022, 023 or 024 (Controlled Substance Crimes in the 1st to 4th Degree). **(gross misdemeanor)**

Enhancement: If the endangerment results in substantial harm to the child's physical, mental, or emotional health, the defendant is guilty of a **felony**. "Substantial harm" is not defined by statute; consult with your county attorney for clarification.

Note: The above section does not prevent a parent, legal guardian or caretaker from causing or permitting a child to engage in activities that are appropriate to the child's age, stage of development and experience, or from selecting health care in good faith which depends upon spiritual means or prayer for treatment or care of disease or remedial care of the child.

Defense: It is a defense to a prosecution under the above section that at the time of the neglect there was a reasonable apprehension in the mind of the defendant that acting to stop or prevent the neglect would result in substantial bodily harm to the defendant or the child in retaliation.

OR

> **Child Endangerment by Firearm Access**
> (1)   No person shall
> (2)   intentionally or recklessly cause a child under 14 years of age
> (3)   to be placed in a situation likely to substantially harm the child's physical health or cause the child's death
> (4)   as a result of the child's access to a loaded firearm.   **(gross misdemeanor)**
>
> Enhancement: If the endangerment results in substantial harm to the child's physical health, defendant is guilty of a **felony**.
>
> Cross Reference: See also "NEGLIGENT STORAGE OF FIREARMS", chapter 9, section C.

Jurisdiction - Gross misdemeanor: In Anoka, Carver, Dakota, Hennepin, Ramsey, Scott and Washington Counties, the county attorney shall prosecute all felony and gross misdemeanor violations of any of the above sections (M.S. § 388.051, Subd. 2(a), (b)).

Jurisdiction - Child victim: If the victim is a child (under 18 years), violations of the above section may be prosecuted in either the county where the incident occurred or where the child was found (M.S. § 627.15).

C.   DEFINITIONS:
(1)   **Caretaker** (M.S. § 609.376, subd. 3)
             "Caretaker" is defined in chapter 21 (Kidnapping and False Imprisonment), section C.
(2)   **Controlled substance** (M.S. § 152.01, subd. 4)
             "Controlled substance" is defined in chapter 4 (Controlled Substance Crimes), section X.
(3)   **Great bodily harm** (M.S. § 609.02, subd. 8)
             "Great bodily harm" is defined in chapter 2 (Assaults), section U.
(4)   **Substantial bodily harm** (M.S. § 609.02, subd. 7a)
             "Substantial bodily harm" is defined in chapter 2 (Assaults), section U.

MOTOR VEHICLE TAMPERING
M.S. § 609.546 (1),(2) (Misdemeanor)
Name
Date and Time of Offense
Location (Venue)

(1)	No person shall intentionally
(2)	ride in or on
(3)	a motor vehicle
(4)	knowing that the vehicle was taken and is being driven by another
(5)	without the owner's permission.

OR

(1)	No person shall intentionally
(2)	tamper with or enter into or on
(3)	a motor vehicle
(4)	without the owner's permission.

25. MURDER AND MANSLAUGHTER

A. MURDER IN THE FIRST DEGREE
M.S. § 609.185 (Felony)

Name
Date and Time of Offense
Location (Venue)

(1)	No person shall
(2)	cause the death of a human being
(3)	with premeditation
(4)	and with intent to effect the death of the person or of another.

Definition of **"premeditation"** (M.S. § 609.18 - CRIMJIG 11.02) - means that a defendant considered, planned, prepared for or determined to commit the act before defendant committed it. Premeditation, being a process of the mind, is wholly subjective and hence not always susceptible to proof by direct evidence. It may be inferred from all the circumstances surrounding the event. It is not necessary that premeditation exist for any specific length of time. A premeditated decision to kill may be reached in a short period of time. However, an unconsidered or rash impulse, even though it includes an intent to kill, is not premeditated.

OR

(1)	No person shall
(2)	cause the death of a human being
(3)	while committing or attempting to commit Criminal Sexual Conduct in the 1st or 2nd Degree (M.S. § 609.342 or § 609.343)
(4)	with force or violence
(5)	either upon or affecting the person or another.

OR

(1)	No person shall	
(2)	cause the death of a human being	
(3)	with intent to effect the death of the person or another	
(4)	while committing or attempting to commit:	
	a.	Burglary (M.S. § 609.582)
	b.	Aggravated Robbery (M.S. § 609.245)
	c.	Kidnapping (M.S. § 609.25)
	d.	Arson in the 1st or 2nd Degree (M.S. § 609.561 and § 609.562)
	e.	A drive by shooting (M.S. § 609.66)

f.		Tampering With a Witness in the 1st Degree (M.S. § 609.498)
g.		Escape From Custody (M.S. § 609.485), or
h.		any felony violation of Chapter 152 involving the unlawful sale of a controlled substance.

OR

(1)	No person shall
(2)	cause the death of a peace officer, prosecuting attorney, judge or a guard employed at a Minnesota state or local correctional facility
(3)	with intent to effect the death of that person or another
(4)	while the peace officer or guard
(5)	is engaged in the performance of official duties.

Definition of **"prosecuting attorney"** (M.S. § 609.185, subd. 2(c)(4)) – means an attorney, with criminal prosecution or civil responsibilities, who is the attorney general, a political subdivision's elected or appointed county or city attorney, or a deputy, assistant, or special assistant of any of these.

Definition of **"judge"** (M.S. § 609.185, subd. 2(c)(5)) – means a judge or justice of any court of this state that is established by the Minnesota Constitution.

OR

(1)	No person shall
(2)	cause the death of a minor (under 18 years of age)
(3)	while committing child abuse
(4)	when the perpetrator has engaged in a past pattern of child abuse upon a child
(5)	and the death occurs under circumstances manifesting an extreme indifference to human life.

Definition of **"child abuse"** (M.S. § 609.185) - means an act committed against a minor victim that constitutes a violation of the following laws of this state or any similar laws of the United States or any other state: M.S. § 609.221, § 609.222, § 609.223, § 609.224 (Assault in the 1st, 2nd, 3rd, or 5th Degree); § 609.2242 (Domestic Assault); § 609.342, § 609.343, § 609.344, § 609.345 (Criminal Sexual Conduct in the 1st, 2nd, 3rd, or 4th Degree; § 609.377 (Malicious Punishment of a Child); § 609.378 (Neglect or Endangerment of a Child); or § 609.713 (Terroristic Threats).

<u>Definition</u> of **"past pattern of child abuse"** - this term is not defined by statute. Contact your county attorney's office for clarification.

OR

(1)	No person shall
(2)	cause the death of a human being
(3)	while committing domestic abuse
(4)	when the perpetrator has engaged in a past pattern of domestic abuse upon the victim or upon another family or household member
(5)	and the death occurs under circumstances manifesting an extreme indifference to human life

<u>Definition</u> of **"domestic abuse"** (M.S. § 609.185) - means an act that constitutes a violation of M.S. § 609.221, 222, 223, 224 (Assault in the 1st, 2nd, 3rd, or 5th Degree); § 609.2242 (Domestic Assault); § 609.342 through 345 (Criminal Sexual Conduct in the 1st, 2nd, 3rd, or 4th Degree); or § 609.713 (Terroristic Threats), or any similar laws of the United States or any other state, and is committed against the victim who is a family or household member as defined below.

<u>Definition</u> of **"family or household members"** (M.S. § 518B.01, subd. 2, paragraph (b)) - means spouses, former spouses, parents and children, persons related by blood, and persons who are presently residing together or who have resided together in the past, and persons who have a child in common regardless of whether they have been married or have lived together at any time. It also includes a man and woman if the woman is pregnant and the man is alleged to be the father, regardless of whether they have been married or have lived together at any time.

<u>Definition</u> of **"past pattern of domestic abuse"** - this term is not defined by statute. Contact your county attorney's office for clarification.

OR

(1)	No person shall
(2)	cause the death of a human being
(3)	while committing, conspiring to commit, or attempting to commit a felony crime to further terrorism
(4)	and the death occurs under circumstances manifesting an extreme indifference to human life

Minn. Stat. § 609.185(a)(7)

Definition of **"further terrorism"** (M.S. § 609.714, subd.1) means a crime is committed to "further terrorism" if the crime is a felony and is a premeditated act involving violence to persons or property that is intended to:

(1) terrorize, intimidate, or coerce a considerable number of members of the public in addition to the direct victims of the act; and
(2) significantly disrupt or interfere with the lawful exercise, operation, or conduct of government, lawful commerce, or the right of lawful assembly.

Note: If the murder victim is an unborn child, see M.S. § 609.2661 (Murder of an Unborn Child in the 1st Degree).

B. MURDER IN THE SECOND DEGREE
M.S. § 609.19 (Felony)
Name
Date and Time of Offense
Location (Venue)

INTENTIONAL MURDER

(1)	No person shall
(2)	cause the death of a human being
(3)	with intent to effect the death of that person or another
(4)	but without premeditation.

OR

DRIVE-BY SHOOTING - UNINTENTIONAL DEATH

(1)	No person shall
(2)	cause the death of a human being
(3)	without intent to effect the death of any person
(4)	while committing or attempting to commit
(5)	a drive-by shooting in violation of M.S. § 609.66, subd. 1e (see chapter 9, B. "Dangerous Weapons", 7th box).

OR

```
UNINTENTIONAL MURDER - Felony Murder
(1)      No person shall
(2)      cause the death of a human being
(3)      without intent to effect the death of any person
(4)      while committing or attempting to commit
(5)      a felony offense other than Criminal Sexual Conduct in the
         1st or 2nd Deg. with force or violence or a drive-by shooting.
```

OR

```
UNINTENTIONAL MURDER - Order for Protection
(1)      No person shall
(2)      cause the death of a human being
(3)      without intent to effect the death of any person
(4)      while intentionally inflicting or attempting to inflict bodily harm
         upon the victim
(5)      when the perpetrator is restrained under an order for
         protection (as defined below) and the victim is a person
         designated to receive protection under the order.
```

Definition of **"order for protection"** (M.S. § 609.19(3)) - As used in the above section, "order for protection" includes an order for protection issued under chapter 518B; a harassment restraining order issued under section 609.748; a court order setting conditions of pretrial release or conditions of a criminal sentence or juvenile court disposition; a restraining order issued in a marriage dissolution action; and any order issued by a court of another state or of the United States that is similar to any of these orders.

Note: If the murder victim is an unborn child, see M.S. § 609.2661 (Murder of an Unborn Child in the 2nd Degree).

C.   MURDER IN THE THIRD DEGREE
M.S. § 609.195 (Felony)

Name
Date and Time of Offense
Location (Venue)

```
(1)      No person shall
(2)      without intent to effect the death of any person
(3)      cause the death of another
```

(4)   by perpetrating an act imminently dangerous to others and evincing a depraved mind

(5)   without regard for human life.

OR

(1)   No person shall

(2)   without intent to cause death

(3)   proximately cause the death of a human being

(4)   by, directly or indirectly, unlawfully selling, giving away, bartering, delivering, exchanging, distributing, or administering a controlled substance classified in Schedule I or II (as defined in chapter 4, section X, "Definitions".)

Note: If the murder victim is an unborn child, see M.S. § 609.2663 (Murder of an Unborn Child in the 3rd Degree).

D.   MANSLAUGHTER IN THE FIRST DEGREE
   M.S. § 609.20 (Felony)

Name

Date and Time of Offense

Location (Venue)

(1)   No person shall

(2)   intentionally cause the death of another person

(3)   in the heat of passion

(4)   provoked by such words or acts of another as would provoke a "person of ordinary self-control" under like circumstances.

Note: The crying of a child does not constitute provocation.

Note: As used in this section, a "person of ordinary self-control" does not include a person under the influence of intoxicants or a controlled substance (M.S. § 609.20(5)).

OR

(1)   No person shall

(2)   violate M.S. § 609.224 (Assault 5th Degree)

(3)   and cause the death of another

OR

(1)	No person shall
(2)	cause the death of another
(3)	in committing or attempting to commit a misdemeanor or gross misdemeanor offense
(4)	with such force and violence that death of or great bodily harm to any person was reasonably foreseeable
(5)	and Murder in the 1st or 2nd Degree was not committed thereby.

OR

(1)	No person shall
(2)	intentionally cause the death of another person
(3)	because the actor is coerced by threats
(4)	made by someone other than the actor's co-conspirator
(5)	and which caused the actor reasonably to believe that the act performed by the actor is the only means of preventing imminent death to the actor or another.

Note: The statutory defense of duress does not apply to violations of the above section. (M.S. § 609.08).

OR

(1)	No person shall
(2)	proximately cause the death of another
(3)	without intent to cause death
(4)	by, directly or indirectly, unlawfully selling, giving away, bartering, delivering, exchanging, distributing, or administering a controlled substance classified in Schedule III, IV or V (as defined in chapter 4, section X, "Definitions".)

OR

(1)	No person shall
(2)	cause the death of another
(3)	in committing or attempting to commit
(4)	a violation of M.S. § 609.377 (Malicious Punishment of a Child - see Chapter 23, section A), and Murder in the 1st, 2nd or 3rd Degree is not committed thereby.

Note: If the victim is an unborn child, see M.S. § 609.2664 (Manslaughter of an Unborn Child in the 1st Degree).

E. MANSLAUGHTER IN THE SECOND DEGREE
M.S. § 609.205 (Felony)

Name
Date and Time of Offense
Location (Venue)

(1)	No person shall cause the death of another
(2)	by the person's culpable negligence
(3)	whereby the person creates an unreasonable risk and consciously takes chances of causing death or great bodily harm to another.

Definition of **"culpable negligence"** (CRIMJIG 11.24) - means more than ordinary or gross negligence and means intentional conduct which the defendant may not have intended to be harmful but which an ordinary, reasonably prudent person would recognize as involving a strong probability of injury to others.

OR

(1)	No person shall cause the death of another
(2)	by shooting another with a firearm or other dangerous weapon
(3)	as a result of negligently believing the other to be a deer or other animal.

OR

(1)	No person shall cause the death of another
(2)	by setting a spring gun, pitfall, deadfall, snare or other like dangerous weapon or device.

OR

(1)	No person shall cause the death of another
(2)	by negligently or intentionally permitting any animal
(3)	known by the person to have vicious propensities or to have caused great or substantial bodily harm in the past
(4)	to run uncontrolled off the owner's premises or negligently failing to keep it properly confined.

Defense: It shall be an affirmative defense to criminal liability that the victim provoked the animal to cause the victim's death.

Note: If the victim is an unborn child, see M.S. § 609.2665 (Manslaughter of an Unborn Child in the 2nd Degree).

26. OBSTRUCTING LEGAL PROCESS

A. OBSTRUCTING LEGAL PROCESS, ARREST OR FIREFIGHTING
M.S. § 609.50 (Misdemeanor - Gross Misdemeanor - Felony)

Name

Date and Time of Offense

Location (Venue)

(1)   No person shall intentionally

(2)   a.   obstruct, hinder or prevent the lawful execution of any legal process, civil or criminal, or apprehension of another on a charge or conviction of a criminal offense.
         or

         b.   obstruct, resist or interfere with a peace officer while the officer is engaged in the performance of official duties.
         or

         c.   interfere with or obstruct a firefighter while the firefighter is engaged in the performance of official duties.
         or

         d.   interferes with or obstructs a member of an ambulance service personnel crew who is providing, or attempting to provide, emergency care.
         or

         e.   by force or threat of force endeavor to obstruct any employee of the Department of Revenue while the employee is lawfully engaged in the performance of official duties for the purpose of deterring or interfering with the performance of those duties.

Penalty:

a.   If any of the above acts were committed with:

         (i)   the person knowing or having reason to know that the act created a risk of death, substantial bodily harm or serious property damage; or

         (ii)   the act caused death, substantial bodily harm, or serious property damage defendant is guilty of a **felony**.
         or

b.   if the act was accompanied by force or violence or the threat thereof, and is not covered by paragraph (a) above, defendant is guilty of a **gross misdemeanor**.
         or

c.   in all other cases, defendant is guilty of a **misdemeanor**.

B.   DISARMING A PEACE OFFICER
M.S. § 609.504 (Felony)

Name
Date and Time of Offense
Location (Venue)

(1)   No person shall intentionally
(2)   take possession of a defensive device being carried by a peace officer or from the area within the officer's immediate control
(3)   without the officer's consent
(4)   while the officer is engaged in the performance of official duties.

Definition: **"Defensive Device"**, as used in this section, includes a firearm; a dangerous weapon; an authorized tear gas compound, as defined in § 624.731, subd. 1; an electronic incapacitation device, as defined in § 624.731, subd. 1; a club or baton; and any item issued by a peace officer's employer to the officer to assist in the officer's protection.

C.   AIDING AN OFFENDER
M.S. § 609.495, subd. 1, 3 (Felony)

Name
Date and Time of Offense
Location (Venue)

Aiding Offender
(1)   No person shall
(2)   harbor, conceal, aid or assist by words or acts, another person
(3)   whom the defendant knows or has reason to know has committed a crime under the laws of this or another state or of the United States
(4)   IF the crime committed or attempted by the other person is a felony.

OR

Aiding Person on Probation, Parole, or Supervised Release
(1)   No person shall
(2)   knowingly harbor, conceal or aid
(3)   a person who is on probation, parole, or supervised release because of a felony level conviction and for whom an arrest and detention order has been issued
(4)   with intent that the person evade or escape being taken into custody under the order.

Definition of **"Arrest and Detention Order"** - A written order to take and detain a probationer, parolee, or supervised releasee that is issued under section 243.05, subd. 1; 260.311, subd. 3a; or 401.02, subd. 4.

Accomplice After the Fact

(1) No person shall
(2) intentionally aid another person
(3) whom the defendant knows or has reason to know has committed a criminal act (as defined below)
(4) by destroying or concealing evidence of a crime, providing false or misleading information about that crime, receiving the proceeds of that crime, or otherwise obstructing the investigation or prosecution of that crime.

Definition: **"Criminal act"** for purposes of the above section, includes the following offenses and/or attempts to commit the following offenses:

a. Murder in the 1st, 2nd, or 3rd Degree (M.S. § 609.185 to § 609.195).
b. Assault in the 1st, 2nd, or 3rd Degree (M.S. § 609.221 to § 609.223).
c. Burglary (M.S. § 609.582)
d. Kidnapping (M.S. § 609.25)
e. False Imprisonment (M.S. § 609.255)
f. Manslaughter in the 1st or 2nd Degree (M.S. § 609.20, § 609.205)
g. Aggravated Robbery (M.S. § 609.245)
h. Simple Robbery (M.S. § 609.24)
i. Criminal Sexual Conduct in the 1st, 2nd, or 3rd Degree, excluding those sections requiring "significant relationships". (M.S. § 609.342, subd. 1(a) to (f); § 609.343, subd. 1(a) to (f); § 609.344, subd. 1(a) to (e) and (h) to (j)).
j. Escape From Custody (M.S. § 609.485)
k. Arson in the 1st, 2nd, or 3rd Degree (M.S. § 609.561 to § 609.563)
l. Any felony level controlled substance offense (M.S. Chapter 152)

Jurisdiction: "An offense committed under subdivision 1 or 3 may be prosecuted in:
(1) the county where the aiding or obstructing behavior occurred; or
(2) the county where the underlying criminal act occurred."

Taking Responsibility for Criminal Acts:
1.   Unless the person is convicted of the underlying crime, no person shall
2.   assume responsibility for a criminal act
3.   with the intent to obstruct, impede, or prevent a criminal investigation.

Exception (no longer valid): There used to be an exception in which the above statute did not apply to persons related to the offender as spouse, parent, or child. That exception was repealed by the 1996 legislature effective August 1, 1996.

D.   FALSELY REPORTING CRIME
     M.S. § 609.505, Subd. 1, 2 (Misdemeanor - Gross Misdemeanor)
Name
Date and Time of Offense
Location (Venue)

(1)	No person shall
(2)	inform a law enforcement officer
(3)	that a crime has been committed, or otherwise provides information to an on-duty peace officer, knowing that the person is a peace officer, regarding the conduct of others, knowing that it is false and intending that the officer shall act in reliance upon it **(misdemeanor)**.

Enhancement: Whoever violates the above section a second or subsequent time is guilty of a **gross misdemeanor**.

Note: (M.S. § 609.5051) Whoever uses the criminal alert network under M.S. § 299A.61 to disseminate information regarding the commission of a crime, knowing that it is false or misleading, is guilty of a **misdemeanor**.

OR

(1)	No person shall
(2)	inform a peace officer, whose responsibilities include investigating or reporting police misconduct
(3)	that a peace officer has committed an act of police misconduct , knowing that the information is false, is guilty of a **misdemeanor**, if the false information does not allege a criminal act; or a **gross misdemeanor** if the false information alleges a criminal act.

- 163 -

E.   **DEFINITIONS:**

(1)   **Peace Officer (M.S. § 609.505, Subd. 1, 2)**
an employee or an elected or appointed official of a political subdivision or law enforcement agency who is licensed by the board, charged with the prevention and detection of crime and the enforcement of the general criminal laws of the state and who has the full power of arrest, and shall also include the Minnesota State Patrol, agents of the Division of Alcohol and Gambling Enforcement, state conservation officers, Metropolitan Transit police officers, Department of Corrections Fugitive Apprehension Unit officers, and Department of Commerce Insurance Fraud Unit officers; and a peace officer who is employed by a law enforcement agency of a federally recognized tribe, as defined in United States Code, title 25, section 450b(e), and who is licensed by the board.

27. ORDER FOR PROTECTION VIOLATION

ORDER FOR PROTECTION VIOLATION
M.S. § 518B.01, subd. 14 (Misdemeanor - Gross Misdemeanor - Felony)
Name
Date and Time of Offense
Location (Venue)
(1)   No person
(2)   who knows of the existence of the order
(3)   shall violate an existing court order for protection **(misdemeanor)**.

Enhancement to Gross Misdemeanor: Whoever violates the above section within ten years of a previous *"qualified domestic violence-related offense"* conviction or adjudication of delinquency is guilty of a **gross misdemeanor**. M.S. § 518B.01, subd. 14(c).

Enhancement to Felony (previous convictions): Whoever violates the above section within ten years of the first of two or more previous *"qualified domestic violence-related offense"* convictions or adjudications of delinquency is guilty of a **felony**.
M.S. § 518B.01, subd. 14(d)(1).

Enhancement to Felony (dangerous weapons): Whoever violates the above section while possessing a dangerous weapon, as defined in M.S. § 609.02, subd. 6, is guilty of a **felony**.
M.S. § 518B.01, subd. 14(d)(2)

Jurisdiction: An offense may be prosecuted
(1) where any call is made or received; or
(2) in the case of wireless or electronic communication or any communication made through available technologies, where the actor or victim resides; or
(3) in the jurisdiction of the victim's designated address if the victim participates in the address confidentiality program.

DEFINITIONS:

(1)   **Qualified Domestic Violence-Related Offense** (M.S. § 609.02, subd. 16)

"Qualified domestic violence-related offense" includes a violation of or an attempt to violate: § 518B.01, subd. 14 (Violation of Domestic Abuse Order for Protection); § 518B.01, subd. 22 (Violation of a Domestic Abuse No

Contact Order); § 609.185 (First-Degree Murder); § 609.19 (Second-Degree Murder); § 609.221 (First Degree Assault); § 609.22 (Second Degree Assault); § 609.223 (Third Degree Assault); § 609.2231 (Fourth Degree Assault); § 609.224 (Fifth Degree Assault); § 609.2242 (Domestic Assault); § 609.2245 (Female Genital Mutilation); § 609.2247 (Domestic Assault by Strangulation); § 609.342 (First Degree Criminal Sexual Conduct); § 609.343 (Second Degree Criminal Sexual Conduct); § 609.344 (Third Degree Criminal Sexual Conduct); § 609.345 (Fourth Degree Criminal Sexual Conduct); § 609.377 (Malicious Punishment of a Child); § 609.713 (Terroristic Threats); § 609.748, subd. 6 (Violation of Harassment Restraining Order); § 609.749 (Harassment/Stalking); and § 609.78, subd. 2 (Interference with an Emergency Call); and similar laws of other states, the United States, the District of Columbia, tribal lands, and United States territories.

28. VIOLATION OF A DOMESTIC ABUSE NO CONTACT ORDER

VIOLATION OF A DOMESTIC ABUSE NO CONTACT ORDER
M.S. § 629.75, subd. 2 (Misdemeanor – Gross Misdemeanor – Felony
Name
Date and Time of Offense
Location (Venue)
(1)   No person
(2)   who knows of the existence of the no contact order against that person
(3)   shall violate the no contact order **(misdemeanor)**.

Enhancement to Gross Misdemeanor: Whoever violates the above section within ten years of a previous "*qualified domestic violence-related offense*" conviction or adjudication of delinquency is guilty of a **gross misdemeanor**.
M.S. § 629.75, subd. 2(c)

Enhancement to Felony (previous convictions): Whoever violates the above section within ten years of the first of two or more previous "*qualified domestic violence-related offense*" convictions or adjudications of delinquency is guilty of a **felony**.
M.S. § 629.75, subd. 2(d)(1)

Enhancement to Felony (dangerous weapons): Whoever violates the above section while possessing a dangerous weapon, as defined in M.S. § 609.02, subd. 6, is guilty of a **felony**.
M.S. § 629.75, subd. 2(d)(2)

Jurisdiction: An offense may be prosecuted
      (1) where any call is made or received; or
      (2) in the case of wireless or electronic communication or any communication made through available technologies, where the actor or victim resides; or
      (3) in the jurisdiction of the victim's designated address if the victim participates in the address confidentiality program.

DEFINITIONS:
(1)   **Arrest:** A peace officer shall arrest without a warrant and take into custody a person whom a peace officer has probable cause to believe has violated a domestic abuse no contact order, even if the violation of the order was not in the presence of the peace officer, if the existence of the order can be verified by the officer.

(2)   **Domestic Abuse No Contact Order** (M.S. § 629.75, subd. 1(a)

"Domestic abuse no contact order" is an order issued by the court against a defendant in a criminal proceeding for:

(a)   domestic abuse;

(b)   harassment or stalking under § 609.749 when committed against a family or household member;

(c)   violation of an order for protection under § 518B.01, subd. 14; or

(d)   violation of a prior domestic abuse no contact order under M.S § 629.75 or M.S. § 518B.01, subd. 22.

(3)   **Qualified Domestic Violence-Related Offense** (M.S. § 609.02, subd. 16)

"Qualified domestic violence-related offense" includes a violation of or an attempt to violate: § 518B.01, subd. 14 (Violation of Domestic Abuse Order for Protection); § 518B.01, subd. 22 (Violation of a Domestic Abuse No Contact Order); § 609.185 (First-Degree Murder); § 609.19 (Second-Degree Murder); § 609.221 (First Degree Assault); § 609.22 (Second Degree Assault); § 609.223 (Third Degree Assault); § 609.2231 (Fourth Degree Assault); § 609.224 (Fifth Degree Assault); § 609.2242 (Domestic Assault); § 609.2245 (Female Genital Mutilation); § 609.2247 (Domestic Assault by Strangulation); § 609.342 (First Degree Criminal Sexual Conduct); § 609.343 (Second Degree Criminal Sexual Conduct); § 609.344 (Third Degree Criminal Sexual Conduct); § 609.345 (Fourth Degree Criminal Sexual Conduct); § 609.377 (Malicious Punishment of a Child); § 609.713 (Terroristic Threats); § 609.748, subd. 6 (Violation of Harassment Restraining Order); § 609.749 (Harassment/Stalking); and § 609.78, subd. 2 (Interference with an Emergency Call); and similar laws of other states, the United States, the District of Columbia, tribal lands, and United States territories.

29. POSSESSION OF AMMUNITION, PISTOLS, FIREARMS, SEMIAUTOMATIC MILITARY-STYLE ASSAULT WEAPONS, RIFLES OR SHOTGUNS

A. **CERTAIN PERSONS NOT TO HAVE AMMUNITION, PISTOLS OR SEMIAUTOMATIC MILITARY-STYLE ASSAULT WEAPONS OR ANY OTHER FIREARM**
M.S. § 624.713, subds. 1(a),(b), 1a, 2, 3 (Felony)

Name
Date and Time of Offense
Location (Venue)

Persons under 18

(1)   No person under the age of 18 years

(2)   may carry or possess ammunition, or a pistol or semiautomatic military-style assault weapon

UNLESS

(3)   a.   in the actual presence or under the direct supervision of the person's parent or guardian.

or

b.   for the purpose of military drill under the auspices of a legally recognized military organization and under competent supervision.

or

c.   for the purpose of instruction, competition or target practice on a firing range approved by the chief of police or county sheriff in whose jurisdiction the range is located and under direct supervision.

or

d.   if the person has successfully completed a course designed to teach marksmanship and safety with a pistol or semiautomatic military-style assault weapon and approved by the Commissioner of Natural Resources.

Note: **Possession in a public place** - A person under the age of 21 who carries a semiautomatic military style assault weapon on or about the person in a public place is guilty of a **felony** (M.S. § 624.7181, subd. 2).

OR

Crime of violence

(1)   No person who has been convicted of, or adjudicated delinquent or convicted as an extended jurisdiction juvenile for committing, in this state or elsewhere

(2)   a crime of violence

(3)   may carry or possess ammunition, or a pistol or semiautomatic military-style assault weapon or any other firearm

Note: For purposes of the above section, **"crime of violence"** includes crimes in other states or jurisdictions which would have been crimes of violence if they had been committed in this state. **"Crime of violence"** is defined in this chapter, section I., "Definitions."

Exception: The criminal penalty for a person who has been convicted of Certain Persons Not to Have Firearms - Crime of Violence, does not apply to any person who has received a relief of disability under United States Code, title 18, section 925, or whose ability to possess firearms has been restored under M.S. § 609.165, subd. 1d.

Enlargement of Firearm Prohibition Time Period: If defendant is convicted in this state or elsewhere of assaulting a family or household member (as defined in chapter 2, section U. "Definitions") and the court determines that he used a firearm in any way during commission of the assault, the court may prohibit defendant from possessing any type of firearm for any period longer than 3 years or for the remainder of defendant's life. A violation of this provision is a **gross misdemeanor**. (M.S. § 609.2242, subd. 3(c); § 624.713, subd. 1(8), (9)).

Note: The lifetime prohibition on possessing, receiving, shipping, or transporting firearms for persons convicted or adjudicated delinquent of a crime of violence in this section applies only to offenders who are discharged from sentence or court supervision for a crime of violence on or after August 1, 1993.

B.   POSSESSION OF FIREARMS AND AMMUNITION - Crime of Violence
        M.S. § 609.165, subd. 1b (Felony)

Name

Date and Time of Offense

Location (Venue)

(1)   No person who has been convicted

(2)   of a crime of violence (as defined in section I. "Definitions")

(3) may ship, transport, possess, or receive a firearm or ammunition (as defined in chapter 9, section F.)

Note: A discharge from sentence may be (1) by order of the court following stay of sentence or stay of execution of sentence, or (2) upon expiration of sentence.

Note: A conviction and sentencing under this section shall be construed to bar a conviction and sentencing for any violation of M.S. § 624.713.

Note: The lifetime prohibition on possessing, receiving, shipping, or transporting firearms or ammunition for persons convicted or adjudicated delinquent of a crime of violence in this section applies only to offenders who are discharged from sentence or court supervision for a crime of violence on or after August 1, 1993.

Exemption: Sections A and B above do not apply to antique firearms which are carried or possessed as curiosities or for their historical significance or value or to ammunition or primers, projectiles, or propellant powder designed solely for use in an antique firearm (M.S. § 624.715). Also, the criminal penalty for a person who has been convicted of Certain Persons Not to Have Firearms - Crime of Violence, does not apply to any person who has received a relief of disability under United States Code, title 18, section 925, or whose ability to possess firearms has been restored under M.S. § 609.165, subd. 1d.

C. **CERTAIN PERSONS NOT TO HAVE AMMUNITION, PISTOLS OR SEMIAUTOMATIC MILITARY-STYLE ASSAULT WEAPONS OR ANY OTHER FIREARM**
M.S. § 624.713, subd. 1(3), (4), (5), (6), (7), (8), (9), (10), (11), (12), (13), subd. 1a, 2; M.S. § 609.224, subd. 3(b); § 609.2242 (Gross Misdemeanor)

Name
Date and Time of Offense
Location (Venue)

Mentally Ill Persons - Not Committed
(1) No person who is or who has ever been committed to a treatment facility in Minnesota or elsewhere
(2) by a judicial determination that the person is mentally ill, developmentally disabled, or mentally ill and dangerous to the public (as defined in Section I. "Definitions" below), or who has ever been found incompetent to stand trial or not guilty by reason of mental illness

---

(3)   may carry or possess ammunition or any type of firearm
UNLESS
(4)   the person has had his or her eligibility to possess firearms and ammunition restored by court order.

OR

Drug Conviction and/or Drug Treatment
(1)   No person who has been convicted in Minnesota or else-where:
(2)   a.   of a misdemeanor or gross misdemeanor controlled substance violation of M.S. Chapter 152.
           or
          b.   a person who is or who has ever been hospitalized or committed for treatment for the habitual use of a controlled substance or marijuana, as defined in M.S. § 152.01, and 152.02
(3)   may carry or possess ammunition or any type of firearm.

Defense: The above section does not apply to a person who was hospitalized or committed for treatment under (2)b. above, if the person possesses a certificate from a medical doctor or psychiatrist licensed in Minnesota or other satisfactory proof that the person has not abused a controlled substance or marijuana during the previous two years.

Definition of **"conviction"**: Any conviction which has been expunged, or set aside, or for which a person has been pardoned or has had civil rights restored shall not be considered a conviction for purposes of the above section, unless such pardon, expungement, or restoration of civil rights expressly provides that the person may not ship, transport, possess, or receive firearms and ammunition.

OR

Chemically Dependent Persons
(1)   No person who has been confined or committed to a treatment facility in Minnesota or elsewhere
(2)   as "chemically dependent" (as defined in section I. "Definitions" below)
(3)   may carry or possess ammunition or any type of firearm
           UNLESS
(4)   the person has completed treatment.

OR

Peace Officers

(1) No peace officer who is informally admitted to a treatment facility pursuant to M.S. § 253B.04 for chemical dependency

(2) may carry or possess ammunition or any type of firearm
UNLESS

(3) the officer possesses a certificate from the head of the treatment facility discharging or provisionally discharging the officer from the treatment facility.

OR

Pretrial Divisionary Program

(1) No person, including a person under the jurisdiction of the juvenile court, who has been charged with committing a crime of violence (as defined in section I. below) and has been placed in a pretrial diversion program by the Court before disposition

(2) may carry or possess ammunition or any type of firearm
UNTIL

(3) the person has completed the diversion program and the charge of committing the crime of violence has been dismissed.

OR

Previous Assault Conviction

(1) No person who has been convicted after August 1, 1992,

(2) of Assault in the 5th Degree

(3) may possess ammunition or a pistol

(4) if the offense was committed within three years

(5) of a previous conviction under M.S. § 609.221 to § 609.224 (Assault in the 1st through 5th Degree)
UNLESS

(6) three years have elapsed from the date of conviction and, during that time, the person has not been convicted of any other violations of M.S. § 609.224 (Assault in the 5th Degree). **(gross misdemeanor)** (M.S. § 609.224, subd. 3(b)).

OR

Assault in the 5th Degree or Domestic Assault - Family or Household Member
(1)   No person who has been convicted of Assault in the 5th Degree (M.S. § 609.224) or Domestic Assault (M.S. § 609.2242)
(2)   and the victim was a family or household member (as defined in Chapter 2, Section U. "Definitions")
(3)   may possess ammunition or a pistol for 3 years from the date of conviction. (**gross misdemeanor**) (M.S. § 609.2242, subd. 3(d)).

OR

Family or Household Member - after August 1, 1992.
(1)   No person who has been convicted after August 1, 1992,
(2)   of Assault in the 5th Degree (M.S. § 609.224) or Domestic Assault (M.S. § 609.2242).
(3)   and the assault victim was a family or household member (as defined in chapter 2, section U. "Definitions")
(4)   may possess ammunition or a pistol
        UNLESS
(5)   three years have elapsed from the date of conviction and, during that time, the person has not been convicted of any other violation of M.S. § 609.224 (Assault in the 5th Degree) or Domestic Assault (M.S. § 609.2242, subd. 3(e)). (**gross misdemeanor**)

Note: It is also a **gross misdemeanor** if a person has been convicted in another state of committing an offense similar to the above section and then, while in Minnesota, possesses ammunition, or a pistol, or semiautomatic military-
style assault weapon or any other firearm, in violation of the above section. (M.S. § 624.713, subd. 1(9)).

Increasing firearm prohibition from 3 years to life - use of firearm:
If the person is convicted in this state or elsewhere of assaulting a family member or household member and the court determines that the person used a firearm in any way during commission of the assault, the court may order that the person is prohibited from possessing ammunition or any type of firearm for any period longer than 3 years or for the remainder of the person's life. A violation of this provision is a **gross misdemeanor**. (M.S. § 624.713, subd. 1(9);
M.S. § 609.2242, subd. 3(c)).

OR

Stalking Conviction or Violation of Order for Protection
(1)	No person convicted of Stalking (M.S. § 609.749) or violation of order for protection; (M.S. § 518B.01)
(2)	may possess ammunition or a pistol for 3 years from the date of conviction. **(gross misdemeanor).** (M.S. § 609.749, subd. 8(b); (M.S. § 518B.01, subd. 14(a)).

Note - after the first 3 years: If defendant is convicted of Stalking or Violation of Order for Protection after August 1, 1996, he may not possess ammunition or a pistol unless 3 years have elapsed from the date of conviction and, during that time, the person has not been convicted of any other violation of this section. **(gross misdemeanor)** (M.S. § 609.749, subd. 8(c)); M.S. § 518B.01, subd. 14(j).

Increasing firearm prohibition from 3 years to life - use of firearm:
If defendant is convicted of Stalking or Violation of Order for Protection and the Court determines that the defendant used a firearm in any way during commission of the crime, the Court may order that the defendant be prohibited from possessing ammunition or any type of firearm for any period longer than 3 years or for the remainder of the person's life. **(gross misdemeanor)** (M.S. § 609.749, subd. 8(a)); M.S. § 518B.01, subd. 14(h), (i).

OR

Previous Felony Conviction - Non-crime of violence
(1)	No person who has been convicted in any court of a crime punishable by imprisonment for a term exceeding one year
	(as defined below)
(2)	may possess ammunition or any type of firearm. (M.S. § 624.713, subd. 1(10)(i)).

Definition of **"crime punishable by imprisonment for a term exceeding one year"** (M.S. § 624.712, subd. 10) does not include:
a.	any federal or state offense pertaining to antitrust violations, unfair trade practices, restraints of trade, or other similar offenses relating to the regulation of business practices; or

b.   any state offense classified by the laws of this state or any other state as a misdemeanor and punishable by a term of imprisonment of two years or less.

Definition of **"conviction"** - What constitutes a conviction of a crime shall be determined in accordance with the law of the jurisdiction in which the proceedings were held. Any conviction which has been expunged, or set aside, or for which a person has been pardoned or has had civil rights restored shall not be considered a conviction for purposes of this definition, unless such pardon, expungement, or restoration of civil rights expressly provides that the person may not ship, transport, possess, or receive firearms.

Note: If the conviction is for a "crime of violence" as defined in section I. "Definitions" below, then the person is guilty of a **felony**. See section A. above (2nd box) "crime of violence".

OR

Fugitive from Justice
(1)   No person who is a fugitive from justice as a result of having fled from any state to avoid prosecution for a crime or to avoid giving testimony in any criminal proceeding
(2)   may possess ammunition or any type of firearm (M.S. § 624.713, subd. 1(10)(ii)).

OR

Controlled Substance User
(1)   No person who is an unlawful user of any controlled substance as defined in M.S. § 152
(2)   may possess ammunition or any type of firearm (M.S. § 624.713, subd. 1(10)(iii)).

OR

Mentally Ill Persons - Committed
(1)   No person who has been judicially committed to a treatment facility in Minnesota or elsewhere as a "mentally ill", "mentally retarded" or "mentally ill and dangerous to the public" person as defined in this chapter, section I, "Definitions".
(2)   may possess ammunition or any type of firearm. (M.S. § 624.713 subd. 1(10)(iv)).

OR

Illegal Alien
(1)   No person who is an alien who is illegally or unlawfully in the United States
(2)   may possess ammunition or any type of firearm. (M.S. § 624.713 subd. 1(10)(v)).

OR

Dishonorable Military Discharge
(1)   No person who has been discharged from the armed forces of the United States under dishonorable conditions
(2)   may possess ammunition or any type of firearm. (M.S. § 624.713 subd. 1(10)(vi)).

OR

Renounced U.S. Citizenship
(1)   No person who has renounced the person's citizenship having been a citizen of the United States
(2)   may possess ammunition or any type of firearm. (M.S. § 624.713, subd. 1(10)(vii)).

OR

Pending Felony Charge
(1)   No person who is presently charged with a crime punishable by imprisonment for a term exceeding one year (as defined below)
(2)   shall be entitled to receive, ship, or transport any pistol or semi-automatic military-style assault weapon or ammunition designed for use in a pistol or semi-automatic military-style assault weapon (M.S. § 624.713, subd. 1a).

Note: The above provision does not prohibit the possession of "any other firearms.

Definition of **"crime punishable by imprisonment for a term exceeding one year"** (M.S. § 624.712, subd. 10) does not include:
a.   any federal or state offense pertaining to antitrust violations, unfair trade practices, restraints of trade, or other similar offenses relating to the regulation of business practices; or
b.   any state offense classified by the laws of this state or any other state as a misdemeanor and punishable by a term of imprisonment of two years or less.

OR

Certain Gross Misdemeanor Convictions
(1)   No person who has been convicted
(2)   of any of the following gross misdemeanor offenses:
    (a)   crimes committed for the benefit of a gang, M.S. § 609.229;
    (b)   assaults motivated by bias, M.S. § 609.2231, subd. 4;
    (c)   false imprisonment, M.S. § 609.255;
    (d)   neglect or endangerment of a child, M.S. § 609.378;
    (e)   burglary in the fourth degree, M.S. § 609.582, subd. 4;
    (f)   setting a spring gun, M.S. § 609.665;
    (g)   riot, M.S. § 609.71;
    (h)   stalking, M.S. § 609.749
    (i)   or crimes committed in other states which would have been gross misdemeanors if conviction occurred in this state, M.S. § 624.713, subd. 1(11).
(3)   may carry ammunition or possess any type of firearm.
    UNLESS
(4)   three years have elapsed since the date of conviction, and
(5)   during that time, the person has not been convicted of any other violation of these sections.

Note: For purposes of this crime, the specified gross misdemeanor convictions include crimes committed in other states or jurisdictions.

Exemption: None of the above sections apply to antique firearms which are carried or possessed as curiosities or for their historical significance or value or to ammunition or primers, projectiles, or propellant powder designed soley for use in an antique firearm (M.S. § 624.715).

D.   PURCHASING FIREARM ON BEHALF OF INELIGIBLE PERSON
    M.S § 624.7133 (Gross Misdemeanor)

Name
Date and Time of Offense
Location (Venue)

(1)   No person may purchase or otherwise obtain a firearm
(2)   on behalf of or for transfer to
(3)   a person known to be ineligible to possess or purchase a firearm pursuant to federal or state law.

E. **CARRYING OF WEAPONS (PISTOLS) WITHOUT PERMIT**
M.S. § 624.714, subds. 1a, 1b, (Misdemeanor - Gross Misdemeanor - Felony)

Name
Date and Time of Offense
Location (Venue)

(1)   No person, other than a peace officer, as defined in section 626.84, subd. 1,

(2)   shall carry, hold, or possess a pistol

(3)   (a)   in a motor vehicle
        (b)   snowmobile or boat
        (c)   or on or about the person's clothes or the person
        (d)   or otherwise in possession or control in a public place, as defined in section 624.7181, subd. 1(c)

(4)   without first having obtained a permit to carry the pistol. **(gross misdemeanor)**

Enhancement to Felony: Whoever violates the above section a second or subsequent time is guilty of a **felony.**

Note: The holder of a permit to carry must have the permit card and a driver's license, state identification card, or other government-issued photo identification in immediate possession at all times when carrying a pistol and must display the permit card and identification document upon lawful demand by a peace officer. Failure to do so is a petty misdemeanor, punishable by a fine for a first time offense of not more than $25. M.S. § 624.714, subd. 1b. A firearm carried in violation of this M.S. § 624, 714, subd. 1b, is not subject to forfeiture. Also, a citation under M.S. § 624.714, subd. 1b, must be dismissed if the person demonstrates, in court or in the office of the arresting officer, that the person was authorized to carry the pistol at the time of the alleged violation. The permit holder, upon request of a peace officer, must also write a sample signature in the officer's presence to aid in verifying the person's identity.

Note: A person who gives or causes to be given any false material information in applying for a permit to carry, knowing or having reason to know the information is false, is guilty of a **gross misdemeanor** (M.S. § 624.714, subd. 10).

Carrying Pistols About One's Premises or For Purposes of Repair, Target Practice: A permit to carry is not required of a person:

        (1)   To keep or carry about the person's place of business, dwelling house, premises or on land possessed by the person a pistol;

(2)   To carry a pistol from a place of purchase to the person's dwelling house or place of business or from the person's dwelling house or place of business to or from a place where repairing is done, to have the pistol repaired;

(3)   To carry a pistol between the person's dwelling house and place of business;

(4)   To carry a pistol in the woods or fields or upon the waters of this state for the purpose of hunting or for target shooting in a safe area; or

(5)   To transport a pistol in a motor vehicle, snowmobile or boat if the pistol is unloaded, contained in a closed and fastened case, gun box or securely tied package (M.S. § 624.714, subd. 9).

Exemption: Adult correctional facility officers - A permit to carry a pistol is not required of any officer of a state adult correctional facility when on guard duty or otherwise engaged in an assigned duty (M.S. § 624.714, subd. 13).

Exemption: None of the above sections apply to antique firearms which are carried or possessed as curiosities or for their historical significance or value to ammunition or primers, projectiles, or propellant powder designed solely for use in an antique firearm (M.S. § 624.715).

F.   CARRYING WHILE UNDER THE INFLUENCE OF ALCOHOL OR A CONTROLLED SUBSTANCE
M.S. § 624.7142 (Misdemeanor - Gross Misdemeanor)

Name
Date and Time of Offense
Location (Venue)

(1)   No person shall

(2)   carry a pistol

(3)   on or about the person's clothes or person

(4)   in a public place;

(5)   when the person:

      (a)   is under the influence of a controlled substance, as defined in section 152.01, subd. 4; or

      (b)   is under the influence of a combination of any two or more of the elements of a controlled substance and/or alcohol; or

      (c)   is knowingly under the influence of any chemical compound or combination of chemical compounds that is listed as a hazardous substance in rules adopted under section 182.655 and that affects the nervous system, brain, or muscles of the person so as to impair the person's clearness of intellect or physical control; or

(d)   is under the influence of alcohol; or

(e)   when the person's alcohol concentration is 0.10 or more; or

(f)   when the person's alcohol concentration is less than 0.10 but more than 0.04.

Note: **Penalties:** - A violation of the above (5)(a) through (5)(e) is a misdemeanor. A second or subsequent violation is a gross misdemeanor. A violation of (5)(f) is a misdemeanor.

Arrest - A peace officer may arrest a person for a violation of carrying while under the influence without a warrant upon probable cause, without regard to whether the violation was committed in the officer's presence.

Preliminary Screening Test - When an officer has reason to believe that a person may be carrying while under the influence, the officer may require the person to provide a breath sample for a preliminary screening test using a device approved by the commissioner of public safety for this purpose. Following the preliminary screening test, additional tests may be required of the person under M.S. § 624.7143. (See M.S. § 624.7143 "Chemical Testing" including mandatory chemical testing and civil penalties for refusal). A person who refuses a breath sample is subject to the provisions of M.S. § 624.7143 unless, in compliance with that section, the person submits to a blood, breath, or urine test to determine the presence of alcohol or a controlled substance.

G.   ALLOWING AN INELIGIBLE PERSON ACCESS TO FIREARMS
M.S. § 624.7144 (Gross Misdemeanor)

Name

Date and Time of Offense

Location (Venue)

(1)   No person shall

(2)   accept a transferred firearm from an abusing party or offender ordered to transfer the firearm pursuant to an order under

       a.   M.S. § 260C.201, subd. 3 (domestic child abuse order for protection)

       b.   M.S. § 518B.01B, subd. 6 (domestic abuse order for protection)

       c.   M.S. § 609.2242, subd. 3 (domestic assault), or

       d.   M.S. § 609.749, subd. 8 (stalking)

(3)   and allow the abusing party or offender to obtain possession of the transferred firearm while the person is prohibited from possessing firearms.

Defense: It is an affirmative defense to a violation of this section that the third party who accepted the transferred firearm exercised due care to ensure the abusing party or offender could not access the firearm.

Note: The third party shall not return the firearm to the abusing party or offender until the prohibiting time period has expired and the abusing party or offender presents a current, valid transferee permit or passes a federal background check.

H.   RIFLES AND SHOTGUNS IN PUBLIC PLACES
M.S. § 624.7181, subd. 1, 2, 3 (Gross Misdemeanor - Felony)
Name
Date and Time of Offense
Location (Venue)
(1)   No person shall
(2)   carry (as defined in section I, "Definitions" below) a BB gun, rifle, or shotgun
(3)   on or about the person in a public place (as defined in section I, "Definitions" below).

Exceptions: The above section does not apply to officers, employees, or agents of law enforcement agencies or the armed forces of the state or the United States, or private detectives or protective agents, to the extent that these persons are authorized by law to carry firearms and are acting in the scope of their official duties.

Definition of **"BB gun"** (M.S. § 624.7181, subd. 1) - "BB gun" means a device that fires or ejects a shot measuring .18 of an inch or less in diameter.

Enhancement: A person under the age of 21 who carries a semi-automatic military-style assault weapon on or about the person in a public place is guilty of a **felony**.

I.   DEFINITIONS:

(1)   **Ammunition** (M.S. § 609.02, subd. 17))
                "Ammunition" means ammunition or cartridge case, primers, bullets, or propellant powder designed for use in any firearm. Ammunition does not include ornaments, curiosities, or souvenirs constructed from or resembling ammunition or

- 182 -

ammunition components that are not operable as ammunition.

(2) **Antique Firearm** (M.S. § 624.712, subd. 3)

"Antique firearm" means any firearm, including any pistol, with a matchlock, flintlock, percussion cap, or similar type of ignition system, manufactured before 1899 and any replica of any firearm described herein if such replica is not designed or redesigned, made or remade, or intended to fire conventional rimfire or conventional centerfire ammunition, or uses conventional rimfire or conventional centerfire ammunition which is not readily available in the ordinary channels of commercial trade.

(3) **Carry** (M.S. § 624.7181, subd. 1)

"Carry" does not include:

a. the carrying of a BB gun, rifle, or shotgun to, from, or at a place where firearms are repaired, bought, sold, traded, or displayed, or where hunting, target shooting, or other lawful activity involving firearms occurs, or at funerals, parades, or other lawful ceremonies;

b. the carrying by a person of a BB gun, rifle, or shotgun that is unloaded and in a gun case expressly made to contain a firearm, if the case fully encloses the firearm by being zipped, snapped, buckled, tied, or otherwise fastened, and no portion of the firearm is exposed;

c. the carrying of a BB gun, rifle, or shotgun by a person who has a permit under section 624.714;

d. the carrying of an antique firearm as a curiosity or for its historical significance or value; or

e. the transporting of a BB gun, rifle, or shotgun in compliance with section 97B.045.

(4) **Chemically dependent person** (M.S. § 253B.02, subd. 2)

"Chemically dependent person" means any person (a) determined as being incapable of self-management or management of personal affairs by reason of the habitual and excessive use of alcohol, drugs or other mind-altering substances and (b) whose recent conduct as a result of habitual and excessive use of alcohol, drugs, or other mind-altering substances; poses a substantial likelihood of physical harm to self or others as demonstrated by (i) a recent attempt or threat to physically harm self or others, (ii) evidence of recent serious physical problems or (iii) a failure to obtain necessary food, clothing, shelter or medical care. "Chemically dependent" person also means a pregnant

- 183 -

woman who has engaged during the pregnancy in habitual or excessive use for a nonmedical purpose of any of the following controlled substances or their derivatives: cocaine, heroin, phencyclidine (PCP), methamphetamine or amphetamine.

(5)   **Crime of violence** (M.S. § 624.712, subd. 5)

"Crime of violence" means felony convictions or felony attempt convictions for the following offenses:

a.   Aggravated Robbery
b.   Aiding Suicide and Aiding Attempted Suicide
c.   Arson in the 1st and 2nd Degree
d.   Assault in the 1st, 2nd, 3rd, 4th and 5th Degree
e.   Burglary in the 1st, 2nd Degree
f.   Commission of a Crime While Wearing or Possessing a Bullet-Resistant Vest
g.   Crimes Committed for the Benefit of a Gang
h.   Criminal Sexual Conduct in the 1st, 2nd, 3rd, and 4th Degree
i.   Domestic Assault
j.   Domestic Assault by Strangulation
k.   Drive-By Shooting
l.   Drugs and Controlled Substances
m.   False Imprisonment
n.   Harassment and Stalking
o.   Kidnapping
p.   Malicious Punishment of a Child
q.   Manslaughter in the 1st and 2nd Degree
r.   Murder in the 1st, 2nd, and 3rd Degree
s.   Neglect or Endangerment of a Child
t.   Riot
u.   Shooting at a Public Transit Vehicle or Facility
v.   Simple Robbery
w.   Solicitation, Inducement, and Promotion of Prostitution; Sex Trafficking
x.   Stalking
y.   Terroristic Threats
z.   Theft Involving the Theft of a Controlled Substance, an Explosive, or an Incendiary Device
aa.   Theft of Firearm
bb.   Unlawfully Owning, Possessing, Operating a Machine Gun or Short-Barreled Shotgun
cc.   Use of Drugs to Injure of Facilitate a Crime

(6)   **Mentally ill person** (M.S. § 253B.02, subd. 13)
        (a)   "Mentally ill person" means any person who has an organic disorder of the brain or a substantial psychiatric disorder of thought, mood, perception, orientation or memory which grossly impairs judgment, behavior, capacity to recognize reality or to reason or understand, which is manifested by instances of grossly disturbed behavior or faulty perceptions and poses a substantial likelihood of physical harm to self or others as demonstrated by: (i) a failure to obtain necessary food, clothing, shelter or medical care as a result of the impairment, or (ii) a recent attempt or threat to physically harm self or others.
        (b)   A person is not mentally ill under this section if the impairment is solely due to:
                (1) epilepsy; (2) mental retardation; (3) brief periods of intoxication caused by alcohol, drugs, or other mind-altering substances; or (4) dependence upon or addiction to any alcohol, drugs, or other mind-altering substances.
(7)   **Mentally ill and dangerous to the public** (M.S. § 253B.02, subd. 17)
        A person "mentally ill and dangerous to the public" is a person (a) who is mentally ill; and (b) who, as a result of that mental illness, presents a clear danger to the safety of others as demonstrated by the fact that (i) the person has engaged in an overt act causing or attempting to cause serious physical harm to another; and (ii) there is a substantial likelihood that the person will engage in acts capable of inflicting serious physical harm on another.
(8)   **Mentally retarded person** (M.S. § 253B.02, subd. 14)
        "Mentally retarded person" means any person: (a) who has been diagnosed as having significantly subaverage intellectual functioning existing concurrently with demonstrated deficits in adaptive behavior and who manifests these conditions prior to the person's 22nd birthday; and (b) whose recent conduct is a result of mental retardation and poses a substantial likelihood of physical harm to self or others in that there has been (i) a recent attempt or threat to physically harm self or others or (ii) a failure and inability to obtain necessary food, clothing, shelter, safety or medical care.
(9)   **Pistol**   (M.S. § 624.712, subd. 2)
        "Pistol" includes a weapon designed to be fired by the use of a single hand and with an overall length less than 26 inches, or having a barrel or barrels of a length less than 18 inches in

the case of a shotgun or having a barrel of a length less than 16 inches in the case of a rifle (a) from which may be fired or ejected one or more solid projectiles by means of a cartridge or shell or by the action of an explosive or the igniting of flammable or explosive substances; or (b) for which the propelling force is a spring, elastic band, carbon dioxide, air or other gas or vapor.

"Pistol" does not include a device firing or ejecting a shot measuring .18 of an inch or less in diameter and commonly known as a BB gun, a scuba gun, a stud gun or nail gun used in the construction industry or children's pop guns or toys.

(10)   **Public place** (M.S. § 624.7181, subd. 1)

"Public place" means property owned, leased, or controlled by a governmental unit and private property that is regularly and frequently open to or made available for use by the public in sufficient numbers to give clear notice of the property's current dedication to public use but does not include: a person's dwelling house or premises, the place of business owned or managed by the person, or land possessed by the person; a gun show, gun shop, or hunting or target shooting facility; or the woods, fields, or waters of this state where the person is present lawfully for the purpose of hunting or target shooting or other lawful activity involving firearms.

(11)   **Semiautomatic military-style assault weapon**   (M.S. § 624.712, subd. 7)

"Semiautomatic military-style assault weapon" means any of the following firearms:

(a)   Avtomat Kalashnikov (AK-47) semiautomatic rifle type;

(b)   Beretta AR-70 and BM-59 semiautomatic rifle types;

(c)   Colt AR-15 semiautomatic rifle type;

(d)   Daewoo Max-1 and Max-2 semiautomatic rifle types;

(e)   Famas MAS semiautomatic rifle type;

(f)   Fabrique Nationale FN-LAR and FN-FNC semiautomatic rifle types;

(g)   Galil semiautomatic rifle type;

(h)   Heckler & Koch HK-91, HK-93, and HK-94 semiautomatic rifle types;

(i)   Ingram MAC-10 and MAC-11 semiautomatic pistol and carbine types;

(j)   Intratec TEC-9 semiautomatic pistol type;

(k)   Sigarms SIG 550SP and SIG 551SP semiautomatic rifle types;

(l)   SKS with detachable magazine semiautomatic rifle type;

(m)   Steyr AUG semiautomatic rifle type;

(n)   Street Sweeper and Striker-12 revolving-cylinder shotgun types;

(o)   USAS-12 semiautomatic shotgun type;

(p)   Uzi semiautomatic pistol and carbine types; or

(q)   Valmet M76 and M78 semiautomatic rifle types;

(r)   any firearm that is another model made by the same manufacturer as one of the firearms listed in (a) to (q) above, and has the same action design as one of the listed firearms, and is a redesigned, renamed, or renumbered version of one of the firearms listed in (a) to (q) above, or has a slight modification or enhancement, including but not limited to a folding or retractable stock; adjustable sight; case deflector for left-handed shooters; shorter barrel; wooden, plastic, or metal stock; larger clip size; different caliber; or a bayonet mount; and

(s)   any firearm that has been manufactured or sold by another company under a licensing agreement with a manufacturer of one of the firearms listed in (a) to (q) above entered into after August 1, 1993, to manufacture or sell firearms that are identical or nearly identical to those listed in (a) to (q) above, or described in (r) above, regardless of the company of production or country of origin.

30. RECEIVING STOLEN PROPERTY

RECEIVING STOLEN PROPERTY
M.S. § 609.53, subd. 1; M.S. § 609.52, subd. 3 (Misdemeanor, Gross Misdemeanor, Felony)

Name
Date and Time of Offense
Location (Venue)

(1)   No person shall
(2)   receive, possess, transfer, buy or conceal
(3)   any stolen property or property obtained by robbery
(4)   knowing or having reason to know
(5)   the property was stolen or obtained by robbery.

SENTENCING CONSIDERATIONS:
20-Year Felony

(1)   If the property stolen is a firearm.

10-Year Felony

(1)   If the value of the property stolen is more than $5,000;
       or
(2)   the property stolen was an article representing a trade secret;
       or
(3)   the property stolen was an explosive or incendiary device;
       or
(4)   the property stolen was a controlled substance listed in Schedule I or II pursuant to M.S. § 152.02, with the exception of marijuana.

5-Year Felony

(1)   If the value of the property stolen is more than $1,000 but not more than $5,000;
       or
(2)   the property stolen was a controlled substance listed in Schedule III, IV or V pursuant to M.S. § 152.02;
       or
(3)   the value of the property stolen is more than $500, but not more than $1,000 and the person has been convicted of and received a felony or gross misdemeanor sentence within the preceding five years for any of the following offenses:
       a.   any theft or theft-related offense (M.S. § 609.52)
       b.   Welfare Fraud (M.S. § 256.98)
       c.   Unemployment Compensation Fraud (M.S. § 268.18, subd. 3)
       d.   Simple Robbery (M.S. § 609.24)

e.	Aggravated Robbery (M.S. § 609.245)
f.	Receiving Stolen Property (M.S. § 609.53)
g.	Burglary (M.S. § 609.582, subd. 1, 2 or 3)
h.	Aggravated Forgery (M.S. § 609.625)
i.	Forgery (M.S. § 609.63)
j.	Check Forgery; Offering a Forged Check (M.S. § 609.631)
k.	Financial Transaction Card Fraud (M.S. § 609.821)
l.	or a statute from another state in conformity with any of the above sections.

or

(4) If the value of the property stolen is not more than $1,000, and:

    a. the property is taken from the person of another or from a corpse or grave or coffin containing a corpse; or

    b. the property is a record of a court or officer or a writing, instrument or record kept, filed or deposited according to law with or in the keeping of any public officer or office; or

    c. the property is taken from a burning building or upon its removal therefrom, or from an area of destruction caused by civil disaster, riot, bombing or the proximity of battle; or

    d. the property consists of public funds belonging to the state or to any political subdivision or agency thereof; or

    e. the property stolen is a motor vehicle.

Gross Misdemeanor

(1) If the value of the property stolen is more than $500 but not more than $1,000.

Misdemeanor

(1) In all other cases where the value of the property stolen is $500 or less.

31. ROBBERY

A. ROBBERY
M.S. § 609.24 (Felony)

Name
Date and Time of Offense
Location (Venue)

(1) No person shall
(2) having knowledge of not being entitled thereto
(3) take personal property from the person or in the presence of another
(4) and use or threaten the imminent use of force against any person
(5) to overcome the person's resistance or powers of resistance to, or to compel acquiescence in
(6) the taking or carrying away of the property.

B. AGGRAVATED ROBBERY IN THE FIRST DEGREE
M.S. § 609.245, subd. 1 (Felony)

Name
Date and Time of Offense
Location (Venue)

(1) No person shall
(2) while committing a robbery (as defined above, section A)
(3) a. be armed with a dangerous weapon (as defined in chapter 2 (Assaults), section U, "Definitions".)
   or
   b. any article used or fashioned in a manner to lead the victim to reasonably believe it to be a dangerous weapon.
   or
   c. inflict bodily harm upon another ("bodily harm" is defined in chapter 2 (Assaults), section U, "Definitions".)

C. AGGRAVATED ROBBERY IN THE SECOND DEGREE
M.S. § 609.245, subd. 2 (Felony)

Name
Date and Time of Offense
Location (Venue)

(1) No person shall
(2) while committing a robbery (as defined above, section A)
(3) imply, by word or act, possession of a dangerous weapon (as defined in chapter 2 (Assaults), section U, "Definitions".)

32. STALKING , WINDOW PEEPING, AND NONCONSENSUAL DISSEMINATION OF SEXUAL IMAGES

A.   STALKING
         M.S. § 609.749, subds. 1, 2 (Gross Misdemeanor)
Name
Date and Time of Offense
Location (Venue)
(1)   No person shall
(2)   stalk another by committing any of the following acts:

Note: "Stalking" is defined in Section G, "Definitions" below.

(a)   Directly or indirectly, or through third parties, manifests a purpose or intent to injure the person, property, or rights of another by the commission of an unlawful act.

OR

(b)   Follows, monitors, or pursues another, whether in person or through any available technological or any other means. Jurisdiction: The conduct may be prosecuted where the actor or victim resides. Note: The above section does not impair the right of any individual or group to engage in speech protected by the federal constitution, the state constitution, or federal or state law, including peaceful and lawful handbilling and picketing.

OR

(c)   Returns to the property of another if the actor is without claim of right to the property or consent of one with authority to consent.

OR

(d)   Repeatedly makes telephone calls, sends text messages, or induces a victim to make telephone calls to the actor, whether or not conversation ensues.

Jurisdiction: Violations of the above section may be prosecuted at the place where any call is either made or received or, additionally, in the case of wireless or electronic communication or any communication made through available technologies, where the actor or victim resides or in the jurisdiction of the victim's designated address if the victim participates in an address confidentiality program.

OR

(e) Makes or causes the telephone of another repeatedly or continuously to ring.

Jurisdiction: Violations of the above section may be prosecuted at the place where any call is either made or received or, additionally, in the case of wireless or electronic communication or any communication made through available technologies where the actor or victim resides or in the jurisdiction of the victim's designated address if the victim participates in an address confidentiality program.

OR

(f) Repeatedly mails or delivers or causes the delivery of letters, telegrams, messages, packages, through assistive devices for people with vision impairments or hearing loss, or communication made through any available technologies, or other objects.

Jurisdiction: Violations of the above section may be prosecuted where any letter, telegram, message, package, or other object is either sent or received or, additionally, in the case of wireless or electronic communication or communication made through other available technologies, where the actor or victim resides or in the jurisdiction of the victim's designated address if the victim participates in an address confidentiality program.

OR

(g)	Knowingly makes false allegations against a peace officer concerning the officer's performance of official duties with intent to influence or tamper with the officer's performance of official duties.
	Note: A peace officer may not make a warrantless custodial arrest of any person for a violation of this section.

OR

(h)	Uses another's personal information, without consent, to invite, encourage, or solicit a third party to engage in a sexual act with the person.

Penalty:

A person violating any of the provisions above in Section A is guilty of a **gross misdemeanor** if the violation is not subject to enhancement to a felony under Section B. below or the offense is not a "second or subsequent violation" as defined below.

B.   STALKING
M.S. § 609.749, subds. 3, 4 (Felony)

Name

Date and Time of Offense

Location (Venue)

(1)   No person shall

(2)   stalk another by committing any of the acts in Section A above:

(a)	Because of the victim's or another's actual or perceived race, color, religion, sex, sexual orientation, disability, age, or national origin.

OR

(b)	By falsely impersonating another.

OR

(c)	And possesses a dangerous weapon at the time of the offense.

OR

(d)	With intent to influence or otherwise tamper with a juror or a judicial proceeding or with intent to retaliate against a judicial officer (as defined in Section F, "Definitions" below) or prosecutor, defense attorney, or officer of the court, because of that person's performance of official duties in connection with a judicial proceeding.

OR

- 193 -

(e)	When the victim is under the age of 18, if the defendant is more than 36 months older than the victim.

OR

(f)	When the victim is under the age of 18, if the defendant is more than 36 months older than the victim and the act is committed with sexual or aggressive intent.

Penalty:
A person violating any of the provisions above in Section B. is guilty of a **felony.**

Second or subsequent violations: A person is guilty of a **felony** who commits any of the acts in Section A. above within ten years of a previous qualified domestic violence-related offense conviction or adjudication of delinquency "Qualified domestic violence-related offense" is defined in section F. below.

A person is guilty of a **felony** with an increased penalty who commits any of acts in Section A. above within ten years of the first of two or more previous qualified domestic violence-related offense convictions or adjudications of delinquency. "Qualified domestic violence-related offense" is defined in section F. below.

C. **PATTERN OF STALKING**
   (Felony)
Name
Date and Time of Offense
Location (Venue)

(1)	Whoever engages in a pattern conduct with respect to a single victim or one or more members of a single household which the actor knows or has reason to know would cause the victim under the circumstances to feel terrorized or to fear bodily harm and which does cause this reaction on the part of the victim is guilty of a **felony.** Note: "Pattern of stalking conduct" is defined in section G, "Definitions" below.

Venue: When acts constituting a violation of these stalking provisions (Section A, B, or C) are committed in two or more counties, the accused may be prosecuting in any county in which one of the acts was committed for all acts in violation of this section.

Arrest: For all violations of the stalking statute (Sections A, B, and C above) with the exception of knowingly making false allegations against a peace officer (Section A(9) above), a peace officer may make a warrantless, custodial arrest under the provisions of M.S. § 629.34.

D.   **EXCEPTIONS/DEFENSES:** Conduct is not a crime under any of the above sections if it is performed:

(1)   Under terms of a valid license.

OR

(2)   To ensure compliance with a court order.

OR

(3)   To carry out a specific lawful commercial purpose or employment duty.

OR

(4)   Is authorized or required by a valid contract.

OR

(5)   Is authorized, required, or protected by state or federal law or the state or federal constitutions.

Note: No proof of specific intent required - In a prosecution under any of the above sections, the state is not required to prove that the actor intended to cause the victim to feel frightened, threatened, oppressed, persecuted, or intimidated, or except as otherwise provided in M.S. § 609.749, subd. 3(a) (Judicial Proceedings – Section B.2(d)) or M.S. § 609.749, subd. 3(b) (victim under age 18 with sexual or aggressive intent – Section B 2(f), that the actor intended to cause any other result (M.S. § 609.749, subd. 1a).

E. INTERFERENCE WITH PRIVACY - Window peeping
M.S. § 609.746, subd. 1 (Gross Misdemeanor - Felony)

Name
Date and Time of Offense
Location (Venue)

(1)	No person shall
(2)	enter upon another's property
(3)	and surreptitiously gaze, stare or peep
(4)	in the window or any other aperture of a house or place of dwelling of another
(5)	with intent to intrude upon or interfere with the privacy of a member of the household. **(Gross Misdemeanor)**

OR

(1)	No person shall
(2)	enter upon another's property
(3)	and surreptitiously install or use any device for observing, photographing, recording, amplifying, or broadcasting sounds or events through the window or any other aperture of a house or place of dwelling of another
(4)	with intent to intrude upon or interfere with the privacy of a member of the household. **(Gross Misdemeanor)**

Exclusion - Law Enforcement: The above section does not apply to law enforcement officers or corrections investigators, or to those acting under their direction, while engaged in the performance of their lawful duties.

OR

(1)	No person shall
(2)	surreptitiously gaze, stare, or peep
(3)	in the window or other aperture or a sleeping room in a hotel (as defined in M.S. § 327.70, subd. 3), a tanning booth, or other place where a reasonable person would have an expectation of privacy and has exposed or is likely to expose their intimate parts (i.e. the primary genital area, groin, inner thigh, buttocks, or breast of a human being - M.S. § 609.341, subd. 5), or the clothing covering the immediate area of the intimate parts

(4)   and does so with intent to intrude upon or interfere with the privacy of the occupant. (Gross Misdemeanor)

Exclusion - Medical Facility or Commercial Establishment: The above section does not apply to conduct in: (1) a medical facility; or (2) a commercial establishment if the owner of the establishment has posted conspicuous signs warning that the premises are under surveillance by the owner or the owner's employees.

OR

(1)   No person shall
(2)   surreptitiously install or use any device for observing, photographing, recording, amplifying, or broadcasting sounds or events
(3)   through the window or other aperture of a sleeping room in a hotel (as defined in M.S. § 327.70, subd. 3), a tanning booth, or other place where a reasonable person would have an expectation of privacy and has exposed or is likely to expose their intimate parts (i.e. primary genital area, groin, inner thigh, buttocks, or breast of a human being - M.S. § 609.341, subd. 5), or the clothing covering the immediate area of the intimate parts
(4)   and does so with intent to intrude upon or interfere with the privacy of the occupant. **(Gross Misdemeanor)**

Exclusion - Law Enforcement: The above section does not apply to law enforcement officers or corrections investigators, or to those acting under their direction, while engaged in the performance of their lawful duties.

Exclusion - Medical Facility or Commercial Establishment: The above section does not apply to conduct in: (1) a medical facility; or (2) a commercial establishment if the owner of the establishment has posted conspicuous signs warning that the premises are under surveillance by the owner or the owner's employees.

Enhancement to Felony: A person is guilty of a felony if the person:
(a)   violates any of the above sections after a previous conviction of any of the above sections or M.S. § 609.749 (Stalking);
      or
(b)   violates any of the above sections against a minor under the age of 18, knowing or having reason to know that the minor is present.

F.   **NONCONSENSUAL DISSEMINATON OF**
       PRIVATE SEXUAL IMAGES
       M.S. § 617.261 (Gross Misdemeanor and Felony)

Name

Date and Time of Offense

Location (Venue)

(1)   No person shall

(2)   intentionally disseminate an image of another person who is depicted
       in a sexual act or whose intimate parts are exposed, in whole or in part,
       when

    a.   the person is identifiable

        i.   from the image itself, by the person depicted in the
       image or by another person

            or

        ii.   from personal information displayed in connection with
       the image

    b.   the actor knows or reasonably should know that the person
       depicted in the image did not consent to the dissemination
       and

(3)   the image was obtained or created under circumstances in which the actor
       knew or reasonably should have known the person depicted had a
       reasonable expectation of privacy. **(gross misdemeanor)**

Enhancement to Felony: Whoever violates the provisions above and

    (1)   the person depicted in the image suffers financial loss
       due to the dissemination of the image

        or

    (2)   the actor disseminates the image with intent to profit
       from the dissemination

        or

    (3)   the actor maintains an internet web site, online service,
       online application, or mobile application for the
       purpose of disseminating the image

        or

    (4) the actor posts the image on a website

        or

    (5)   the actor disseminates the image with intent to harass
       the person depicted in the image

        or

    (6)   the actor obtained the image by committing theft,
       interference with privacy, computer theft, or
       unauthorized computer access

        or

    (7)   the actor had previously been convicted under this
       section.

• No defense: It is not a defense if the person consented to the capture or possession of the image.

Venue: An offense may be prosecuted in

(1)	the county where the offense occurred
(2)	the county of residence of the actor or victim or in the jurisdiction of the victim's designated address if the victim participates in the address confidentiality program **or**
(3)	if the venue cannot be located in any of the above, in the county where any image is produced, reproduced, found, stored, or possessed.

Exemptions: This section does not apply when

(1)	the dissemination is made for purpose of a criminal investigation or prosecution that is otherwise lawful **or**
(2)	the dissemination is for the purpose of, or in connections with, the reporting of unlawful conduct **or**
(3)	the dissemination is made in the course of seeking or receiving medical or mental health treatment and the image is protected from further dissemination **or**
(4)	the image involves exposure in pubic or was obtained in a commercial setting for the purpose of the legal sale of goods or services, including the creation of artistic products for sale or display **or**
(5)	the image relates to a matter of public interest and dissemination serves a lawful public purpose
(6)	**or**
(7)	the dissemination is for legitimate scientific research or educational purposes **or**
(8)	the dissemination is made for legal proceedings and is consistent with common practice in civil proceedings necessary for the proper functioning of the criminal justice system, or protected by court order which prohibits any further dissemination.

Immunity: If the content or information is provided solely by another person, nothing in this section shall be construed to impose liability upon

(1)	an internet computer service **or**

(2)   a provider of public mobile services or private radio services

or

(3)   a telecommunications network or broadband provider.

Definitions:

(1)   "Dissemination" means distribution to one or more persons, other than the person depicted in the image, or publication by any publicly available medium.

(2)   "Harass" means an act that would cause a substantial adverse effect on the safety, security, or privacy of a reasonable person.

(3)   "Image" means a photograph, film, video recording, or digital photograph or recording.

(4)   "Intimate parts" means the genitals, pubic area, or anus of an individual, or if the individual is female, a partially or fully exposed nipple.

(5)   "Personal information" means any identifier that permits communication or in-person contact with a person, including

  a.   a person's first and last name, first initial and last name, first name and last initial, or nickname

  b.   a person's home, school, or work address

  c.   a person's telephone number, e-mail address, or social media account information

  or

  d.   a person's geolocation information.

(6)   "Sexual act" means either sexual contact or sexual penetration.

(7)   "Sexual contact" means the intentional touching of intimate parts or intentional touching with seminal fluid or sperm onto another person's body.

(8)   "Sexual penetration" means

  a.   sexual intercourse, cunnilingus, fellatio, or anal intercourse

  or

  b.   any intrusion, however slight, into the genital or anal openings of an individual by another's body part or an object used by another for this purpose.

9)   "Social media" means any electronic medium, including interactive computer service, telephone network, or data network, that allows users to create, share, and view user-generated content.

G. DEFINITIONS

(1) **Dangerous weapon** (M.S. § 609.02, subd. 6)

"Dangerous weapon" is defined in chapter 2 (Assaults), section U, "Definitions".

(2) **Judicial Officer** (M.S. § 609.415, subd. 1(3))

"Judicial officer" means a judge, court commissioner, referee, or any other person appointed by a judge or court to hear or determine a cause or controversy.

(3) **Pattern of Stalking Conduct** (M.S. § 609.749, subd. 5)

"Pattern of stalking conduct" means two or more acts within a five-year period that violate or attempt to violate the provisions of any of the following:

a. any of the above Stalking sections (M.S. § 609.749);

b. First to Third Degree Murder and First and Second Degree Manslaughter (M.S. § 609.185 to 609.205)

c. Terroristic Threats (M.S. § 609.713);

d. Assault in the 5th Degree (M.S. § 609.224);

e. Domestic Assault (M.S. § 609.2242);

f. Violation of Domestic Abuse Order for Protection (M.S. § 518B.01, Subd. 14);

g. Violation of Harassment Restraining Order (M.S. § 609.748, Subd. 6);

h. Trespass (M.S. § 609.605, Subd. 1(b) clauses (3), (4) and (7))

"Returns to the property of another with the intent to abuse, disturb, or cause distress in or threaten another, after being told to leave the property and not to return, if the actor is without claim of right to the property or consent of one with authority to consent";

i. Interference with Emergency Calls (M.S. § 609.78, subd. 2);

j. Obscene or Harassing Telephone Calls (M.S. §609.79);

k. Illegal Letter, Telegram, or Package Opening (M.S. § 609.795);

l. Burglary (M.S. § 609.582);

m. Damage to Property (M.S. § 609.595);

n. Criminal Defamation (M.S. § 609.765);

o. Criminal Sexual Conduct in the 1st, 2nd, 3rd, 4th, and 5th Degree (M.S. § 609.342 to § 609.3451);

p. Violations of Domestic Abuse No Contact Orders (M.S. § 629.75, subd. 2).

(4)   **Personal Information** (M.S. § 617.261, subd. 7(f))
        "Personal Information" is defined in chapter 32, section G, Definitions

(5)   **Qualified Domestic Violence-Related Offense** (M.S. § 609.02, subd. 16)
        "Qualified domestic violence-related offense" includes a violation of or an attempt to violate: § 518B.01, subd. 14 (Violation of Domestic Abuse Order for Protection); §518B.01, subd 22 (Violation of a Domestic Abuse No Contact Order); § 609.185 (First Degree Murder); § 609.19 (Second Degree Murder; § 609.221 (First Degree Assault); § 609.22 (Second Degree Assault); § 609.223 (Third Degree Assault); § 609.2231 (Fourth Degree Assault); § 609.224 (Fifth Degree Assault); § 609.2242 (Domestic Assault); § 609.2245 (Female Genital Mutilation); § 609.2247 (Domestic Assault by Strangulation); § 609.342 (First Degree Criminal Sexual Conduct); § 609.343 (Second Degree Criminal Sexual Conduct); § 609.344 (Third Degree Criminal Sexual Conduct); § 609.345 (Fourth Degree Criminal Sexual Conduct); § 609.377 (Malicious Punishment of a Child); § 609.713 (Terroristic Threats); § 609.748, subd. 6 (Violation of Harassment Restraining Order); § 609.749 (Harass-ment/Stalking); and § 609.78, subd. 2 (Interference with an Emergency Call); and similar laws of other states, the United States, the District of Columbia, tribal lands, and United States territories.

(6)   **Sexual Act** (M.S. § 617.261, subd. 7(g))
        "Sexual Act" is defined in chapter 32, section G, Definitions

(7)   **Stalking** (M.S. § 609.749, subd. 1)
        "Stalking" means to engage in intentional conduct which:
        a.   the actor knows or has reason to know would cause the victim under the circumstances to feel frightened, threatened, oppressed, persecuted, or intimidated; and
        b.   causes this reaction on the part of the victim regardless of the relationship between the actor and victim.

33. STOLEN OR COUNTERFEIT CHECK

POSSESSION OR SALE OF STOLEN OR COUNTERFEIT CHECK
M.S. § 609.528, subds. 1, 2, 3   (Misdemeanor - Gross Misdemeanor - Felony)
Name
Date and Time of Offense
Location (Venue)
(1)   No person shall
(2)   sell, possess, receive, or transfer a check that is stolen or counterfeit
(3)   knowing or having reason to know that the check is stolen or counterfeit

<u>Definition</u> of **"Direct victim"** means any person or entity from whom a check is stolen and whose name or other identification information is contained in a counterfeit check.

<u>Definition</u> of **"Indirect victim"** means any person or entity other than a direct victim.

<u>Definition</u> of **"Loss"** means value obtained and expenses incurred by a direct or indirect victim as a result of a violation of this section.

<u>Penalties:</u> If the offense involves a single direct victim and the total, combined loss to the direct victim and any indirect victims is $250 or less, the penalty is a **misdemeanor**. If the offense involves a single direct victim and the total, combined loss to the direct victim and any indirect victims is more than $250 but not more than $500, the penalty is a **gross misdemeanor**. If the offense involves two or three direct victims or the total, combined loss to the direct and indirect victims is more than $500 but not more than $2,500, the penalty is a **five-year felony**. If the offense involves four or more direct victims, or if the total, combined loss to the direct and indirect victims is more than $2,500, the penalty is a **ten-year felony**.

34. THREATS OF VIOLENCE

THREATS OF VIOLENCE
M.S. § 609.713, subds. 1, 2, 3 (Felony)
Name
Date and Time of Offense
Location (Venue)

(1)	No person shall
(2)	threaten, directly or indirectly,
(3)	to commit any crime of violence (as defined below) under the following circumstances:
	a. with purpose to terrorize another; **or**
	b. to cause evacuation of a building, place of assembly, vehicle or facility of public transportation; **or**
	c. otherwise to cause serious public inconvenience; **or**
	d. in a reckless disregard of the risk of causing such terror or inconvenience.

OR

(1)	No person shall
(2)	communicate to another
(3)	with purpose to terrorize another or in reckless disregard of the risk of causing such terror
(4)	that explosives or an explosive device or any incendiary device
(5)	is present at a named place or location
(6)	whether or not the same is in fact present.

OR

(1)	No person shall
(2)	display, exhibit, brandish or otherwise employ
(3)	a replica firearm or a BB gun (as defined below)
(4)	in a threatening manner
(5)	if, in doing so, the person either:
	a. causes or attempts to cause terror in another person; **or**
	b. acts in reckless disregard of the risk of causing terror in another person.

DEFINITIONS:

(1)   **BB gun** (M.S. § 609.713, subd. 3)

"BB gun" means a device that fires or ejects a shot measuring .18 of an inch or less in diameter. See also definition of "pistol", chapter 29, section I, "Definitions".

(2)   **Crime of violence** (M.S. § 609.1095, subd. 1(d))

"Violent crime" means a violation of or an attempt or conspiracy to violate any of the following laws of this state or any similar laws of the United States or any other state:

a.   Methamphetamine-related crimes involving children and vulnerable adults (M.S. § 152.137)

b.   Possession of firearms (M.S. § 609.165)

c.   Murder in the 1st, 2nd, or 3rd Degree (M.S. § 609.185, 19, 195)

d.   Manslaughter in the 1st or 2nd Degree (M.S. § 609.20, 205)

e.   Criminal Vehicular Operation (M.S. § 609.21)

f.   Assault in the 1st, 2nd, or 3rd Degree (M.S. § 609.221, 222, 223)

g.   Great Bodily Harm Caused by Distribution of Drugs (M.S. § 609.228)

h.   Use of Drugs to Injure or Facilitate Crime (M.S. § 609.235)

i.   Simple Robbery or Aggravated Robbery (M.S. § 609.24, 245)

j.   Kidnapping (M.S. § 609.25)

k.   False Imprisonment (M.S. § 609.255)

l.   Murder, Unborn Child, 1st, 2nd, 3rd Degree (M.S. § 609.2661, 2662, 2663)

m.   Manslaughter, Unborn Child, 1st, 2nd Degree (M.S. § 609.2664, 2665)

n.   Assault, Unborn Child, 1st, 2nd Degree (M.S. § 609.267, 2671)

o.   Injury or Death of an Unborn Child in Commission of Crime (M.S. § 609.268)

p.   Crim. Sex. Conduct, 1st to 4th Degree (M.S. § 609.342 to 345)

q.   Tampering with a Witness in the 1st Degree (M.S. § 609.498, subd. 1)

r.   Arson in the 1st or 2nd Degree (M.S. § 609.561, 562)

s.   Burglary in the 1st Degree (M.S. § 609.582, subd. 1)

t.   Drive-by Shooting (M.S. § 609.66, subd. 1e)

u.   Adulteration (M.S. § 609.687)

v.	Shooting at Public Transit Vehicle or Facility (M.S. § 609.855, subd. 5)
w.	Crime Committed for Benefit of a Gang (M.S. § 609.229, all provisions)
x.	Malicious Punishment of a Child (M.S. § 609.377)
y.	Neglect or Endangerment of a Child (M.S. § 609.378)
z.	Harassment - Stalking (M.S. § 609.749)
aa.	Felony Possession of Firearms (M.S. § 624.713, all felony provisions)
bb.	Controlled Substance Crime, 1st to 4th Degree (i.e. includes all provisions of M.S. § 152 punishable by a maximum sentence of 15 years or more).
cc.	Solicitation, Inducement, and Promotion of Prostitution; Sex Trafficking (M.S. § 609.322)

(2)   **Replica firearm** (M.S. § 609.713, subd. 3)

"Replica firearm" means a device or object that is not defined as a dangerous weapon and that is a facsimile or toy version of, and reasonably appears to be a pistol, revolver, shotgun, sawed-off shotgun, rifle, machine gun, rocket launcher, or any other firearm. The term replica firearm includes, but is not limited to, devices or objects that are designed to fire only blanks.

CRIMES COMMITTED IN FURTHERANCE OF TERRORISM
M.S. § 609.714, subd. 2 (Felony)
Name
Date and Time of Offense
Location (Venue)
(1) No person shall
(2) commit any felony crime
(3) to further terrorism (as defined below)

Definition of **"Further terrorism"** (M.S. § 609.714, subd. 1) means a crime is committed to "further terrorism" if the crime is a felony and is a premeditated act involving violence to persons or property that is intended to: terrorize, intimidate, or coerce a considerable number of members of the public in addition to the direct victims of the act; and significantly disrupt or interfere with the lawful exercise, operation, or conduct of government, lawful commerce, or the right of lawful assembly.

Penalty: The penalty for the above crime is 50 percent longer than the statutory maximum for the underlying crime. (M.S. § 609.714, subd. 2)

36. THEFT AND RELATED OFFENSES

A.   **THEFT - Permanently Deprive**
M.S. § 609.52, subd. 2(a)(1) (Misdemeanor - Gross Misdemeanor Felony)

Name
Date and Time of Offense
Location (Venue)
(1)   No person shall
(2)   intentionally and without claim of right
(3)   take, use, transfer, conceal or retain possession
(4)   of movable property of another
(5)   without the other's consent
(6)   and with intent to deprive the owner permanently of possession of the property.

Penalty: To determine if offense is a misdemeanor, gross misdemeanor or felony, see Section Q, "Special Sentencing Considerations".

B.   **THEFT - Superior Right of Possession**
M.S. § 609.52, subd. 2(a)(2) (Misdemeanor - Gross Misdemeanor Felony)

Name
Date and Time of Offense
Location (Venue)
(1)   No person shall
(2)   with or without having a legal interest in movable property
(3)   intentionally and without consent
(4)   take the property out of the possession
(5)   of a pledgee or other person having a superior right of possession
(6)   with intent thereby
(7)   to deprive the pledgee or other person permanently of the possession of the property.

Penalty: To determine if offense is a misdemeanor, gross misdemeanor or felony, see Section Q, "Special Sentencing Considerations".

C. **THEFT - False Representation**
M.S. § 609.52, subd. 2(a)(3) (Misdemeanor - Gross Misdemeanor Felony)

Name
Date and Time of Offense
Location (Venue)

(1)   No person shall
(2)   obtain for the actor or another
(3)   the possession, custody or title to property of or performance of services by a third person
(4)   by intentionally deceiving the third person
(5)   with a false representation
(6)   which is known to be false
(7)   made with intent to defraud
(8)   and which does defraud the person to whom it is made.

Penalty: To determine if offense is a misdemeanor, gross misdemeanor or felony, see Section Q, "Special Sentencing Considerations".

Definition of **"false representation"** (M.S. § 609.52, subd. 2(a)(3)) - includes without limitation:

a.   the issuance of a check, draft or order for the payment of money, except a forged check as defined in M.S. § 609.631 (Check Forgery - Chapter 16, Section C), or the delivery of property knowing that the defendant is not entitled to draw upon the drawee therefore or to order the payment or delivery thereof; or

b.   a promise made with intent not to perform. Failure to perform is not evidence of intent not to perform unless corroborated by other substantial evidence; or

c.   the preparation or filing of a claim for reimbursement, a rate application or a cost report used to establish a rate or claim for payment for medical care provided to a recipient of medical assistance under M.S. § 256B, which intentionally and falsely states the costs of or actual services provided by a vendor of medical care; or

d.   the preparation or filing of a claim for reimbursement for providing treatment or supplies required to be furnished to an employee under M.S. § 176.135 which intentionally and falsely states the costs of or actual treatment or supplies provided; or

e.   the preparation or filing of a claim for reimbursement for providing treatment or supplies required to be furnished to an employee under M.S. § 176.135 for treatment or supplies that the provider knew were medically unnecessary, inappropriate or excessive.

D.   THEFT - Swindling
M.S. § 609.52, subd. 2(a)(4) (Misdemeanor - Gross Misdemeanor Felony)

Name
Date and Time of Offense
Location (Venue)

(1)   No person shall
(2)   by swindling, whether by artifice, trick, device or any other means
(3)   obtain property or services from another person.

Penalty: To determine if offense is a misdemeanor, gross misdemeanor or felony, see Section Q, "Special Sentencing Considerations".

E.   THEFT - Temporary Control
M.S. § 609.52, subd. 2(a)(5) (Misdemeanor - Gross Misdemeanor Felony)

Name
Date and Time of Offense
Location (Venue)

(1)   No person shall
(2)   intentionally commit any theft or theft-related offense listed in this chapter, "Theft and Related Offenses", Sections A - P (M.S. § 609.52, subd. 2(a))
(3)   with intent to exercise temporary control only
           AND
(4)   a.   the control exercised manifests an indifference to the rights of the owner or the restoration of the property to the owner.
          or
        b.   the actor pledges or otherwise attempts to subject the property to an adverse claim.
          or
        c.   the actor intends to restore the property only on condition that the owner pay a reward or buy back or make other compensation.

Penalty: To determine if offense is a misdemeanor, gross misdemeanor or felony, see Section Q, "Special Sentencing Considerations".

Definition of **"value"** (M.S. § 609.52, subd. 1(3)) - for a theft committed in violation of the above section, elements (4) a and b, if the property has been restored to the owner, **"value"** means the value of the use of the property or the damage which it sustained, whichever is greater, while the owner was deprived of its possession.

F.   THEFT - Lost Property
M.S. § 609.52, subd. 2(a)(6) (Misdemeanor - Gross Misdemeanor Felony)

Name

Date and Time of Offense

Location (Venue)

(1)   No person shall

(2)   find lost property

(3)   and, knowing or having reasonable means of ascertaining the true owner

(4)   appropriate it to the finder's own use or to that of another not entitled thereto

(5)   without first having made a reasonable effort to find the owner

(6)   and offer and surrender the property to the owner.

Penalty: To determine if offense is a misdemeanor, gross misdemeanor or felony, see Section Q, "Special Sentencing Considerations".

G.   THEFT - Coin-Operated Machines
M.S. § 609.52, subd. 2(a)(7) (Misdemeanor - Gross Misdemeanor Felony)

Name

Date and Time of Offense

Location (Venue)

(1)   No person shall

(2)   intentionally obtain property or services

(3)   offered upon the deposit of a sum of money or tokens

(4)   in a coin or token-operated machine or other receptacle

(5)   without making the required deposit or otherwise obtaining the consent of the owner.

Penalty To determine if offense is a misdemeanor, gross misdemeanor or felony, see Section Q, "Special Sentencing Considerations".

H.   THEFT - Trade Secrets
M.S. § 609.52, subd. 2(a)(8) (Misdemeanor - Gross Misdemeanor Felony)

Name
Date and Time of Offense
Location (Venue)

(1)   No person shall
(2)   intentionally and without claim of right
(3)   convert any article representing a trade secret knowing it to be such
(4)   to the actor's own use or that of another person or make a copy of an article representing a trade secret knowing it to be such
(5)   and intentionally and without claim of right
(6)   convert the same to the actor's own use or that of another person.

Penalty: To determine if offense is a misdemeanor, gross misdemeanor or felony, see Section Q, "Special Sentencing Considerations".

Defense: It shall be a complete defense to any prosecution under this clause for the defendant to show that information comprising the trade secret was rightfully known or available to the defendant from a source other than the owner of the trade secret.

I.   THEFT - Leased/Rental Property
M.S. § 609.52, subd. 2(a)(9) (Misdemeanor - Gross Misdemeanor - Felony)

Name
Date and Time of Offense
Location (Venue)

(1)	No person shall
(2)	lease or rent personal property under a written instrument
(3)	and who, with intent to place the property beyond the control of the lessor conceals or aides or abets the concealment of the property or any part thereof.

OR

- 212 -

| (1) | any lessee of the property who sells, conveys or encumbers the property or any part thereof without the written consent of the lessor without informing the person to whom the lessee sells, conveys or encumbers that the same is subject to such lease or rental contract with intent to deprive the lessor of possession thereof. |

OR

| (1) | does not return the property to the lessor at the end of the lease or rental term, plus agreed upon extensions, with intent to wrongfully deprive the lessor of possession of the property and the value of the property must be at least $100. |

OR

| (1) | returns the property to the lessor at the end of the lease or rental term, plus agreed upon extensions, but does not pay the lease or rental charges agreed upon in the written instrument, with intent to wrongfully deprive the lessor of the agreed upon charges and the value of the property must be at least $100. |

Penalty: To determine if offense is a misdemeanor, gross misdemeanor or felony, see Section Q, "Special Sentencing Considerations".

Note: Evidence that a lessee used a false, fictitious or not current name, address, or place of employment in obtaining the property or fails or refuses to return the property or pay the rental contract charges to lessor within five days after written demand for the return has been served personally in the manner provided for service of process of a civil action or sent by certified mail to the last known address of the lessee, whichever shall occur later, shall be evidence of intent to violate this clause. Service by certified mail shall be deemed to be complete upon deposit in the U.S. mail of such demand, post-paid and addressed to the person at the address for the person set forth in the lease or rental agreement, or, in the absence of the address, to the person's last known place of residence.

J. **THEFT - Alteration/Removal of Identification Numbers**
M.S. § 609.52, subd. 2(a)(10)(11) (Misdemeanor - Gross Misdemeanor - Felony)

Name
Date and Time of Offense
Location (Venue)

(1)   No person shall
(2)   alter, remove or obliterate
(3)   numbers or symbols placed on movable property for purposes of identification by the owner or person who has legal custody or right to possession thereof
(4)   with the intent to prevent identification
(5)   if the person who alters, removes or obliterates the numbers or symbols is not the owner and does not have the permission of the owner to make the alteration, removal or obliteration.

OR

(1)   No person shall
(2)   with the intent to prevent the identification of property involved
(3)   so as to deprive the rightful owner of possession thereof
(4)   alter or remove any permanent serial number, permanent distinguishing number or manufacturer's identification number
(5)   on personal property
(6)   or possess, sell or buy any personal property
(7)   knowing or having reason to know that the permanent serial number, permanent distinguishing number or manufacturer's identification number has been removed or altered.

Penalty: To determine if offense is a misdemeanor, gross misdemeanor or felony, see Section Q, "Special Sentencing Considerations".

K. **THEFT - Cable Television Charges**
M.S. § 609.52, subd. 2(a)(12) (Misdemeanor - Gross Misdemeanor - Felony)

Name
Date and Time of Offense
Location (Venue)

(1)   No person shall
(2)   intentionally deprive another
(3)   of a lawful charge for cable television service
(4)   a.   by making or using or attempting to make or use an unauthorized external connection outside the individual

dwelling unit whether physical, electrical, acoustical, inductive or other connection.

or

b.   by attaching any unauthorized device to any cable, wire, microwave or other component of a licensed cable communications system as defined in Chapter 238.

Penalty: To determine if offense is a misdemeanor, gross misdemeanor or felony, see Section Q, "Special Sentencing Considerations".

Note: Nothing herein shall be construed to prohibit the electronic video re-recording of program material transmitted on the cable communications system by a subscriber for fair use as defined by Public Law No. 94-553, Section 107.

L.   THEFT - Telecommunications Service
M.S. § 609.52, subd. 2(a)(14) (Misdemeanor - Gross Misdemeanor - Felony)

Name
Date and Time of Offense
Location (Venue)

(1)   No person shall

(2)   intentionally deprive another of a lawful charge

(3)   for telecommunications service

(4)   a.   by making, using or attempting to make or use an unauthorized connection whether physical, electrical, by wire, microwave, radio or other means to a component of a local telecommunications system as provided in Chapter 237.

    or

    b.   by attaching an unauthorized device to a cable, wire, microwave, radio or other component of a local telecommunications system as provided in Chapter 237.

Penalty: To determine if offense is a misdemeanor, gross misdemeanor or felony, see Section Q, "Special Sentencing Considerations".

Note: The existence of an unauthorized connection is prima facia evidence that the occupier of the premises:

    a.   made or was aware of the connection; and

    b.   was aware that the connection was unauthorized.

M.   **THEFT - Obtaining Services of Another**
M.S. § 609.52, subd. 2(a)(13) (Misdemeanor - Gross Misdemeanor - Felony)

Name
Date and Time of Offense
Location (Venue)

(1)   No person shall
(2)   except as provided in Sections K and L above (Cable Television and Telecommunications Service)
(3)   obtain the services of another
(4)   with the intention of receiving those services without making the agreed or reasonably expected payment of money or other consideration.

Penalty: To determine if offense is a misdemeanor, gross misdemeanor or felony, see Section Q, "Special Sentencing Considerations".

N.   **THEFT - Diverting Corporate Property and Fraudulent Corporate Distributions**
M.S. § 609.52, subd. 2(a)(15),(16) (Misdemeanor - Gross Misdemeanor - Felony)

Name
Date and Time of Offense
Location (Venue)

(1)	No person shall
(2)	with intent to defraud
(3)	divert corporate property
(4)	other than in accordance with general business purposes or for purposes other than those specified in the corporation's articles of incorporation.

OR

(1)	No person shall
(2)	with intent to defraud
(3)	authorize or cause a corporation
(4)	to make a distribution in violation of Section 302A.551 or any other state law in conformity with it.

Penalty: To determine if offense is a misdemeanor, gross misdemeanor or felony, see Section Q, "Special Sentencing Considerations".

- 216 -

O.   **THEFT - Motor Vehicle Use Without Consent**
         M.S. § 609.52, subd. 2(a)(17) (Felony)

Name
Date and Time of Offense
Location (Venue)
(1)   No person shall
(2)   take or drive a motor vehicle
(3)   without the consent of the owner or an authorized agent of the owner
(4)   knowing or having reason to know that the owner or an authorized
        agent of the owner did not give consent.

Penalty: Whoever violates the above section is guilty of a **felony**.

P.   **THEFT - Motor Vehicle Fuel**
         M.S. § 609.52, subd. 2(a)(18)
         (Misdemeanor - Gross Misdemeanor - Felony)

Name
Date and Time of Offense
Location (Venue)
(1)   No person shall
(2)   intentionally, and without claim of right
(3)   take motor fuel from a retailer
(4)   without the retailer's consent
(5)   with intent to deprive the retailer permanently of possession of the
        fuel
(6)   by driving a motor vehicle from the premises of the retailer without
        having paid for the fuel dispensed into the vehicle

Note: Proof that the driver of a motor vehicle into which motor fuel was
dispensed permits the fact finder to infer that the driver acted intentionally and
without claim of right, and that the driver intended to deprive the retailer
permanently of possession of the fuel.

Note: This paragraph does not apply if:
(1)   payment has been made to the retailer within 30 days of the
        receipt of notice of nonpayment under M.S. § 604.15; or
(2)   a written notice as described in M.S. § 604.15, subd. 4,
        disputing the retailer's claim, has been sent.

This paragraph also does not apply to the owner of a motor vehicle if
the vehicle or the vehicle's license plate has been reported stolen
before the theft of the fuel.

Q.   THEFT - SPECIAL SENTENCING CONSIDERATIONS

20-Year Felony
(1)   If the property stolen is a firearm;
         or
(2)   the value of the property or services stolen is more than $35,000 and the conviction is for a violation of section C (Theft - False Representation), or section D (Theft - Swindling), or section N (Theft - Diverting Corporate Property or Fraudulent Corporate Distributions).

10-Year Felony
(1)   If the value of the property or services stolen is more than $5,000;
         or
(2)   the property stolen was an article representing a trade secret;
         or
(3)   the property stolen was an explosive or incendiary device;
         or
(4)   the property stolen was a controlled substance listed in Schedule I or II pursuant to M.S. § 152.02, with the exception of marijuana.

5-Year Felony
(1)   If the value of the property or services stolen is more than $1,000 but not more than $5,000;
         or
(2)   the property stolen was a controlled substance listed in Schedule III, IV or V pursuant to M.S. § 152.02;
         or
(3)   the value of the property or services stolen is more than $500 but not more than $1,000, and the person has been convicted of and received a felony or gross misdemeanor sentence, within the preceding five years, for any of the following offenses:
         a.   Theft (sections A. to P. above) (M.S. § 609.52)
         b.   Welfare Fraud (M.S. § 256.98)
         c.   Unemployment Comp. Fraud (M.S. § 268.18, subd. 3)
         d.   Simple Robbery (M.S. § 609.24)
         e.   Aggravated Robbery (M.S. § 609.245)
         f.   Receiving Stolen Property (M.S. § 609.53)
         g.   Burglary, 1st, 2nd, 3rd Degree (M.S. § 609.582)
         h.   Aggravated Forgery (M.S. § 609.625)
         i.   Forgery (M.S. § 609.63)
         j.   Check Forgery; Offering a Forged Check (M.S. § 609.631)
         k.   Financial Transaction Card Fraud (M.S. § 609.821)
                 or a statute from another state, the United States, or a foreign jurisdiction, in conformity with any of the above sections.
         or

(4)   If the value of the property or services stolen is not more than $1,000, and:

     a.   the property is taken from the person of another or from a corpse or grave or coffin containing a corpse; or

     b.   the property is a record of a court or officer, or a writing, instrument or record kept, filed or deposited according to law with or in the keeping of any public officer or office; or

     c.   the property is taken from a burning, abandoned, or vacant building or upon its removal therefrom, or from an area of destruction caused by civil disaster, riot, bombing or the proximity of battle; or

     d.   the property consists of public funds belonging to the state or to any political subdivision or agency thereof; or

     e.   the property stolen is a motor vehicle.

Gross Misdemeanor

(1)   If the value of the property or services stolen is more than $500 but not more than $1,000.

Misdemeanor

(1)   In all other cases where the value of the property or services stolen is $500 or less.

Aggregation: In any prosecution for theft under section A (Theft -Permanent Deprivation), section B (Theft - Superior Right of Possession), section C (Theft - False Representation), section D (Theft - Swindling), or section M (Theft - Obtaining Services of Another), the value of the money or property or services received by the defendant in violation of any one or more of the above provisions within any six-month period may be **aggregated** and the defendant charged accordingly in applying the provisions of this section.

Jurisdiction: When two or more offenses are committed by the same person in two or more counties, the accused may be prosecuted in any county in which one of the offenses was committed for all of the offenses aggregated under the above paragraph.

Enhancement to a Felony: If a violation of this section creates a reasonably foreseeable risk of bodily harm to another, and the penalty is a misdemeanor or gross misdemeanor, the person is guilty of a felony and may be sentenced to imprisonment for not more than 3 years or to payment of fine of not more than $5000 or both.

Enhanced Felony: If a violation of this section creates a reasonably foreseeable risk of bodily harm to another, and the penalty is a felony, the statutory maximum sentence for the offense is 50 percent longer than for the underlying crime.

R.   **DEFINITIONS:**

(1)   **Motor fuel** (M.S. § 609.52, subd. 1(11))

> "Motor fuel" means a liquid, regardless of its properties, used to propel a vehicle.

(2)   **Motor vehicle** (M.S. § 609.52, subd. 1(10))

> "Motor vehicle" means a self-propelled device for moving persons or property or pulling implements from one place to another, whether the device is operated on land, rails, water or in the air.

(3)   **Movable property** (M.S. § 609.52, subd. 1(2))

> "Movable property" is property whose physical location can be changed, including without limitation things growing on, affixed to or found in land.

(4)   **Property** (M.S. § 609.52, subd. 1(1))

> "Property" means all forms of tangible property, whether real or personal, without limitation including documents of value, electricity, gas, water, corpses, domestic animals, dogs, pets, fowl, and heat supplied by pipe or conduit by municipalities or public utility companies and articles, as defined in M.S. § 609.52, subd. 1(4), representing trade secrets, which articles shall be deemed for the purposes of Extra Session Laws 1967, Chapter 15, to include any trade secret represented by the article.

(5)   **Property of another** (M.S. § 609.52, subd. 1(8))

> "Property of another" includes property in which the actor is co-owner or has a lien, pledge, bailment or lease or other subordinate interest, property transferred by the actor in circumstances which are known to the actor and which make the transfer fraudulent as defined in M.S. § 513.44, ("Transfers Fraudulent as to Present and Future Creditors") - property possessed pursuant to a short-term rental contract, and property of a partnership of which the actor is a member, unless the actor and the victim are husband and wife. It does not include property in which the actor asserts in good faith a claim as a collection fee or commission out of property or funds recovered, or by virtue of a lien, set off or counterclaim.

(6)   **Retailer** (M.S. 609.52, subd. 1(12)

> "Retailer" means a person that sells motor fuel at retail.

(7)   **Services** (M.S. § 609.52, subd. 1(9))

"Services" include but are not limited to labor, professional services, transportation services, electronic computer services, the supplying of hotel accommodations, restaurant services, entertainment services, advertisement services, telecommunication services, and the supplying of equipment for use, including rental of personal property or equipment.

(8)   **Trade secret** (M.S. § 609.52, subd. 1(6))

"Trade secret" means information, including a formula, pattern, compilation, program, device, method, technique or process that:

a. derives independent economic value, actual or potential, from not being generally known to, and not being readily ascertainable by proper means by, other persons who can obtain economic value from its disclosure or use, and

b. is the subject of efforts that are reasonable under the circumstances to maintain its secrecy.

(9)   **Value** (M.S. § 609.52, subd. 1(3))

"Value" means the retail market value at the time of the theft, or if the retail market value cannot be ascertained, the cost of replacement of the property within a reasonable time after the theft, or in the case of a theft or the making of a copy of an article representing a trade secret, where the retail market value or replacement cost cannot be ascertained, any reasonable value representing the damage to the owner which the owner has suffered by reason of losing an advantage over those who do not know of or use the trade secret.

For a check, draft, or other order for the payment of money, "value" means the amount of money promised or ordered to be paid under the terms of the check, draft, or other order.

For a theft committed under section E, elements (4) a. and b., "Theft - Temporary Control", if the property has been restored to the owner, "value" means the value of the use of the property or the damage which it sustained, whichever is greater, while the owner was deprived of its possession, but not exceeding the value otherwise provided herein.

For a theft committed under Section I. (theft of leased/rental property), if the property has been restored to the owner, "value" means the rental value of the property, determined at the rental rate contracted by the defendant or, if no rental rate was contracted, the rental rate customarily charged by the owner for use of the property, plus any damage that occurred to the property while the owner was deprived of its possession, but not exceeding the total retail value of the property at the time of rental.

37. TRESPASS

A.   TRESPASS - Domestic Animals or Fowls
M.S. § 609.605, subd. 1(b)(1) (Misdemeanor)

Name
Date and Time of Offense
Location (Venue)

(1)   No person shall intentionally
(2)   permit domestic animals or fowls
(3)   under the actor's control
(4)   to go on the land of another
(5)   within a city.

B.   TRESPASS - Monuments, Signs or Pointers
M.S. § 609.605, subd. 1(b)(2) (Misdemeanor)

Name
Date and Time of Offense
Location (Venue)

(1)   No person shall intentionally
(2)   interfere unlawfully
(3)   with a monument, sign or pointer
(4)   erected or marked to designate
(5)   a point of a boundary, line or a political subdivision, or a tract of land.

C.   TRESPASS - Property of Another
M.S. § 609.605, subd. 1(b)(3),(7),(8) (Misdemeanor)

Name
Date and Time of Offense
Location (Venue)

Refusal to Depart (1)   No person shall intentionally (2)   trespass on the premises of another (3)   and without claim of right (4)   refuse to depart from the premises (5)   on demand of the lawful possessor.

OR

Return to Property
(1) No person shall return to the property of another
(2) with the intent to abuse, disturb, or cause distress in, or threaten another
(3) after being told to leave the property and not to return
(4) if the actor is without claim of right to the property or consent of one with authority to consent.

OR

Return within One Year
(1) No person shall return to the property of another
(2) within one year after being told to leave the property and not to return
(3) if the defendant is without claim of right to the property or consent of one with authority to consent.

D. TRESPASS - Dwelling or Building of Another
M.S. § 609.605, subd. 1(b)(4) (Misdemeanor)

Name

Date and Time of Offense

Location (Venue)

(1) No person shall occupy or enter
(2) the dwelling or locked or posted building of another
(3) without claim of right or consent of the owner or the consent of one who has the right to give consent

Exception: Emergency situations.

E. TRESPASS - Fruits, Fruit Trees or Vegetables
M.S. § 609.605, subd. 1(b)(5) (Misdemeanor)

Name

Date and Time of Offense

Location (Venue)

(1) No person shall enter the premises of another
(2) with intent to take or injure any fruit, fruit tree or vegetable
(3) growing on the premises
(4) without the permission of the owner or occupant.

F.   TRESPASS - Public or Private Cemetery
M.S. § 609.605, subd. 1(b)(6) (Misdemeanor)

Name

Date and Time of Offense

Location (Venue)

(1)   No person shall enter or be found on the premises

(2)   of a public or private cemetery

(3)   without authorization

(4)   during hours the cemetery is posted as closed to the public.

G.   TRESPASS - Construction Site
M.S. § 609.605, subd. 1(b)(9) (Misdemeanor)

Name

Date and Time of Offense

Location (Venue)

(1)   No person shall enter the locked or posted construction site (as defined in section N. below) of another

(2)   without the consent of the owner or lawful possessor (as defined in section N. below)

(3)   unless the person is a business licensee (as defined in section N. below).

H.   TRESPASS – Mining Site
M.S. § 609.605, subd. 1(b)(10) (Misdemeanor)

Name

Date and Time of Offense

Location (Venue)

(1)   No person shall enter the locked or posted aggregate mining site (as defined in section N. below) of another

(2)   without the consent of the owner or lawful possessor

(3)   unless the person is a business licensee (as defined in section N. below).

I.   TRESPASS – Law Enforcement Cordon
M.S. § 609.605, subd. 1(b)(11) (Misdemeanor)

Name

Date and Time of Offense

Location (Venue)

(1)   No person shall cross or enter into any public or private area

(2)   lawfully cordoned off by or at the direction of a peace officer

(3)   engaged in the performance of official duties

Note: For purposes of this clause, an area may be "cordoned off" through the use of tape, barriers, or other means conspicuously placed and identifying the area as being restricted by a peace officer and identifying the responsible authority.

Defense: It is an affirmative defense to a charge under the above clause that a peace officer permitted entry into the restricted area.

J. TRESPASS - Facility for Battered Women
M.S. § 609.605, subd. 2 (Gross Misdemeanor)

Name
Date and Time of Offense
Location (Venue)

(1)   No person shall trespass upon the grounds
(2)   of a facility providing emergency shelter services for battered women, as defined under M.S. § 611A.31, subd. 3, or of a facility providing transitional housing for battered women and their children
(3)   without claim of right or consent of one who has right to give consent
(4)   and refuse to depart from the grounds of the facility on demand of one who has right to give consent.

K. TRESPASS - School Property
M.S. § 609.605, subd. 4 (Misdemeanor - Gross Misdemeanor)

Name
Date and Time of Offense
Location (Venue)

Misdemeanor
(1)   No person shall
(2)   enter or be found in a public or nonpublic elementary, middle, or secondary school building
UNLESS THE PERSON:

    a.   is an enrolled student in, a parent or guardian of an enrolled student in, or an employee of the school or school district;
       or

    b.   has permission or an invitation from a school official to be in the building;
       or

c.		is attending a school event, class, or meeting to which the person, the public, or a student's family is invited;
or		
d.		has reported the person's presence in the school building in the manner required for visitors to the school.

OR

Misdemeanor
(1) No person shall
(2) enter or be found on school property (as defined in section N, "Definitions" below)
(3) within one year after being told by the school principal or the principal's designee to leave the property and not to return
UNLESS:
a. the principal or the principal's designee has given the person permission to return to the property.

OR

Misdemeanor
(1) No person shall
(2) be on the roof of a public or nonpublic elementary, middle, or secondary school building
UNLESS THE PERSON:
a. has permission from a school official to be on the roof of the building.

OR

Gross Misdemeanor
(1) It is a gross misdemeanor for a group of three or more persons
(2) to enter or be found in a public or nonpublic elementary, middle, or secondary school building UNLESS ONE OF THE PERSONS:
a. is an enrolled student in, a parent or guardian of an enrolled student in, or an employee of the school or school district; •
b. has permission or an invitation from a school official to be in the building;
c. is attending a school event, class, or meeting to which the person, the public, or a student's family is invited; or

> d. has reported the person's presence in the school building in the manner required for visitors to the school.

<u>Detaining Suspect</u> - A school principal or a school employee designated by the school principal to maintain order on school property, who has reasonable cause to believe that a person is violating the above section may detain the person in a reasonable manner for a reasonable period of time pending the arrival of a peace officer. (See also M.S. § 609.06(7) "Authorized Use of Force".)

<u>Warrantless Arrest (preceding 4 hours)</u> - A peace officer may arrest a person without a warrant if the officer has probable cause to believe the person violated the above section within the preceding four hours. The arrest may be made even though the violation did not occur in the peace officer's presence.

L. TRESPASS – School Bus
M.S. § 609.605, subd. 4a (Misdemeanor)

Name
Date and Time of Offense
Location (Venue)

> (1) No person who boards a school bus shall refuse to leave the bus on demand of the bus operator
>
>> (a) when the bus is on its route or otherwise in operation; or
>> (b) while the bus has pupils on it.

M. TRESPASS - Hunting
See M.S. § 97B.001, subd. 1, 2, 3, 4, 5, 6 for misdemeanor provisions.

N. TRESPASS ON CRITICAL PUBLIC SERVICE FACILITY; UTILITY; OR PIPELINE
M.S. § 609.6055 Subd. 2(a), (b) (Gross Misdemeanor)
Name
Date and Time of Offense
Location (Venue)

(1)	No person shall
(2)	enter or be found
(3)	upon property containing a critical public service facility, utility, or pipeline

(4)	without claim of right or consent of one who has the right to give consent to be on the property, **IF**
	(a) the person refuses to depart from the property on the demand of one who has the right to give consent to; or
	(b) within the past six months, the person had been told by one who had the right to give consent to leave the property and not to return, unless a person with the right to give consent has given the person permission to return; or
	(c) the property is posted.

OR

(1)	No person shall
(2)	enter without claim of right or consent of one who has the right to give consent to be in the underground structure
(3)	an underground structure that
(4)	(a) contains a utility line or pipeline
	and
	(b) is not open to the public for pedestrian use.

O.   DEFINITIONS:

(1) **Building** (M.S. § 609.605, subd. 1; 609.581, subd. 2)
> "Building" means a structure suitable for affording shelter for human beings, including any appurtenant or connected structure.

(2) **Business licensee - construction site** (M.S. § 609.605, subd. 1(vi))
> "Business licensee" includes a representative of a building trades labor or management organization.

(3) **Construction site** (M.S. § 609.605, subd. 1(iii))
> "Construction site" means the site of the construction, alteration, painting, or repair of a building or structure.

(4) **Critical public service facility** (M.S. § 609.594, Subd. 1(1))
> "Critical public service facility" includes railroad yards and stations, bus stations, airports, and other mass transit facilities; oil refineries; storage areas or facilities for hazardous materials, hazardous substances, or hazardous wastes; and bridges.

(5) **Disability** (M.S. § 363.01)
> "Disability" is defined in chapter 2 (Assaults), section U.

(6) **Dwelling** (M.S. § 609.605, subd. 1(a)(ii))
> "Dwelling" means the building or a part of a building used by an individual as a place of residence on either a full-time or part-time basis. A dwelling may be part of a multi-dwelling or multi-purpose building, or a manufactured home as defined in M.S. § 168.011, subd. 8.

(7)   **Owner or lawful possessor - construction site** (M.S. § 609.605, subd. 1 (iv))

> "Owner or lawful possessor" means the person on whose behalf a building or dwelling is being constructed, altered, painted, or repaired and the general contractor or subcontractor engaged in that work.

(8)   **Pipeline** (M.S. § 609.594, Subd. 1(2) and § 609.6055, subd. 1(c))

> "Pipeline" includes an aboveground pipeline, a belowground pipeline housed in an underground structure, and any equipment, facility, or building located in this state that is used to transport natural or synthetic gas, crude petroleum or petroleum fuels or oil or their derivatives, or hazardous liquids, to or within a distribution, refining, manufacturing, or storage facility that is located inside or outside of this state. Pipeline does not include service lines.

(9)   **Posted construction site** (M.S. § 609.605, subd. 1(v)(A))

> "Posted construction site" means the placement of a sign at least 11 inches square in a conspicuous place on the exterior of the building that is under construction, alteration, or repair, and additional signs in at least two conspicuous places for each ten acres being protected. The sign must carry an appropriate notice and the name of the person giving the notice, followed by the word "owner" if the person giving the notice is the holder of legal title to the land on which the construction site is located or by the word "occupant" if the person giving the notice is not the holder of legal title but is a lawful occupant of the land.

(10)   **Posted Mining Site** (M.S. § 609.605, subd. 1(v)(B))

> "Posted Mining Site" means the placement of signs that state "no trespassing" or similar terms with letters at least 2 inches high that state Minnesota law prohibits trespassing on the property. The signs must be posted in a conspicuous place and at intervals of 500 feet or less.

(11)   **Posting** (M.S. § 609.6055, subd. 3)

> "Posting " means a critical public service facility, utility, or pipeline is posted if there are signs that: (1) state "no trespassing" or similar terms; (2) display letters at least two inches high; (3) state that Minnesota law prohibits trespassing on the property; and; (4) are posted in a conspicuous place and at intervals of 500 feet or less.

(12)   **Premises** (M.S. § 609.605, subd. 1(a)(i))

> "Premises" means real property and any appurtenant building or structure.

(13)   **Pupils** (M.S. § 609.605, subd. 4a(b))

> "Pupils" means persons in grades prekindergarten through grade 12.

(14) **School Bus** (M.S. § 609.605, subd. 4a(a))
"School Buss" has the meaning given in section 169.011, subd. 71.

(15) **School Property** (M.S. § 609.605, subd. 4(b); 152.01, subd. 14a, (1), (3))

"School property" means

a. any property owned, leased, or controlled by a school district or an organization operating a nonpublic school, as defined in section 123.932, subdivision 3, where an elementary, middle, secondary school, secondary vocational center or other school providing educational services in grade one through grade 12 is located, or used for educational purposes, or where extracurricular or cocurricular activities are regularly provided;

b. the area within a school bus when that bus is being used to transport one or more elementary or secondary school students.

(16) **Utility** (M.S. § 609.594, Subd. 1(3))

"Utility " includes: (i) any organization defined as a utility in section 216C.06, subdivision 5; (ii) any telecommunications carrier or telephone company regulated under chapter 237; and (iii) any local utility or enterprise formed for the purpose of providing electrical or gas heating and power, telephone, water, sewage, wastewater, or other related utility service, which is owned, controlled, or regulated by a town, a statutory or home rule charter city, a county, a port development authority, the metropolitan council, a district heating authority, a regional commission or other regional government unit, or a combination of these governmental units. The term does not include property located above buried power or telecommunications lines or property located below suspended power or telecommunications lines, unless the property is fenced in or otherwise enclosed.

(17) **Utility Line** (M.S. § 609.6055, subd. 1(e))

"Utility line" includes power, telecommunications, and transmissions lines as well as related equipment owned or controlled by a utility.

38. WORTHLESS - DISHONORED CHECKS

ISSUANCE OF DISHONORED CHECKS
M.S. § 609.535, subds. 1, 2, 2a, 3, 4, 5 (Misdemeanor - Gross Misdemeanor - Felony)
Name
Date and Time of Offense
Location (Venue)

(1)   No person shall
(2)   issue a check
(3)   which, at the time of issuance,
(4)   the issuer intends shall not be paid, if:
(5)   a.   the value of the dishonored check or aggregated checks is not more than $250 **(misdemeanor).**
                    or
              b.   the value of the dishonored check or aggregated checks is more than $250 but not more than $500 **(gross misdemeanor).**
                    or
              c.   the value of the dishonored check or aggregated checks is more than $500 **(felony).**

<u>Aggregation:</u> In a prosecution under the above section, the value of dishonored checks issued by the defendant in violation of the above section within any six-month period may be aggregated and the defendant charged accordingly in applying this section.

<u>Jurisdiction:</u> When two or more offenses are committed by the same person in two or more counties, the accused may be prosecuted in any county in which one of the dishonored checks was issued for all of the offenses aggregated under the above paragraph.

<u>Proof of Intent:</u> Any of the following is evidence sufficient to sustain a finding that the person at the time the person issued the check intended it should not be paid:

        a.   Proof that, at the time of issuance, the issuer did not have an account with the drawee;
        b.   Proof that, at the time of issuance, the issuer did not have sufficient funds or credit with the drawee and that the issuer failed to pay the check within five business days after mailing of notice of nonpayment or dishonor as provided in the section below titled "<u>Notice by Certified Mail</u>"; or

c.   Proof that, when presentment was made within a reasonable time, the issuer did not have sufficient funds or credit with the

drawee and that the issuer failed to pay the check within five business days after mailing of notice of nonpayment or dishonor as provided in the section below titled "Notice by Certified Mail."

Notice by Certified Mail or Regular Mail With Affidavit of Service:

a.   Notice of nonpayment or dishonor that includes a citation to and a description of the penalties in this section shall be sent by the payee or holder of the check to the maker or drawer by certified mail, return receipt requested, or by regular mail, supported by an affidavit of service by mailing, to the address printed on the check. Refusal by the maker or drawer of the check to accept certified mail notice or failure to claim certified or regular mail notice is not a defense that notice was not received.

b.   The notice may state that unless the check is paid in full within five business days after mailing of the notice of nonpayment or dishonor, the payee or holder of the check will or may refer the matter to proper authorities for prosecution under this section.

c.   An affidavit of service by mailing shall be retained by the payee or holder of the check.

Exceptions: The above sections do not apply to a post-dated check or to a check given for a past consideration, except a payroll check or a check issued to a fund for employee benefits.

Cross reference: See "THEFT - False Representation" (i.e. issuance of a check, etc.) chapter 36, section C.

Definition of **"check"** (M.S. § 609.535, subd. 1(a)) - means a check, draft, order of withdrawal or similar negotiable or non-negotiable instrument.

Definition of **"credit"** (M.S. § 609.535, subd. 1(b)) - means an arrangement or understanding with the drawee for the payment of a check.

APPENDIX A

ANTICIPATORY CRIMES - ATTEMPTS AND CONSPIRACY

A.   ATTEMPTS
M.S. § 609.17, subd. 1,2,3 (Misdemeanor - Gross Misdemeanor Felony)

Name
Date and Time of Offense
Location (Venue)
(1)   No person shall
(2)   with intent to commit a crime
(3)   do an act which is a substantial step toward, and more than mere preparation for, the commission of the crime.

Penalty: Whoever violates the above section may be sentenced to not more than one-half of the maximum sentence provided for the crime attempted (except Murder in the 1st Degree), but the maximum sentence in any case shall not be less than imprisonment for 90 days or a fine of $100.

Defense of Impossibility: The defense of impossibility only applies if the impossibility of committing the crime would have been obvious to a person of normal understanding (subd. 2; CRIMJIG 5.03).

Defense of Abandonment: It is a defense to a charge of attempt that the crime was not committed because the accused desisted voluntarily and in good faith and abandoned the intention to commit the crime, even though the defendant had already taken a substantial step toward the commission of the crime (subd. 3, CRIMJIG 5.04).

B.   CONSPIRACY
M.S. § 609.175, subd. 1,2,3 (Misdemeanor - Gross Misdemeanor - Felony)

Name
Date and Time of Offense
Location (Venue)
(1)   No person shall
(2)   conspire with another to commit a crime
(3)   and, in furtherance of the conspiracy, one or more of the parties does some overt act in furtherance of the conspiracy.

Penalty: If the crime intended is a misdemeanor, then defendant is guilty of a **misdemeanor**. If the crime intended is any gross misdemeanor or felony offense (except Murder in the 1st Degree or Treason), then defendant may be sentenced to one-half of the maximum sentence provided for that **felony** or **gross misdemeanor**.

Note: Whoever conspires with another to cause a third person to be arrested or prosecuted on a criminal charge, knowing the charge to be false, is guilty of a **misdemeanor**.

Jurisdiction: The above section applies even if:
    (1) The defendant in this state conspires with another outside of this state; or
    (2) The defendant outside of this state conspires with another in this state; or
    (3) The defendant outside of this state conspires with another outside of this state and an overt act in furtherance of the conspiracy is committed within this state by either of them; or
    (4) The defendant in this state conspires with another in this state.

Controlled Substance Crimes: Whoever (person, firm or corporation) conspires to commit any controlled substance crime (M.S. Chapter 152), except possession or distribution for no remuneration of a small amount of marijuana, is guilty of a **felony**. (M.S. § 152.096; CRIMJIG 5.06)

Defense of Withdrawal: A person who has conspired with another to commit a crime but who withdraws from the agreement and communicates such withdrawal to the other person(s) <u>before</u> an overt act is committed is not guilty of conspiracy. In other words, the crime of conspiracy is complete as soon as the overt act is done and withdrawal thereafter is too late. (M.S. § 609.05, subd. 3; CRIMJIG 5.15)

Note: A person may be guilty of a conspiracy if he/she agrees with another person to commit a crime, even though the other person does not actually intend that the crime will be committed. (CRIMJIG 5.12)

APPENDIX B

CRIMINAL DEFENSES

---

1. ABANDONMENT OF A CRIME
   a.   Attempts
   b.   Crime Committed by Accomplice

2. DURESS OR COERCION

3. ENTRAPMENT

4. IMPOSSIBILITY

5. INTOXICATION
   a.   Voluntary Intoxication
   b.   Involuntary Intoxication

6. MENTAL ILLNESS OR MENTAL DEFICIENCY

7. SELF DEFENSE
   a.   Causing Death
   b.   Not Causing Death

1. ABANDONMENT OF A CRIME

a. Attempts (M.S. § 609.17, subd. 3; CRIMJIG 5.04)
It is a defense to a charge of attempt that the crime was not committed because the accused desisted voluntarily and in good faith and abandoned the intention to commit the crime, even though the defendant had already taken a substantial step toward the commission of the crime.

b. Crime Committed by Accomplice (M.S. § 609.05, subd. 3):
A person who intentionally aids, advises, hires, counsels, or conspires with or otherwise procures another to commit a crime and thereafter abandons that purpose and makes a reasonable effort to prevent the commission of the crime prior to its commission is not liable if the crime is thereafter committed.

2. DURESS OR COERCION (M.S. § 609.08; CRIMJIG 7.01)

The defendant is not guilty of a crime if defendant participated in the crime only because of a reasonable belief from the threats by another person engaged in the commission of the crime that defendant would be immediately killed if he/she refused to participate in the commission of the crime.

Note: Defendant's reasonable fear of instant death must continue throughout the time the crime is being committed, and it must not have been possible for defendant to withdraw in safety. Threats of future danger to defendant's life is not a defense.

Exception: The above defense does not apply to prosecutions under M.S. § 609.20, clause (3) (Manslaughter in the 1st Degree - crime committed because of coercion) (see Chapter 25, Section D, 4th box).

3. **ENTRAPMENT** (CRIMJIG 7.02)

Defendant is not guilty of a crime when the defendant commits an act or engages in conduct otherwise criminal, if the criminal design does not originate with defendant, but is conceived in the mind of a government agent and defendant is by coercion, persuasion, deceitful representation, or inducement lured into committing an act which the defendant otherwise would not have committed and had no intention of committing. If a person is willing and ready to commit the crime, the fact that the government agent has provided what appears to be a favorable opportunity is not an excuse. The State must prove beyond a reasonable doubt that defendant had the ready willingness (was predisposed) to commit the act.

4. **IMPOSSIBILITY** (M.S. § 609.17, subd. 2; CRIMJIG 5.03)

Even though the commission of a crime was not possible because of the circumstances under which the act was performed or because of the inadequacy of the means employed, a person can still be guilty of an attempt to commit that crime, if the person intended to commit the crime and took a substantial step toward its commission. The defense of impossibility only applies if the impossibility of committing the crime would have been obvious to a person of normal understanding.

5. **INTOXICATION**

   a. Voluntary Intoxication (M.S. § 609.075; CRIMJIG 7.03):
   It is not a defense to a crime that defendant was intoxicated at the time of the act if defendant voluntarily became intoxicated. However, if a specific intent or purpose is an essential element of the crime, the fact of intoxication may be taken into consideration in determining whether defendant was capable of forming the required intent.

   Note: Because an assault involving actual bodily injury is not a specific intent crime, the defense of voluntary intoxication does not apply.

   b. Involuntary Intoxication (CRIMJIG 7.04):
   A defendant is not guilty of any crime if defendant's actions were unintentional and non-negligent because of involuntary intoxication. However, involuntary intoxication is a defense only if it causes temporary insanity (see Mental Illness below).

- 238 -

6. **MENTAL ILLNESS OR MENTAL DEFICIENCY**
(M.S. § 611.026; CRIMJIG 6.02)

The M'Naghten Rule - Under the statutes of Minnesota, a person is not criminally liable for an act when, at the time of committing the act, the person did not know the nature of the act, or did not know that it was wrong because of a defect of reason caused by a mental illness or cognitive impairment.

7. **SELF DEFENSE**

a. Causing Death (M.S. § 609.065; CRIMJIG 7.05)
No crime is committed when a person takes the life of another person, even intentionally, if defendant's action is taken in resisting or preventing an offense which defendant reasonably believes exposes defendant (or another) to death or great bodily harm, or if defendant's action is taken in preventing the commission of a felony in defendant's place of abode.

Note: In order for a killing to be justified under the above section, three conditions must be met:
i. the killing must have been done in the belief that it was necessary to avert death or great bodily harm.
ii. the judgment of defendant as to the gravity of the peril to which (he) (she) (or another) was exposed must have been reasonable under the circumstances.
iii. defendant's election to defend must have been such as a reasonable person would have made in light of the danger perceived and the existence of any alternative way of avoiding the peril.

b. Not Causing Death (M.S. § 609.06(3); CRIMJIG 7.06)
Defendant is not guilty of a crime, if defendant used reasonable force to resist (or to aid another in resisting) an offense against the person, and such an offense was being committed or defendant reasonably believed that it was.

WARRANTLESS MISDEMEANOR ARRESTS

GENERAL RULE - A peace officer can only arrest for a misdemeanor or gross misdemeanor without a warrant if the offense was committed in the officer's presence:

EXCEPTIONS - A peace officer may arrest a suspect on probable cause without a warrant for the following misdemeanor or gross misdemeanor offenses even though not committed in the officer's presence.

1. **Domestic Assault**
   M.S. § 629.341, subd. 1

   "A peace officer may arrest a person anywhere without a warrant, including at the person's residence, if the peace officer has probable cause to believe that within the preceding 72 hours, exclusive of the day probable cause was established, the person has committed non-felony domestic abuse (as defined below). The arrest may be made even though the assault did not take place in the presence of the peace officer."

   Definition of **"Domestic Abuse"** (M.S. § 518B.01, subd. 2) - means: (i) physical harm, bodily injury, assault, or the infliction of fear of imminent physical harm, bodily injury or assault, between family or household members; or (ii) terroristic threats, within the meaning of M.S. § 609.713, subd. 1, or criminal sexual conduct, within the meaning of M.S. § 609.342, § 609.343, § 609.344, or § 609.345, committed against a family or household member by a family or household member, or interference with an emergency call within the meaning of M.S. § 609.78, subd. 2.

2. **Fifth Degree Assault on School Property**
   M.S. § 629.343

   "Not withstanding section 629.34, a peace officer, as defined in M.S. § 626.84, subdivision 1, paragraph (c), who is on or off duty within the jurisdiction of the appointing authority or on duty outside the jurisdiction of the appointing authority pursuant to M.S. § 629.40, may arrest a person without a warrant if the peace officer has probable cause to believe that the person within the preceding four hours has committed a fifth-degree assault, as defined in M.S. § 609.224, on school property, as defined in M.S. § 609.66, subdivision 1d. The arrest may be made even though the crimes were not committed in the presence of the peace officer."

3. **Violation of Restraining Orders - Domestic Abuse Order for Protection (O.F.P.) or Harassment Restraining Order (H.R.O.)**
§ 518B.01, subd. 14; § 609.748, subd. 6

A peace officer must arrest, without a warrant and take into custody, a person violating a restraining order (O.F.P. or H.R.O.) even if the violation did not take place in the presence of the officer, if:

a. The peace officer has probable cause to believe the person has violated the order; and

b. The existence of the order can be verified by the officer.

4. **Violation of No Contact Orders**
M.S. § 629.34, subd. 1(6); Rule of Crim. Proced. 6.03, subd. 2

A peace officer may arrest without a warrant and take into custody, a person violating a no contact order, even if the violation did not take place in the presence of the officer, if:

a. The peace officer has probable cause to believe that a released defendant has violated the no contact order; and

b. It is impracticable to secure a warrant or summons directing the defendant to appear before the District Court.

Note: Under normal circumstances, a peace officer should notify the prosecuting attorney of the violation, and they can then make application to the Court for either an arrest warrant or a summons directing the defendant to appear in court. Arresting a defendant without a warrant should only be done if:

a. It reasonably appears that the arrest or detention is necessary to prevent bodily harm to the accused or another; or

b. To prevent further criminal conduct; or

c. That there is substantial likelihood that the defendant will fail to respond to a citation or summons.

5. **Violation of a Domestic Abuse No Contact Order**
M.S. § 629.75, subd. 3

A peace officer shall arrest without a warrant and take into custody a person whom the peace officer has probable cause to believe has violated a domestic abuse no contact order, even if the violation did not take place in the presence of the peace officer, if the existence of the order can be verified.

6. **Trespass on School Property**
M.S. § 609.605, subd. 4(d)

A peace officer may arrest a person without a warrant if the officer has probable cause to believe the person violated M.S. § 609.605, subd. 4 (Trespass on School Property) within the preceding four hours. The arrest may be made even though the violation did not occur in the peace officer's presence.

7. **All DWI Related Offenses - DWI, Aggravated DWI, Commercial Vehicle DWI, Aircraft DWI, Snowmobile and All-Terrain Vehicle DWI**
M.S. § 169A.20, subd. 1; § 360.0752; § 84.91

Note - Boating DWI: The above list includes Boating While Intoxicated if the defendant was involved in a motor boat accident resulting in death, personal injury or property damage (M.S. § 86B.331, subd. 2).

8. **Theft in Business Establishments: Detaining Suspects (Misdemeanor or Gross Misdemeanor)**
M.S. § 629.366, subd. 2

Upon a charge being made by a merchant or merchant's employee, a peace officer may arrest a person without a warrant, if the officer has reasonable cause for believing that the person has committed or attempted to commit the crime of theft and the defendant is being detained by the merchant or the merchant's employee.

9. **Theft By Swindle**
(Misdemeanor or Gross Misdemeanor)
M.S. § 609.52, subd. 2(4); § 629.364(b)

10. **Any Gross Misdemeanor Theft**
M.S. § 609.52, subd. 2(1) to (17); § 629.34(5)

11. **Gross Misdemeanor Criminal Damage to Property in the 3rd Degree - damage over $500 but not more than $1,000; or under $500 if motivated by bias.**
M.S. § 609.595, subd. 2; § 629.34(5)

12. **Gross Misdemeanor Check Forgery - $250 or Less**
M.S. § 609.631, subd. 4(4); § 629.34(5)

13. **Gross Misdemeanor Stalking - Applies to all sections except gross misdemeanor cases involving false allegations made against peace officers.**
M.S. § 609.749; § 629.34(5)

14. **Gross Misdemeanor Financial Transaction Card Fraud**
M.S. §609.821, subd. 3; § 629.34(5)

15. **Illegal Approach to or Passing of School Bus**
(Misdemeanor or Gross Misdemeanor)
M.S. § 169.444, subd. 1, 1a, 5

16. **Failure to Yield to an Emergency Vehicle (Misdemeanor)**
M.S. § 169.20, subd. 5(c).

A peace officer may arrest the driver of a motor vehicle if the peace officer has probable cause to believe that the driver has failed to yield to an emergency vehicle within the four-hour period following the termination of the emergency incident.

17. **Second conviction for any of the following misdemeanor-level crimes:**
M.S. § 609.153, subd. 1 & 2).

"A peace officer acting without a warrant who has decided to proceed with the prosecution of a person for committing a crime listed below (a-e) may arrest and take the person into custody if the officer has reason to believe the person has a prior conviction for any crime listed below (a-e)."

(a)   prostitution (M.S. § 609.324)
(b)   motor vehicle tampering (M.S. § 609.546)
(c)   damage to property (M.S. § 609.595)
(d)   dangerous weapons (M.S. § 609.66)
(e)   violation of local ordinances prohibiting the unlawful sale or possession of controlled substances

18. **Driving through columns of school children (misdemeanor)**
M.S. § 169.21(c)

A peace officer may arrest the driver of a motor vehicle if the peace officer has probable cause to believe that the driver has operated the vehicle in violation of M.S. 169.21(c) within the past four hours. M.S. § 169.21(c) states:

"It is unlawful for any person to drive a motor vehicle through a column of school children crossing a street or highway or past a member of a school safety patrol or adult crossing guard while the member of the school safety patrol or adult crossing guard is holding an official signal in the stop position."

19. **Driver of vehicle who fails or refuses to stop and submit the vehicle and load to a weighing (misdemeanor)**
M.S. § 169.85, subd. 3,4

"A peace officer may arrest the driver of a motor vehicle if the peace officer has probable cause to believe that the driver has operated the vehicle in violation of M.S. § 169.85, subd. 3, within the past four hours."

20. **Driver who fails to stop for railroad crossing (misdemeanor)**
M.S. § 169.26, subd. 1a.

"A police officer may arrest the driver of a motor vehicle if the police officer has probable cause to believe that the driver has operated the vehicle in violation of M.S. § 169.26, subd. 1, within the past four hours."

Note: Citizen Arrest (M.S. § 629.37)
A peace officer may take into custody any suspect that has been lawfully placed under arrest by a citizen that witnessed the misdemeanor or gross misdemeanor offense.

INDEX
CRIMINAL OFFENSES

A

INDEX - CRIMINAL OFFENSES

INDEX - CRIMINAL OFFENSES

INDEX - CRIMINAL OFFENSES

INDEX - CRIMINAL OFFENSES

INDEX - CRIMINAL OFFENSES

INDEX
DEFINITIONS

D

INDEX - DEFINITIONS

INDEX - DEFINITIONS

H

I

J

L

M

INDEX - DEFINITIONS

INDEX - DEFINITIONS